03

Frock **Rock**

Frock **Rock**

Women
Performing
Popular Music

Mavis Bayton

Oxford   New York

OXFORD UNIVERSITY PRESS

1998

Oxford University Press, Great Clarendon Street, Oxford OX2 6DP
Oxford New York
Athens Auckland Bangkok Bogotá Buenos Aires Calcutta
Cape Town Chennai Dar es Salaam Delhi Florence Hong Kong Istanbul
Karachi Kuala Lumpur Madrid Melbourne Mexico City Mumbai
Nairobi Paris São Paulo Singapore Taipei Tokyo Toronto Warsaw

and associated companies in
Berlin Ibadan

Oxford is a registered trade mark of Oxford University Press

Published in the United States
by Oxford University Press Inc., New York

British Library Cataloguing in Publication Data
Data available

Library of Congress Cataloging in Publication Data
Bayton, Mavis.
Frock rock : women, popular music, and the conditions of
performance / Mavis Bayton.
p. cm.
"Select discography": p.
Includes bibliographical references (p.   ) and index.
1. Women rock musicians—England.   2. Rock music—England—
Performance.   3. Music and society—England.   4. Women rock
musicians—England—Interviews.   I. Title.
ML3492.B39 998   781.66'082'0942—dc21   98–7969
ISBN 0–19–816615–X

1 3 5 7 9 10 8 6 4 2

Typeset by Graphicraft Ltd, Hong Kong
Printed in Great Britain
on acid-free paper by Biddles Ltd
Guildford & Kings Lynn

This book is dedicated to the memory of

BILL BAYTON (1946–1992)
my beloved partner and best friend

'THE MISTAKES' (1978–1982)
Ali West, Georgina Clarke, Judy Parsons,
Linda Gardner, and Penny Wood

Preface

This book is a sociological study of women in contemporary popular music in the UK from the 1970s to the 1990s. Its focus is on instrumentalists, rather than singers; local music-making rather than international stardom. It is written with more than one potential readership in mind. Primarily, it is for students and academics in the fields of popular music, cultural and media studies, women's studies, and sociology. Hopefully, it can also be read as a guide for women considering a career in music-making, to show what the problems are likely to be and to demonstrate how others have successfully resisted and dealt with them. Lastly, it is for the general reader interested in popular music.

The book is based on ethnographic research undertaken for a Ph.D. in the 1980s and updated in 1995–6. In 1978 I became a member of Oxford's first all-women band—the Mistakes. As a sociologist by training, I became increasingly fascinated by the world of rock bands. Gradually moving from observant participation to full 'participant observation', I registered for a research degree at Warwick University and decided to widen the scope of my fieldwork by undertaking in-depth interviews with women musicians at various career stages: starting out, semi-professional, and fully professional. In all, I undertook forty-nine interviews. Most of these were lengthy—over two hours, the longest taking nine hours. They were structured by an interview schedule containing over 200 questions and recorded on tape. Alongside this, I undertook observation at women's music workshops. I also carried out innumerable brief informal unstructured interviews with men and women working in the record business, in recording studios, on music magazines, sound engineers, and so forth. Lastly, I went to hundreds of gigs. (Standard equipment: camera, tape recorder, notebook, and DMs.) The main questions I had in my mind were as follows. First, why were so comparatively few women playing instruments in bands? Second, what was special about those rare individuals who were doing it? Third, what were their experiences in playing music and how did their careers work?

In 1990 I obtained my Ph.D. and should have published a book, but my life partner became seriously ill and soon died. It was 1995 before I felt able to write a book, by which time my original fieldwork had become history, so I decided to repeat the entire research to obtain contemporary comparative data. This gave me two 'snapshots' to compare: one of the early to mid-1980s and one of the mid-1990s. Between 1995 and 1996 I immersed myself in gigs and carried out a further fifty-six interviews. Thus, this book is based on interviews with 105 women, the great majority (seventy-nine) of whom played instruments in bands. The rest include vocalists, sound engineers, music teachers, administrators and participants at women's music projects/workshops, a record distributor, a band manager, and a studio manager.

I diversified my sample in terms of career stage, location, type of music played, instrument, age, social class, sexuality. (See Appendix 2 for the full list.) Ageism is endemic in this field, where a woman is 'old' at 30 since chart success is all to do with youthful bodies and hegemonic masculinist notions of 'attractiveness'. However, although it is true that even at the amateur local band level the majority of players are under 30, since some older women do participate, I deliberately included some 30- and 40-year-olds in my sample. The book is concerned mainly with white female musicians simply because there are few black women (or men) in rock/indie music. For this reason, I made a point of interviewing seven non-white women, including several high-profile performers. I discuss both ethnicity and social class where relevant.

The fieldwork was immensely time-consuming but also rewarding and enjoyable. The majority of the interviews were face to face, whilst a handful were done over the phone (one was transatlantic). They took place backstage, in recording studios, in pubs and cafés, in kitchens, bedrooms, and even on the beach. Although a number of famous women performers refused to be interviewed, most of the musicians I approached responded to my request with interest. For bands starting out, any interviews are welcomed. Stars, however, typically receive three or more requests for interviews per day and, in contrast to journalists, I was not offering useful publicity; those professionals who gave me their time in their busy schedules did so out of a commitment to my project. The main problem was getting to these women, past the layers of management and record company personnel who performed a gatekeeping role. For instance, thirty-four phone-calls and four faxes were required to reach one musician but the resulting interview was exceedingly worthwhile.

My methodological approach, then, is ethnographic and thus my theory is grounded in everyday reality, incorporating women's daily experiences from their grass-roots accounts. In the spirit of the women's movement and believing that 'the personal is political', I have chosen to put myself in the frame. I am a white, heterosexual woman, a sociologist, a feminist, and a musician. Being both a woman and a musician myself was immensely valuable in the research process as there were fewer barriers between me and the musical world which I was researching. I could empathize with my interviewees and many had sympathy for my project. Furthermore, my experience suggested some questions which would probably not have occurred to the non-musician, an advantage which the resulting account reflects. As a feminist, I was concerned not to exploit the women I was interviewing. I tried to make the interviews relaxed and enjoyable and I gave my interviewees the opportunity to ask me questions about my research. At the end of each interview women were given the chance to ask me about my own experiences and views. Indeed, Vi Subversa decided to interview me for half an hour. In my first series of interviews I was, I now feel, unnecessarily sensitive to issues of confidentiality: the interviews were carried out anonymously, in contrast to the 1995–6 sample. Where possible, I have since obtained permission to use the names of those I have traced of my 1980s interviewees. However, because many women proved to be untraceable and a few others wished to remain anonymous, some have pseudonyms, indicated by inverted commas (see Appendix 2).

In preparing for this book, I have had to confront certain problems to do with language and audience. In order to appeal to the general reader I am committed to writing in plain English, although academic credibility seems to demand that I do otherwise. I have tried to censor out any obscure language and unnecessary terminology, but it is impossible to avoid using some sociological concepts and making relevant academic references. I hope that I have managed to reach an effective compromise. It matters to me that this book should be understandable to non-academics.

A more serious problem confronts me with regard to describing the music(s) that I am dealing with. The available terminological categories (rock, pop, and indie) seem highly inadequate and problematic. From the 1960s to the 1980s it was fairly straightforward to use the terms 'rock' and 'pop' to delineate two clearly separated phenomena and 'rock' would have been the appropriate broad term to cover all the types of bands which I have researched (see, for instance, Frith 1983). Since then, both music and language have changed and rock means a narrower style of music. Many of the bands I researched in 1995–6 would loosely describe their music as 'indie', whereas women playing the same type of music in the 1980s would have used the term 'rock'. Since my research covers both periods I have been faced with a problem of language. All but one of the bands I researched contained at least one guitar and many were what have been called 'guitar bands' in the 1990s, yet my investigation has also included jazz, soul, and reggae bands. Furthermore, in the 1970s bands you could dance to played 'dance music', whereas today this term is reserved largely for electronic music. One solution, which you will find in this book, is my use of the term 'popular music', one which is both over-broad and unwieldy to serve this purpose throughout. American books, such as Gaar (1992), often use the term 'rock and roll' or 'rock'n'roll' to define the overall field of bands with guitars in them and it has a growing colloquial use in the UK (as in 'sex and drugs and rock and roll'). However, in the UK this term is still most often used to describe not the breadth of popular music but the very specific style of the 1950s. As Deena Weinstein (1991) observes, 'this confusion is to be expected when treating a bricolage genre and an undisciplined discipline'. There is no perfect solution, so I have chosen to opt most of the time for the term 'rock' despite its drawbacks. Where it is important to make the distinction between 'rock' and 'pop' I have done so. I have also given a specific label to each band's music (see Appendix 2) despite the fact that, significantly, nearly every band I interviewed was unable to label it themselves, saying 'it's difficult to describe'.

In the 1990s journalists and commentators informed us that the world was 'post-feminist'. The battles were supposedly won and feminism no longer necessary. Indeed, feminism was actually being blamed for the role conflicts of contemporary young women and even accused of oppressing *men*. Various implications flow from the unwarranted assumptions of post-feminism which are relevant to my research area. First, the masculine is seen as the universal in rock, the norm, and the absence of women is unnoticed, underestimated, or denied. Likewise, the omnipresence of men is not registered but unconsciously taken for granted. People usually greatly overestimate the number of women in bands and find my statistics surprising, the most common and irritating response being 'Well, what about the Spice Girls?' as if the existence of one phenomenally successful all-female group who sing and dance (but do not play any instruments) means that men and women are equally represented in the field of popular music. Second, if the absence is noted, the social obstacles facing women would-be instrumentalists are often denied and individualistic explanations offered: 'there is nothing stopping women playing in bands these days so why don't they just get on with it?' That is, it is a personal failing of the individual women concerned, who have only themselves to blame. Third, the whole issue is not seen as interesting.

When I began my research, in the early 1980s, little had been written about female popular music-makers. Now, although there are a number of journalistic books on the topic (Steward and Garratt 1984; Cooper 1995; Evans 1994; L. O'Brien 1995; K. O'Brien 1995; Raphael 1995) there is still a lack of academic texts. Overall, the amount of words in print about women musicians is minute compared to the coverage of male musicians and male bands, since for decades all the books have been about men (and should have been subtitled 'a book about men in rock' or 'the story of an all-male band', a tactic which if adopted would make the imbalance startlingly clear). Yet the response to a new book in the field tends to be 'Not another book on women and rock!' as if women's experiences within bands had been comprehensively charted and the topic had been finally exhausted. Nothing could be further from the truth.

I have written this book as a sociologist, a musician, and a feminist, so that, in it, women are centre stage, for a change, displacing the male-as-norm. Moreover, although it includes quotations from some famous female musicians, the main focus of the book is on local music-making, amateur and semi-professional bands, about which very little is known in Britain outside biographies and autobiographies. Apart from shedding light on the hidden world of female musicians at the lower end of the career ladder, I also hope that this book inspires other women to get out there and set up bands and other people (teachers, parents, youth workers) to encourage and facilitate them to do so.

Acknowledgements

This book has only come at last to fruition with the help, support, and encouragement of many people. First I wish to thank all the musicians who gave me hours of their time in order to be interviewed and whose names appear in Appendix 2. However, I must also acknowledge that the insights of many others, whom I spoke to briefly and more informally, have enriched my thinking and thereby fed into this book. Sadly, they are too numerous to list. They include academics and students who have responded to papers I have given and articles I have written. In particular, I wish to acknowledge the interest of my fellow members of IASPM (the International Association for the Study of Popular Music).

On the practical front, I am very grateful to the friendly librarians of my workplace, Ruskin College, in particular Chris Keable, and to Roger Guiste of Virgin Records, Oxford, for helping me compile the discography. Thanks also to Paul Freestone for photographic advice and Gareth Coleman for last-minute computing assistance. I wish to express my appreciation to all those working in the music industry who helped me set up interviews, and to Nick Morpath for letting me use the Zodiac Club, Oxford. Also, Ronan Munro (editor of *Nightshift*) helped me get an initial sense of the local Oxford music scene.

A number of people gave generously of their time in order to read chapters in progress, and variously offer encouragement, suggestions, and rigorous criticism. They include my Ruskin students Andrew Whelan and John Fernandez, my colleagues Dennis Gregory, Hilda Kean, and Jane Thompson, Caroline Hutton of Women's Revolutions Per Minute (WRPM), Lucy Green, Elaine Nicol, Sara Cohen, Dave Harker, Dai Griffiths, and Sarah Thornton.

My greatest thanks goes to those who were dedicated enough to read the whole book in draft, indeed more than once, and spent hours discussing it with me. Anne-Marie Sweeney, Martin Smith, and Piers Mayfield gave this project their painstaking and meticulous attention, as editors, scholars, and friends.

A special thanks goes to Simon Frith, for his enthusiasm at the very start, when this research was just an idea in my head and he was a fan of my band, as well as for his patient encouragement and unwavering support, as my tutor, throughout my part-time Ph.D. He has encouraged me to write and has read the first draft of practically everything I have written. Without him I would never have completed either the doctorate or the book. His influence is everywhere, some-times and inevitably unacknowledged.

I wish to express my deepest appreciation to my friends who, in their different ways, supported and encouraged me through the difficult stages in the writing and to my mother, Daphne Jenkins, for her unwavering belief in my abilities. Finally, I want to acknowledge the enduring inspiration, encouragement, and support of my life partner, Bill, sadly no longer with me.

Contents

List of Figures

1 The Position of Women in Popular Music

The world of popular music is highly structured in terms of gender. Traditionally, women have been positioned as consumers and fans, and in supportive roles (wife, mother, girlfriend) rather than as active producers of music: musicians. When they have been on stage, on TV, on record, it has nearly always been as singers. They have sometimes written their own lyrics, rarely their own music, and there are very few women playing instruments. Currently, women's lives are accompanied by a *male* soundtrack. This has important implications, for popular music permeates modern life and helps to make us the people we are, both reflecting existing gender differences and also actively helping to construct them. Young women and men learn how to be feminine, masculine, and heterosexual through listening to rock[1] music, and observing the clothes, bodily gestures, and general performance of rock musicians as they simultaneously perform gender, sexuality, and music.

All human beings are musical, capable of both appreciating and making music. Because girls are as musical as boys, and women as musical as men, you would expect women to comprise roughly half of the jazz or blues players in the local pub, 50 per cent of instrumentalists on TV, half of all club DJs, and half of the people on stage at music festivals, which is patently not the case and never has been. There have, of course, always been exceptions and these have become more frequent over the last two decades, but the pattern is only slowly beginning to change. I approach music as a music fan, a musician, a feminist, and a sociologist. It is in the latter role that I ask the obvious question: why is there such an imbalance between men and women's involvement? However, before moving on to explanations, it is necessary to paint as clear and broad a picture as possible of the gendered nature of modern popular music-making.

---

[1] Regarding my use of the (inadequate) terms 'rock', 'pop', and 'indie', see the Preface.

Women in Record Companies

Of all the many thousands of bands in the UK, only a small proportion become well known outside their local neighbourhood; few make a record; only a tiny fraction of these reach the charts; and only about one in eight earn enough money from sales to pay back their advance and start making money (Negus 1992). In order to become commercially successful, the musician has to gain access to a series of social institutions: clubs, record companies, the music press, and radio stations. Such access is gained via a series of people in influential positions, often termed 'gatekeepers' (Frith 1983), but whom Negus has called, more accurately, 'cultural intermediaries': promoters, agents, journalists, and DJs. The majority of these are male. Thus the careers of female musicians are dependent on the decisions of a series of men in key positions, who filter out the vast majority of bands (whether male or female) as unworthy of attention.

In terms of paid employment within the record industry, women disproportionately occupy positions of lower pay, status, and power, at the bottom of the hierarchy, doing unskilled and semi-skilled manual jobs, and routine office work. Many young women are attracted to the industry for its glamour, believing they will meet the stars. In reality, the nearest they typically get to their idols is typing their names on envelopes. At the opposite end of the scale, in the UK, very few women are senior executives in the record industry or run their own record companies.

A key task within the record industry is deciding which performers should be offered record contracts and which records should be released. This is called A&R (artists and repertoire) and it involves talent scouting, deciding which numbers bands should record, and which records should be promoted. It is restricted by a perception of public taste, but as no one knows for sure exactly what the public will purchase, the clutch of records which become available in the shops have been chosen for the consumer by A&R. Thus, few roles could exercise more influence over the musician's career. This highly prestigious work is done mainly by men who decide how much money and time to invest in a band. They have to differentiate their acts into potential earnings divisions: major stars and 'serious' music for long-term investment or lightweight novelty acts for investing in the short term (Frith 1983; Negus 1992). All-female bands are accorded cult or novelty status. Women performers, in contrast to men, tend to be placed in a more limited number of categories. A&R is a well-paid, self-sustaining white, male club steeped in traditional 'laddish' rock culture: A&R man Keith Wozencroft signed a new (male) band after 'an ugly A&R scramble that involved one rival sending the band a call girl as a present' (*Guardian*, 8 March 1996).

Apart from that of sex object, this world only allows women the subservient role of secretary-handmaiden, a chauvinistic relationship which can even be reflected in the utilization of office space (Negus 1992).

The one area in record companies where women are present is in the press and public relations departments which have been viewed as female ghettos

(L. O'Brien 1995). This is not surprising, as much of the work requires so-called 'feminine' attributes, since nurturing the fragile egos of rock stars is an important responsibility. Another aspect of the job involves close dealings with (predominantly male) journalists, when women are utilized for their sex appeal and 'charm' in situations which can become institutionalized flirting. On the other hand, women were markedly absent from press and public relations in the 1970s and their current presence is the result of their active attempt to gain access to this field. Moreover, there are some signs (though little substantive research) that women have a higher profile in international marketing, product management, promotion, market research, and video production, with the greatest increase in Britain being in sales and marketing. However, women have not yet secured the decision-making positions within these departments (Negus 1992).

Thus, there is both horizontal and vertical gender differentiation within the record industry.

Media Men

DJs are the most significant of rock's gatekeepers, argued Frith (1983). Airplay is the most effective form of record promotion, but it is not under the control of record companies. Most DJs are male, so that for a long time Anne Nightingale, the only female DJ on Radio One, was faced with the sort of ridicule and hostility which has beset women interlopers in other all-male settings (Steward and Garratt 1984). Today, women DJs on national radio are still the exception.

Music journalists are also central cultural intermediaries, their opinions having an influence beyond their actual readers (Frith 1983). Gig and record reviews are especially significant for unestablished acts, where any publicity can only help. Moreover, reviews influence record companies, alerting them to public taste, possible signings, and which bands to heavily promote. However, female journalists are in a small minority, since women entrants are made to feel unwanted, given the less 'serious' articles because they are considered lightweight and yet often have to work twice as hard as men (Steward and Garratt 1984; Balfour 1986).

As most journalists are male, a hegemonic masculine view tends to predominate in the music press. Women, who are not presented as artists in the way that men are or to be taken seriously as musicians, are often viewed as just puppets, moulded by record companies, rarely asked about playing their instruments and often presented in sexual terms rather than as craftswomen, serious about their work. Laetitia, central to the creativity and musicianship of Stereolab, told me that she is often called 'beautiful', whereas co-band member Tim is not called 'handsome' and, over the years, she has had to learn to contain her anger at the way she is sidelined: 'The guys who do interviews would rather speak to Tim and engage in conversation with him, leaving me aside. So I can easily feel bad about it.' Quite a few musicians whom I interviewed would not read the 'serious' music press because of the emphasis on women's bodies at the expense of the music. As Kathryn (of Frantic Spiders) put it in 1995: 'They like to think they're really right-on, but they're no different from the tabloids.' This emphasis on the female body comes across strikingly in photographs. There are some highly successful female photographers (like Val Wilmer, Pennie Smith, and Annie Leibovitz) but they are still outnumbered by males, male picture editors selecting which shots the paper will use. Choices are influenced by ideas of sexual attractiveness; gender notions help to structure the framework within which they are made. In my personal experience, those who work on local newspapers tend to see women's bands simply in terms of 'glamour shots', often completely out of keeping with a band's music and image. In national music papers, too, women's bodies are routinely prioritized in photographs. According to Manda Rin from Bis:

> There's two boys in the band and me and they always make me stand in the middle and forward from the other two . . . We usually prefer to stand in a row. That's how we do it on stage . . . There's no main person . . . I stand at the side. So it's not as if we are a female-fronted band at all. But I do get that a lot. It's like, 'Oh, Manda, come forward' and 'Manda do this' and it's not very fair on the other two.

Few established female artists have managed to gain control over the processes of their presentation.

Promoters and Agents

When bands start out it is relatively easy to get gigs locally. At a later stage, however, they need an agent, to save time, and to gain access to prestigious venues. Because the majority of agents and promoters are male, they have often in the past been prejudiced against women's bands or, perhaps, against those all-women bands who refuse to present themselves as sex objects. In the pre-war period, direct and open discrimination against women was quite common (Dahl 1984; Vicinus 1979). In my research I uncovered a number of instances of gross sexism on the 'club' circuit, where the Mission Belles were asked to perform in bikinis, with the implication that they might have to play topless. Bunty Murtagh: 'It was worth a fortune. And we wouldn't do it. We'd come to play music, not show our tits.' Today sexist ideology generally works in more subtle ways. However, in the highly competitive process of gaining access to venues, the persistence of gender stereotypes and sexist attitudes can seriously harm a band's career. Women's bands, even in the 1990s, were still seen as a bit of a speciality novelty act, as Delia from Mambo Taxi gives witness: 'There was the obstacle of being a girl-band, turning up at venues and [promoters] saying, "We've already had one girl band on this week and we didn't think it was a good idea having another one in such a short period" '. (Disregarding the fact that Mambo Taxi were pop and the other one had been, say, a metal band.)

Managers

Managers organize finances, get the best deals for the band, and mediate between it and the record company. Because they also help to develop a strategy for commercial success, they are, in that sense, involved in creating the final 'product' (Frith 1983), influencing the band's overall image, the publicity, and the kind of venues played. A manager may attempt to push the band in a certain direction, in terms of both music and audience and may even try to exert influence over who is actually to stay in the band, which provides plenty of scope for sexual prejudice.

Sometimes, with professional bands, the managerial role is split into two, one person dealing with all the financial tasks, while another takes care of the band in a more personal way, organizing their time, encouraging them along, and so forth. Where such role division occurs, quite often a woman performs the latter, more 'motherly' role. However, most managers are men, a female manager being a very rare thing before the end of the 1970s when punk opened the way into band management for some, although they had to deal with sexual prejudice and sheer incredulity from record company staff, promoters sometimes seeing them as 'lightweight'.

STEPH HILLIER (1990s band manager): I never would go into a promoter's office on my own. I've heard stories of people getting harassed behind closed doors when they've gone in to collect the money. Maybe they think, 'I can only give you fifty quid tonight, but I'll give you a shag instead!' That kind of stuff.

Agents find it easier dealing with male managers, because most agents are male themselves and their working lives are interlinked. Men in the rock industry, whether agents or record company employees, find it difficult to take a woman manager seriously: 'They laugh at you. People actually laugh in your face' ('Jayne', a 1990s band manager). The very 'maleness' of the music industry affects women musicians' opportunities and the general shape of their careers. The lack of women in positions of power within the music industry impedes their progress and curtails their numbers.

Backroom Boys

In the recording studio, all the creative and technical roles tend to be done by men. Under 'producers, engineers and programmers' in the British listings in the 1995 edition of *Kemps International Music Book*, there were 649 men and only 13 women (just under 2 per cent of the total). Whilst in 1996, at Red Tape Studios in Sheffield, only 1 per cent of applications for the sound engineering course were from women.

This absence of women in all the important technical roles has serious impli-cations for the career of the female musician because the producer, in particular, mediates between their music and the final commercial product, and since the advent of 'multi-tracking', the producer's role has become incomparably more creative. Indeed, some producers originate more musical ideas than the bands they work with. Sometimes, this may reduce the band to a vehicle for the pro-ducer's characteristic sound, which is privileged over all other aspects (such as lyrics and melody). It can therefore be seen how easily producers can come into conflict with bands. As nearly all producers are male, such conflict can, with women's bands, take on gender characteristics. In this way gender stereotyp-ing affects the innumerable musical and technical choices which must be taken during the recording process. The sound engineer, too, has tremendous power within the creative process of making a record, which can intensify conflict between musicians and technicians, which becomes an important issue when all-female bands are engaged in a struggle with male technicians.

Because of their socialization, young women do not often consider a career in sound technology, whereas boys think in terms of careers both as musicians and as producers (Tobler and Grundy 1982). The main route into production was traditionally via engineering, and most girls have not even considered that as a career choice. Thus, when at some stage a young woman does decide to try and get a job in a studio, she will be hampered if she lacks everyday technical skills which most young men have. As significantly, recording work does not com-bine easily with family life since producers and engineers typically work very long hours, sometimes doing fourteen hours of continuous recording at a stretch. Family life has to take second place so that for women the choice is a stark one between becoming a producer or having children. There is also straightforward prejudice against women, as Moira Sutton (the manager of Red Tape Studios, Sheffield) told me: 'One of the studios actually specifically said they wouldn't have women engineers or studio managers, because artists would feel that they couldn't behave naturally in front of them.'

Finally, if a woman does manage to overcome employer prejudice, and actually get employment in a studio, she will be viewed as an intruder. In the recording studio, men typically exert social control over women just as they do in other male-dominated worlds. Gender and sexuality can get in the way of a simple working relationship between equals (Whitehead 1976; Hearn and Parkin 1986). Sexist jokes abound. This masculinist culture helps to explain the rarity of women studio technicians and also poses problems for female musicians for whom entering a recording studio can be daunting. Alone on the studio floor, the musician's only contact with the world is a set of head-phones, through which she may be asked to redo her part dozens of times and yet not be told why. Lack of confidence may cause her to lose heart since a lack of technical knowledge and techno-jargon puts her in a position of relative powerlessness in a world where strange abbreviations abound. Furthermore, engineers, and even tape-ops, have been heard to make disparaging remarks about women's playing.

'ROBERTA' (1980s music tutor): Sound technology is controlled by men and a lot of men want to keep it for themselves. They don't take you seriously as a woman. Some men are fine but the situation is generally that you are liable, as a woman, to be given wrong information, misleading information. They're so possessive about it. Or, they just won't let you near it.

For these reasons, feminist musicians are concerned about the lack of women technicians, especially as a feminist all-women band with a male producer cannot claim that all the creativity which went into the record was female. Thus, there have been feminist initiatives to create all-women studios (like Ovatones, in London), and courses for women in sound engineering and production.

There is a career route within the studio. Typically, a young man interested in science and technology applies to become a tape-op, and then works his way up from there, via engineer to producer, following a sort of informal apprenticeship. Often women cannot get employment at the initial tape-op stage. This career progression, however, is not always followed as some people go straight into production without any training in studio technology, picking up technical information and skills from the engineers and technicians they have worked with. Such a route depends, of course, on having good relationships with these technicians, which may be difficult for a female producer hampered by gender prejudice. Typically, women enter production in other ways, for example via arranging, particularly of strings, perhaps because many have been classically trained on stringed instruments. However, the most popular route for women has been via self-production, this being the way Joni Mitchell, Carole King, Kate Bush, and Millie Jackson learnt their production skills.

Since the late 1980s more women have entered sound engineering and production because in areas of high unemployment women are availing themselves of state-funded vocational training schemes in sound engineering. Furthermore, there are some indications that changes in computer education in schools are making girls more confident about technology in general. Some schools have even built sound studios. According to Mandy, originally from Liverpool, a live sound engineer and bassist in indie band Ms45 (now the Slingbacks), this has had an effect in the north of England in the 1990s: 'When I left school and I went to work in a studio at 16, I didn't know one other female engineer . . . But now they're training you in school. In my school, the year after I left, they built a studio. It was an all-girls' school . . . I've got loads of friends who've gone into it now.' Moira Sutton says that she has noticed a recent improvement in girls' understanding of technical language: 'Education is improving the way they deal with technology in schools. *All* students do information technology. Whereas, we used to have school visits and you'd talk about a piece of equipment and the boys'd know exactly what it meant, and the girls would hang back . . . But, the women coming in here now, their technical vocabulary is equal with the boys.' Some female producers and engineers are becoming established and respected but such changes will only slowly have an effect on the relative numbers of women entering the musical-technical world.

On the Road

Sound, lighting, and road crews are, with few exceptions, male. When I was gigging in the 1980s, there were, as far as I could see, less than a dozen female sound engineers in the whole of Britain. That picture changed by the mid-1990s but there were still proportionately far fewer than men and they were still being treated as interlopers.

STEPH HILLIER (1990s live sound engineer): Being taken seriously is the main thing . . . most people think that I'm not doing this job for a living; that I'm somebody's girlfriend. The amount of times I've turned up at gigs and people have assumed I'm the girlfriend of somebody in the band or that I'm an accessory. And when you go up to the mixing desk they look at you like 'No way!' It's a look of complete disbelief most of the time.

Women who enter this field find themselves in an even more laddish environment than that of the recording studio. The masculinist subculture, rather than the physical demands of the work, limits women's involvement, and constrains their presence. The sexist jokes and sexual boasting (let alone actual sex) in the van create an uncomfortable atmosphere, and a woman's options in such robust male company are limited. If she ignores or accepts it, trying to become 'one of the lads', she is fighting an uphill battle since a woman can never really be one of the boys. If she, too, tells raunchy stories, they do not work in the same way, for a woman's place in the discourse of sexual relations is structured completely differently. Men behaving like this, regardless of the fact that a woman is present, are saying, 'This is a male club. You do not belong here, so you do not count.' A female sound engineer explained to me why she would not go on tour with a male band:

FRAN RAYNER (Jam Today): I'd probably be the only woman. It would just be horrific. There would be constant sexual bantering, and they'd immediately want to slot me [into a category]—I'd either be the tart who slept with them all, or I'd be a real prude because I wouldn't sleep with any of them. It's very sexist, the straight music business, and the blokes all think they're terribly strong and macho.

As these jobs are seen as endowing masculine status, if women start doing them, such status conferral will be undermined. Stories about life on the road are told with relish, romanticizing its hardness for ideological reasons since, if you can survive, you are a 'real man'.

On the road the most important role is that of live sound engineer as she or he has great influence over what the audience hears, and work shades over from the purely technical into the creative. At big gigs, what the band hears, the 'on-stage mix', or 'monitor mix', comes out of small on-stage speakers placed in front of the band, and is quite distinct from the sound issuing from the main speakers. Two separate sound engineers are involved in these operations. Thus the engineer doing the 'main mix' has enormous power, and, as the band cannot hear or evaluate what she or he is doing, a lot of trust is involved. A unique hidden effect of the male control of live sound is that almost all club PAs are set up with a vocal graphic equalizer (EQ—tone control) mixed for a male voice:

MANDY (Ms45): I used to do monitors all the time. So, when I set the EQ up for 'on-stage', I'd do it for me. 'Cause you're doing it off your own voice, whereas most of your engineers are male. So we don't sound so good on stage, because it's set for a man's voice. Because we have higher frequencies; they dip them all out, so we can't hear the top end of our voices.

During the 1970s and 1980s, sound engineers tended to ignore the instructions of women musicians, behaviour which was less often mentioned by my interviewees in the 1990s, as there has been an increase in the number of women doing sound engineering. In fact, there is some evidence that women these days are even getting into roadying. According to Debbie Smith, guitarist in Echobelly:

When I first started playing professionally, I was surprised to see that many university gigs have female crew, who'll go out and hump all the gear and put the PA together and all that. Especially around the Manchester area. When you go north of Manchester there's tons of girls in the crew all the time, which is really good.

Public Lives and Private Support: Wives, Girlfriends, and Mothers

Traditionally one way in which women gained access to the world of rock is through their relationships with male musicians. For a tiny minority, this has been the gateway to their own performing careers, although, for most, only one kind of activity has been expected of them, personal service. Women set out on rock-related careers of their own but, over time, many of them become just girlfriends and wives giving up their own musical careers in order to further their man's (Balfour 1986). Many women seem simply to retire from music upon marriage (Greig 1989; Dahl 1984; Gaar 1992). In contrast, men are aided in their careers by the unacknowledged, hidden, and taken-for-granted, private services carried out by the women in their lives who perform routine, unpaid, mundane domestic tasks, so as to enable their husbands and sons to concentrate on their careers. Male musicians, with their minds on 'higher things', are often assumed to need a woman to look after their daily existence.

In all the arts (except writing) the assumption has existed that only men are truly creative. Likewise, 'genius' is deemed to be an exclusively male attribute (Battersby 1989). Although there have been as many female as male art students, far fewer women have actually become career artists since they have married and ceased to be creative. 'Hilary', of a 1980s all-female Yorkshire pop band, never managed to become a musician until she left her husband:

> **I'd got this thing about wanting to play blues on the piano . . . I couldn't do it when I lived with him because he was a musician . . . That was his thing and I was just there to watch him. It was very significant that I didn't take it up until he'd gone. Because he was the creative one. We had different roles. I had the kids and he had his job and his guitar. It happened with painting as well, because I could really paint. And I gave that up to get married [and had kids] really soon after that. So I didn't have time to do anything . . . I gave college up to get married. And I stopped painting as well. I just stopped being creative . . . I got married and everything just stopped.**

Childcare does not usually affect the male musician since in the average hetero-sexual couple, the man's career usually comes first. Women are handicapped in their careers by the role they play in the family sphere, and nowhere is this general picture more true than in the world of rock.

Being a professional rock musician requires a greater dedication of time, energy, and concentration than most other careers, and, as money and recognition may be slow in coming, continuance in the career depends on the musician's unshake-able belief in his or her talent and the importance of what he or she is trying to do. On the other hand, expected to tailor their social lives so that they fit around their boyfriends' musical careers, the girlfriends of rock musicians are kept waiting for long periods of time, hanging around at the end of gigs. Judy Parsons (of the Belle Stars) vividly described to me her early experiences as a musician's wife:

> **You're part of the female scene—'the women'. And you've got 'the women's table'. There's the drummer's woman, and the guitarist's woman, and the bass player's woman. And you join the women's table. And you sit there, because they're up there playing for hours. And another thing that the women have to do is get the audience going. The band starts up and it goes down like a ton of lead, and there's no one dancing. Then the group's women have to get up and dance. . . . Every gig you get up and dance in a very loyal way. We knowingly had to make idiots of ourselves on behalf of the band.**

Terry Hunt (of Jam Today) recalled going to gigs with her boyfriend (in the distant past): 'I felt like a bit on the side—you're the lead guitarist's "chick", or something very insignificant. The musicians never took each other's girlfriends seriously.' Further examples of such gender constraints can be found in Kitwood (1980), Cohen (1991), and the biographies of male musicians. See, for instance, Connolly (1981) and Hunter Davies (1969) on the Beatles' wives. The implicit assumption is that nothing a young woman is involved in could be as import-ant as her boyfriend's career, and that her role is to service him, domestically, sexually, and emotionally, so that his special talent is able to flourish to its full capacity. Furthermore, the position of the girlfriends and wives of rock stars is often characterized by dependency and insecurity. The male star, besieged on tour by women, has greater power than his stay-at-home lady.

In stark contrast, the husbands and boyfriends of female musicians do not typically perform support and maintenance services for their partners, and rarely will men consent to being rock and roll widowers. Thus, touring poses more problems for female than for male performers (Archer and Simmonds 1986). Not only does a woman musician miss out by not having a wife, she will be expected to be someone else's. That women are faced with the choice of musical career, or marriage and family, comes out time and again in the biographies and auto-biographies of women musicians, and many of the professional musicians I interviewed were resigned to having no partner whilst pursuing their career.

Lastly, particularly in the past, the woman musician in a male band has often been expected to become the touring surrogate wife, cutting hair and sewing on buttons. There are instances of this cited in Dahl's oral history of jazzwomen (1984). But I also found a contemporary example on the English northern working men's club circuit:

DEE (of the vocal-dance group Every Woman): If you've got four men in the band and one girl, they might like you but they don't take you seriously. They take you seriously when you wash their clothes and you iron their shirts, make brews for them. . . . 'Dee, just iron the stage clothes for us'. For years and years. All the time. Every gig.

Female Consumers and Fans

CAROLINE APPLEYARD (of Treacle): I've never been a fan. I think it's sad. If you want to [play music], then do it yourself, don't try and get someone who is doing it. If you want that sort of lifestyle or whatever, do it for yourself.

Paradoxically, the 'male' music world is dependent on young female consumers, who, although traditionally despised by musicians and rock journalists, are essential for a band's success. Consumer and producer, fan and star: there is a symbiotic relationship between these roles. In written accounts, fans have been typically characterized as pathological and requiring special explanation as 'deviant behaviour', a perspective which has been challenged (Jenson 1992), for in some ways we are all 'fans'. Moreover, both Garratt (1984) and the Vermorels (1985) took issue with existing notions of the fan as passive victim and asserted the positive features of fanhood: 'courage, innovation and daring'. Nevertheless, although it is true that fans are not unthinking record-fodder, for all their adventurousness, they are still consumers and not producers of the music.

In the past, it was male stars (Elvis, the Beatles, the Bay City Rollers) who were notably idolized by female fans. Yet, as Garrett (1984) points out, the Ronnettes and Shangri-Las had some screaming female fans, too. During the 1980s there was an increase in potential female role models, Madonna's rise to stardom launching a national wave of 'wannabes', while in the 1990s a lot of young women in Britain have emulated Justine of Elastica and Louise Wener out of Sleeper.

However, the most significant influence by far has been that of a purely vocal group, the Spice Girls, who in 1997 across the UK are imitated by scores of groups with names like 'Nice'n'Spicy' and 'The Spicey Girls'. The group appears to have captured the imagination and allegiance of pre-teen girls, who identify with the message propounded that girls can take control, express their own sexuality as they wish, lead their own kind of life, and not be dominated by men. A chance to talk to the Spice Girls at the *Daily Star* office apparently crashed the phone system with 300,000 calls in one hour.

The marketing of boy vocal bands encourages girls to fantasize about romance and marriage.

GARY BARLOW (of Take That): **We all had girlfriends throughout the band, but we did our utmost to keep it out of the papers . . . our success was our fanbase—bands like Take That and Boyzone need that core of fans who will do *anything* for them. To build that fanbase they had to build a dream that they'd one day meet us and marry us, so we couldn't be seen to have girlfriends. (*Guardian*, 15 July 1996)**

In contrast, the Spice Girls (who call themselves feminists) encourage girls to do it for themselves. However, like Take That and Boyzone, the Spice Girls are a vocal and dance group, who do not play instruments and were chosen for their looks rather than their musical abilities, so that they cannot inspire young women to become instrumentalists in the way that Elastica might. Being a Spice Girls fan leads to dressing up, dancing, and singing (timeless female activities) but not to playing guitar, drums, or bass. The relative lack of females in this role means that it is more difficult for the girl fan to identify with the instrumental performer and make the essential imaginative leap of picturing herself up there, alongside or instead of her idol.

LOUISE HARTLEY (bass player in Kid Candy): **There's more girls stick as [*sic*] being fans because it's always been blokes in bands. It's always been more male bands and so, if blokes go to a gig, they'll see the band and think, 'I wanna be like the band'. Whereas, girls haven't got that role model and they've got a bigger step to actually go out and do it themselves.**

CHARLEY (guitarist in Frantic Spiders): **The boys are there wanting to be the star and the girls are there just wanting to meet them. And a lot of it is to do with the fact that most of the stars are men at the moment. When there are more women seen to be doing it, then you'll get the girls thinking, 'Oh, I could do that', rather than, 'I think I could go out with him'.**

Singers

The role of singer in popular music-making has been the obvious one for women who have, indeed, a special (rare) space in the professional world of rock as session vocalists, where they anonymously hold their own with (male) session instrumentalists. Nevertheless, this only serves to underline their structural exclusion as instrumentalists. Moreover, with female singers, traditionally, there has been an emphasis on appearance, image, and visual performance and a relative absence of analysis and discussion of vocal technique and the voice-as-instrument.

Within popular music (unlike, perhaps, opera), singing is seen as 'natural' or innate and women are believed to be naturally better singers. Women's singing is seen in contrast with the learnt skills of playing an instrument, a kind of direct female emotional expression, rather than a set of refined techniques. Even Billie Holiday's singing was discussed in terms of an emotional response to her life history of personal suffering, rather than in terms of learnt craft, an assumption which reinforces essentialist notions of biological difference between men and women. Thus it is that the girl vocal group tradition, from the Shirelles in the 1950s to Eternal, Shampoo, and the Spice Girls of the 1990s, has been undervalued, despite being 'the central female tradition within mainstream pop' (Greig 1989). In reality, singing is largely a learnt skill and some of the women I interviewed had had singing lessons; many regularly practised vocal exercises. Girls are encouraged to sing far more than boys, and consequently women generally sing better than men. (Many of my interviewees had sung in school choirs. It is doubtful whether a similar cross-section of male musicians would have done.) Women's musicianship, then, is hidden behind biologically reductionist assumptions.

The *female* voice is unreplicable. It is the only 'instrument' possessed solely by women which is why singing is one of the few rock spaces into which women have been allowed. On the whole, although male musicians see female instrumentalists as trespassers on their patch, they have respected women as singers and exploited their appearance as a 'front' for stage performance, for female singers have not threatened the overall hegemonic masculinity of rock. A woman vocalist in a skirt fronting a band seems perfectly normal and, indeed, 'natural'; whereas a woman in a skirt playing lead guitar or drums is often said to look strange or 'unnatural'. Thus, it does not, in a sense, matter how many women sing in bands, since, even if *all* singers in bands were female, rock itself would remain masculine. A woman does not challenge gender stereotypes by singing in the way that she does if she becomes, say, a drummer. Moreover, many women vocalists present a stereotypical feminine presentation of self, which thereby enhances the 'masculinity' of the male instrumentalists. Moreover, the singer's only 'instrument' is her body. This both confirms and reinforces the long-standing association of women with the body and nature which runs through our culture and contrasts with the image of men as controllers of nature via technology. As Lucy Green states, 'The sight and sound of a woman singing therefore affirms the correctness of the fact of what is absent: the unsuitability of any serious and lasting connection between woman and instrument, woman and technology' (1997: 29).

So much has singing been seen as a woman's place that female musicians have often been steered into it. In the 1950s and early 1960s there were quite a few all-women vocal groups in Britain. However, both the brief 'skiffle' craze and then the more sustained 'beat' music boom made purely vocal groups passé: you had to be able to play your own (electric rock) instruments. All over Britain boys banded together to form groups, whilst all the indications are that girls' skiffle and beat groups were exceedingly rare. Nevertheless, in the 1980s I discovered such a band, which had been consistently playing professionally since the early 1960s. Calling themselves the Intruders, because they were so clearly encroaching on male terrain, they signed to Decca, where there was a sustained campaign to mould them into the traditional girl-group image. Against their expressed wish, A&R changed their name to the Mission Belles, publicized them as 'the female Bachelors', got them to record other people's material rather than their own songs, did not allow them to play their instruments in the recording studio, and tried to get them to cease playing instruments altogether.

Although women's confinement to the role of singer was most obvious in pre-punk days, such pressures still exist. Some women join bands as instrumentalists but, due to competition from male band members and lack of confidence, gradually find themselves singing more and playing less, so that, after a while, the guitar, say, may merely function as a fashion accessory. The same is true in jazz (Dahl 1984.) Anna Power, long-standing member of various Nottingham bands, discussed this (in 1995) in terms of identity:

> A male musician, if he's a guitarist, say, then he'll be a lead guitarist and he'll carry on being a lead guitarist. But, because women are expected to be singers or backing vocalists, then a lot of women, rather than concentrate on what they're good at and going with that, will start thinking, 'I really wish I could sing'. So, I think the limitation on the options available to women in music also limits the way you can appreciate yourself for whatever you do that falls outside of that.

Gender works in other ways. There is nothing natural about the contemporary pop female singing voice, because there is nothing intrinsically natural about any kind of actual vocal expression, voices being governed by changing cultural rules and fashions and varying between genres. With vocals as with music, the record industry works with a set of categories into which it seeks to mould its performers, with the aim of controlling consumer choice (Frith 1983). Gender is inevitably a factor in this categorization process. The categories available for women are restricted, and women's music which cannot be fitted into these may be either rejected outright as unsuitable for signing or altered so that they do fit. Simon Frith furnished me with the example of Suzi Quatro, who was originally in a family group with her sisters, playing strip clubs. Her first record, however, presented her as a folk-singer, with a characteristic folk image. The producer of this record was Mickie Most, who had just produced Julie Felix. With later producers she changed her image yet again, although (like Madonna, Annie Lennox, and Bjork) Suzi Quatro was, apparently, always in control of these image changes. Many women performers in the past have had little influence over their image.

The traditional female classification of 'female folk-singer/singer-songwriter' has been a very conservative category, offering women little scope for experimentation. Because of the lack of role models, many have been packaged as folk, perpetuating the dominance of the female folk image, so that it is not surprising that many of my first batch of interviewees had, in their teenage years, aspired to become folk-singers, whilst very few had, even briefly, entertained the notion of playing rock. During the 1960s and 1970s, Joan Baez, Judy Collins, and, especially, Joni Mitchell acted as important role models for innumerable young women such as 'Brenda': 'I used to love Joni Mitchell, and I'd play her all the time. . . . It was the usual girl-syndrome, playing acoustic guitar. But you never think that you could play electric guitar.' My research suggests that, although the electric guitar is, in many ways, easier for the beginner to play, women guitarists have usually started on acoustic folk guitar. There are a number of possible reasons for this. With folk, you do not require an amplifier and there is no technology to understand. Because an acoustic guitar is light and easy to carry, you do not need a vehicle. A solo folk performer does not have to deal with complex band dynamics, and folk clubs are safer for women. Lastly, there are plenty of female folk-singer role models.[2]

At the very opposite end of the spectrum to folk is the phenomenon of the 'chick singer'. Women are valued in the industry for their glamour, and it is often fashionable to have a female 'fronting' bands, singing backing vocals, playing a bit of percussion and dancing. Thus, Mary Genis (of Dread Warlock) explained her choice of role to me in 1995:

One of the reasons why I decided to be a musician in a band, as opposed to a singer, was because you get taken a bit more seriously. No one takes singers seriously, even now, unless they're a big singer. As a musician, you're treated a little bit more respectfully. . . . Personally, I don't think enough women organize themselves beyond singing and dancing . . . because that's their role. We're all role-playing. So the women sing and dance and the men play the instruments. That's how it is.

As with the long-established clubs tradition and pre-war popular music (Vicinus 1979), physical attractiveness is more important than vocal talent. Whilst it is true that good looks have helped male performers become successful too, men have a wider range of images than is available to female stars. The star system, which is another record company strategy to secure profits (Frith 1983) by creating product loyalty and simplifying record promotion, leads to the objectification of performers, even those who start off as 'serious' musicians. However, there are more pressures on female performers to conform to certain 'right' images than there are on men who seem to have more freedom to play around with masculine stereotypes, such as 'macho', and 'androgynous'. The range of representations available to women is narrower, and women performers often seem trapped by images rather than utilizing them because the pressures on women are greater, reflecting the sexual objectification of women in society in general. Skin, lead singer in the successful 1990s band Skunk Anansie, emphasizes that:

[2] 'The only girl and women performers in either popular music or rock music were singers, and those rare exceptions who did play instruments did so in the way women have done for centuries: plucking strings or playing keyboards to accompany themselves in song' (Green 1997: 75).

> The minute that you are a female fronting a rock band, everybody looks at you sexually. Everybody takes a sexual perspective: do you fancy her, or do you not? I think that's how the industry looks at it. 'Oh, is she good looking? If she is, great. If she's not, Oh, we're not interested then.' The industry is a male-dominated 'laddy' industry and, as a female performer, there's still a lot to fight against. I think it's better now than it was five years ago, but there's still a lot of overtly sexist stuff that goes on.

The emphasis on glamour means that another space allocated to women is disco, Hi-NRG, Eurobeat, dance music, another genre in which they are vocalists rather than instrumentalists. Record companies who signed up all-female bands in the 1980s tried to slot them into this style, favouring a sort of 'girly' sound, emphasizing femininity and youth. Although Bananarama, the Belle Stars, and Amazulu came from completely different backgrounds, and played different types of music, they were made to sound very similar. Instead of doing their own numbers, they made lightweight remakes of old hits with all the emphasis thrown onto the vocals. Women who can sing in tune perfectly well have even been made to sound 'untogether' because it is how their company thinks a gang of 'girls' should sound.

> JUDY PARSONS (Belle Stars): The last two things we've done, we've never sung them before. We go up to the studio and we don't even know the songs. Two days before we go in we're told you'll be doing such and such tomorrow. And we're in the studio and no one knows it properly. And that's the sound they want us to have, that Bananarama untogether-girls-that-can't-sing, singing all different. And we do it.

When dealing with all-women bands, record companies automatically turn to production teams specializing in this type of 'girly' sound—Peter Collins, Jolly and Swain, Stock, Aitken, and Waterman—as happened in the 1960s when Phil Spector produced black female singing groups in which the vocalists became virtually interchangeable, the only constant being Spector himself. The difference in the 1970s and 1980s was that many of the women's bands which were treated in this way were, on signing, fairly autonomous, writing and performing their own compositions, and playing their own instruments. However, because companies have only had this one narrow category in their mind, all-women bands have been marketed as 'all-girl bands' regardless of the differences in age, outlook, and style of music.

Since the crucial moment of punk, however, women have been more directly challenging the sexism which lies behind the processes of marginalization and manipulation which I have described above. Female punk and post-punk vocalists, such as proto-punk Patti Smith, the Raincoats, and Poly Styrene confronted conventional vocal norms head-on, singing in an unconventional and often deliberately 'artificial' way, thereby challenging the very notion of the 'naturalness' of the voice. This was at one with their strategy on clothes, appearance, and image and influenced the use of the voice in grunge bands, Riot Grrrl outfits, and beyond. A similar challenge to the meaning of the female voice has been made by avant-garde singers such as Maggie Nicholls and Diamanda Galas.

Feminism and lesbianism have also had an effect on singers. Because conventional female pop songs usually presumed a male listener, women have been expected to sing in heterosexist terms for the male ear. Frith (1981) noted the variety of voices to be heard on the post-punk 'Making Waves' album of women's bands, the reason being that many of these bands were singing for other women, and thereby breaking the voice codes. There is, in the 1990s, a growing greater variety in women's voices. Images, too, have been more artfully utilized by confident female performers, Annie Lennox and Madonna developing the tactic of presenting a succession of images, in a playfully ironic postmodern way, as a means of avoiding the traditional image trap. Women vocalists have been successfully fighting for more control over their careers within the music industry. What is surprising, however, is the continuing absence of women instrumentalists. This is the issue that most concerns me and it is the one on which I shall now focus.

Instrumental Women

If asked, most people can come up with the names of a number of female singers from the pre-war era, the 1950s, the 1960s, and so on. However, they can rarely name any women playing drums, bass, or electric guitar during those decades, and, even if, like me, they know some names now, they would probably not have known them had they been living at the time. Looking back, the thing which seems so striking to me now is that, in those pre-feminist times, I never dreamed of questioning this seemingly complete absence of women instrumentalists. I now know that there were women musicians there; there have always been women musicians, but they have often been written out of history. For instance, there were women playing saxophones and all manner of traditionally 'male' instruments in the early years of the twentieth century, although their extent and importance were largely forgotten until feminist scholarship 'recovered' them (Dahl 1984; Placksin 1985). This lack of female role models meant that women growing up in the 1950s, 1960s, or early 1970s never considered playing as a possibility:

'BRENDA' (singer and guitarist in 1980s new wave band): I really wanted to [but] I never thought a woman could do it. So I forgot about it for years . . . I never actually decided, 'When I grow up I'm going to be in a rock band'. It's not something that I thought I would ever do.

MARY GENIS (Dread Warlock): As a child, I wanted to be the glamorous, glitzy-frocked, lipsticked, long-nailed Diana Ross type. I also used to see rock bands [but] the only women that were in bands played the tambourine or sang or did backing vocals. I wasn't aware of the shortfall of that. That was what women did. That was their role.

And this was even true of women who were already competent musicians. Candy, growing up in the early 1970s, fantasized about being married to Jimi Hendrix, but she also wanted to be a rock musician herself. Although she was a highly capable classical musician who could have been in a band from the age of 15, she was overawed and intimidated by the male musicians around her and, instead of playing with them, became their fan: 'It was me in a man's world, really. I just used to sit there and never say anything.'

Sadly, like female jazz bands before them (Dahl 1984; Placksin 1985), many of the early women pop/rock musicians and bands were seen as just a passing novelty and ridiculed and trivialized in the music press. Honey Lantree and Goldie and the Gingerbreads (in the 1960s), Fanny (in the early 1970s), and the Runaways (in the mid-1970s) were not taken seriously. Meanwhile, some female musicians who were important within the music industry, we never knew about at the time so that it was a revelation when I learnt about the role of American bassist Carol Kaye in the pop classics of my teenage listening years. Had I known then would I have taken up the bass?

Suzi Quatro, though viewed as male-manipulated, was probably the most important role model of the 1970s. As a raunchy bass player leading a boys' band, she was unique at the time. Suzi Quatro inspired other women rockers, like Joan Jett, and Chrissie Hynde. In turn, Hynde prompted Kat Bjelland and Nina Gordon to play. A few of my older interviewees named Suzi Quatro as their role model; a far larger number claimed Chrissie Hynde. Once punk got fully under way, the number of female instrumentalists increased dramatically and they inspired future generations of young women up to and including the 1990s. Those women in my sample who were teenagers in the late 1970s, 1980s, or early 1990s who later became musicians had far more female musician role models available. My younger interviewees variously mentioned: Chrissie Hynde, Siouxsie Sioux, Debbie Harry, Kate Bush, the Slits, the Au Pairs, Marine Girls, the Go-Go's, the Belle Stars, the Bangles, Bananarama, Alison Moyet, Annie Lennox, the Thompson Twins, Madonna, L7, Bjork, Polly Harvey, and Courtney Love.

DEBBIE SMITH (Echobelly): Susie Quatro was on *Top of the Pops* when I was about 5 and that was a huge revelation. I actually started playing bass guitar because of that, when I decided to play at around 14 . . . that was my huge second influence, I decided I wanted to *be* in Siouxsie and the Banshees. I actually taught myself by listening to their first album. I stayed in my bedroom for about 6 months and learnt. . . . 'Cause about that time I found a tape that had the Au Pairs and the Slits and all those New Wave or punk groups and I was really surprised, because on *Top of the Pops* all you got was Supertramp and Barbara Streisand and stuff. And I thought, 'There's different music out there. Excellent. And there are women in those groups who can play guitar, bass, drums. Right, I can do it as well.'

So far, all of the musicians I have named are reasonably famous and their life stories and place in the history of women's music-making have now been documented

Figure 1: Instrumental women of Oxford in the 1990s.

Left: Ali Smith of Diatribe at The Elm Tree, Oxford, 1995.

Middle: Katherine Garrett of the Mystics, The Zodiac, Oxford, 1996.

Bottom: Soul Devotion, The Chequers, Oxford, 1995. Caroline Scallon in the foreground.

(Steward and Garratt 1984; Gaar 1992; O'Brien 1995). Since doing my research, however, I have discovered others, not recorded in the history books because, although out doing gigs, they were ignored in the music press at the time. The feminist musicians I interviewed in the 1980s told me about the early 1970s women's bands: the Stepney Sisters, the London Women's Liberation Rock Band, the Northern Women's Liberation Rock Band, Fire and Water, the Cosmetics, and Bitch. Through my band's contribution to the 1981 all-female post-punk album *Making Waves*, I discovered the Mission Belles. How many others were there? Many of the women's bands playing in the late 1970s and in the early 1980s are likewise unrecorded. I have a list of fifty-two all-female bands from when I was gigging around the UK and few of them feature in the histories. Thus, in the very process of doing this research I have witnessed the way in which women musicians get lost to history. Given that one of the major reasons for the relative lack of female rock/pop/indie musicians has been the lack of role models, it is vital that those women who do play (and have played) are made visible to future would-be musicians, to inspire them and give them confidence.

OXFORD: A CASE STUDY

In the late 1970s, I became a guitarist in the Mistakes, Oxford's first all-women band. Initially, we had problems finding a woman drummer and, later, when she left (to join the Bodysnatchers and then the BelleStars), we had difficulty replacing her. We were forced to recruit a woman from London who was willing to relocate just to be in our band, which indicates how rare women drummers are. After the demise of the Mistakes I tried, in 1982, to set up another all-female band, but I could not find enough women musicians. Those few who did play were already in bands so, in the end, I joined a short-lived women's band in Coventry, where despite advertising they had been unable to find a female guitarist. This was Coventry's first all-women band. When this band folded I set up a mixed band in Oxford where, although I found a female keyboard player, there simply were no guitarists, drummers, or bass players available. However, it was easy to recruit male musicians. So, from 1978 to 1985 I was thus immersed in the Oxford music scene, yet, in spite of gigging regularly, going to other bands' gigs, and socializing with local musicians, I met hardly any other female instrumentalists.

In 1985 I decided to systematically scan the local music scene to see if there had been any changes. I went to a succession of local gigs, talked to musicians, sound engineers, music journalists, and organizers of local events, including the city council. I only found eleven women who played instruments in local bands. In the local Oxford branch of the Musicians' Union there were 149 male and 35 women members. Thus 19 per cent of the membership was female but, of those 35, most would be classical musicians. In March 1988, no longer playing local gigs, I wondered if things had changed. Dave Newton, the editor of Oxford's music paper *Local Support*, summed up the situation: 'I reckon there's probably one hundred regularly gigging bands in Oxford. . . . But probably no more than

10 per cent of the musicians are women and they're nearly all vocalists. Less than half the bands have some females in them and then it's usually one woman at the most.' This would mean that in Oxford itself there were about 400 to 500 rock band members and, of these, only 40–50 were female. Thus, there were still probably only about 10 to 15 female instrumentalists in Oxford bands.

In the spring of 1995, with the help of musicians, editors of local music magazines, sound engineers, and promoters, I again took a social snapshot of the local music scene. Oxford had about 200 rock bands out gigging, which meant somewhere between 800 and 1,000 rock musicians. There were only twenty-six women in local rock bands, of whom only nineteen played instruments (seven of these female instrumentalists were in Oxford's two all-women bands, both part of the local 'indie' scene). Thus, women still formed only less than 5 per cent of local band musicians. Surprisingly then, despite an increase in absolute numbers, there has been no change in relative terms. This scarcity of female musicians can be illustrated by the experience of all-girl indie band Beaker, who, in 1994, spent nine months trying to find a female bass player, before taking on a guitarist who had to learn the instrument from scratch. Similarly, Death By Crimpers had all met at Oxford Brookes University in the early 1990s when there were lots of male bands but, as for females, 'we were the only ones'.

THE UK

However, what of the national scene? Unfortunately, there are very few secondary sources available on this question, either in Britain or the USA, and no national statistics. Leigh and Frame (1984) note the absence of women in the Liverpool beat bands of the 1960s. Sara Cohen (1991) found very few women musicians in Liverpool, the percentage being, if anything, lower than in Oxford. Ruth Finnegan (1989) found that in Milton Keynes 1982–3, out of 125 rock musicians only eight were female (6 per cent).

With the Mistakes I travelled around the country and performed hundreds of gigs, as far apart as Brighton and Newcastle. In most places there were no all-women bands at all. Indeed, one of the reasons why our band had so many gigs was the sheer absence of women's bands who could play danceable music at all-women bops. Other all-women bands told me of their problems in finding women musicians. One famous band advertised nationally for a female drummer and had only four female applicants, the same number of women applying to another band's advert for a bass player. Some bands, unwillingly, compromised on the all-female agenda and brought a man in.

When I started my research, in 1981, non-musicians were always telling me that there were plenty of all-women bands, a misapprehension based merely on having seen one or two women's bands on television, so I decided, in 1982, to compile a list of women's bands in England. My total was fifty-one all-women bands—fewer than the number of male bands in a small city. For comparison, in 1984, 14 per cent of the total national membership of the Musicians' Union was female. Thus, again, this would imply that Oxford was fairly typical.

Has the picture changed in the 1990s? A spate of books on women and rock has been published, leading to the impression that the days of male-domination in British rock are over. There certainly have been some important changes, not only in the prominence and success of women musicians but also in the way these new young performers choose to present themselves, challenging taken-for-granted gender stereotypes, both in the playing of instruments and in their interaction with audiences. However, I believe that the recent female invasion of rock has been exaggerated. Nearly twenty years ago, punk brought a wave of all-women bands in its wake, although their history has been largely forgotten. At the turn of the 1980s when there was a sudden flurry of media interest in 'women and rock', just as there is now, it seemed that we were on the edge of a breakthrough. Nevertheless, the reality is that in the late 1990s, the proportion is still small and the whole rock-and-roll world remains overwhelmingly male. (This can also be illustrated by looking at women's representation in the media. See Appendix 1.)

Some cities have one or two all-women bands; some have none. I was told that several Nottingham women's bands had advertised for an instrumentalist for a year and a half before anyone phoned up. When my band was gigging in Brighton at the beginning of the 1980s, I knew of only one all-women band there. Later in the 1980s, there was still only one all-women band. In 1995 likewise there was just one: Tampasm. Indeed, when Tampasm were forming (in 1992), they advertised in a music shop for a girl drummer and girl bass player and they had to carry on advertising for over a year.

On the other hand, some of my 1995 interviewees in the north of England reported a recent increase in young teenage girls playing electric instruments. Sara Watts (of Treacle): 'There are so many little 14-year-old girls that can play guitar now. When I was 14 the girls that had learnt to play classical had dropped it. For years, in Sheffield, I was the only female guitarist and now there's hundreds. Right up until probably the last twelve months, I've never known another female guitarist. Now you go into the pub and there's loads all around you.' Moira Sutton (manager of Red Tape Studios, Sheffield) told me that all the young teenage daughters of her friend were in bands: 'Maybe they'll all peter out . . . but I think critical mass will be there in 10 years.' We shall see.

Overall, women's presence in popular music has increased only a little during the last decade and, as in the past, the clear majority of female performers are vocalists. Shampoo and the Spice Girls have achieved worldwide fame and financial success as female singing groups, but there are still hardly any commercially successful British female bands where the women play all the instruments. On the other hand, there has been, over the last decade, an increase in the number of women in bands, including ones which have just one woman playing an instrument (such as Pulp) and where a woman is both playing and doing some vocals (such as the Telstar Ponies). The numbers have increased of mixed bands in which women are powerful and important in terms of songwriting, instrumentation, arranging, and so forth (such as Echobelly and Lush). There are also more of what are usually called 'female-fronted' bands, which can mean that the woman is just in the traditional role of singer and decorative frontperson, or she is a powerful and creative force within the band (such as Skunk Anansie). Furthermore, in the 1990s more women are 'fronting' bands with a guitar in their hands rather than a microphone, and, outside the bands which are visible nationally (in the music press and on TV), there are far more all-women bands and mixed bands lower down the career structure, playing in local pubs and clubs around Britain. In terms of acoustic music, women's presence has been growing, and there has also been a phenomenal increase in the number of women in the African Caribbean community playing steel pans.

Because the success of Elastica, in particular, has made it now more fashionable to have a woman in a band, there seems to be less automatic exclusion of girls by teenage boy musicians and there are now adverts in music shops and papers asking for female guitarists for boys' bands.

SARA WATTS (of Treacle): There's a lot of bands now playing on the fact that if you get a female in the band you look right on. I can honestly say that, because a lot of male bands are advertising now 'female guitarist required'. I don't know why. Obviously when you did [your 1980s research into] female bands there were even less, but when we started we thought 'yeah, there's no female bands'. And just recently they've started to come out. I think [Elastica] are getting more females into it.

Fashions being what they are, it is possible that having a woman in the band may no longer be 'the thing' in a few years time. Liz Naylor (former PR and manager of a record label) is cynical: 'the current thing about having girls in bands will probably pass over, and next it could be about having a disabled person in your band . . . perhaps Asians will be the new tokens' (Cooper 1995). By then, however, there may be a lot more young women out there playing and, in turn, acting as role models for other young women, so I am more optimistic about the future than Liz Naylor, but it will take time to work through.

In sum, *absolute* numbers of female band musicians are greater: we see more women playing instruments. On the other hand, my study of Oxford, my 1996 music media survey (see Appendix 1), and my recent immersion in the music world leads me to the conclusion that there has not been much of a *relative* increase in numbers, for the numbers of male musicians and all-male bands has also risen. The proportion which women make up in the instrument-playing part of the rock world is, by my estimates, less than 15 per cent. Likewise the rock and indie audience is still disproportionately male, in terms of both the audience for rock programmes and the consumers of the more serious music papers.

At the pop end of the spectrum women are present in greater strength than in rock/indie, although they are still a minority (about 25 per cent of all performers) and mainly vocalists and also young. It was quite notable in 1988 that such female performers as Tiffany and Debbie Gibson were the object of much scorn in the 'serious' music papers and the butt of endless jokes. They, and the young girls who bought their records, were denigrated as 'bubblegum rock' and 'teeny-bop fodder'. Some men, like Rick Astley, fell into this category. However most did not, whereas most females did. To be 'laddish', like Status Quo or, in the 1990s, the 60Ft Dolls (one of whom boasted of excreting on the chest of a female fan) has been admired, whereas to be 'girly' (like Bananarama in the 1980s, and like Shampoo, Crush, and Fluffy in the 1990s) was seen as silly, scatterbrained, 'bubbly', and stupid. Such female performers were more likely to be viewed as 'puppets' for male producers (like Stock, Aitken, and Waterman), whether or not this is actually the case. Packaged by the record companies in this way and pushed by the press into a narrow feminine category, these bands were perceived as no threat to the male musical club.

In the 1990s, 'laddism' and 'yob rock' became highly fashionable, arguably as part of the 'backlash' against feminism. With, for example, the launch of *Loaded* magazine, some women (such as Cerys Matthews of Catatonia, Shirley Manson of Garbage, and Louise Wener of Sleeper) were labelled 'ladettes' or 'new lasses'. Late night TV programmes such as *The Girly Show* and *The Pyjama Party* have epitomized this trend, with women showing that they can talk in as sexually an objectifying way about men as men can about women. This has also spread to teenagers' magazines, like *Sugar*. The Spice Girls, a girl-group manufactured by males to be equivalent to 'boy bands' such as Take That, Boyzone, and Upside Down, can also be seen as 'new lasses'. Nevertheless, they seem to have had a genuinely empowering effect on young female fans with their simple individualistic message of 'Girl Power'. Moreover, perhaps because of their phenomenal success, they have been treated more respectfully by the rock press.

What is central, however, for female would-be instrumentalists is that women are rarely discussed as musicians in their own right, in terms of playing an instrument, composing, and arranging. Musicianship is not featured at all in girls' magazines or in the lightweight music publications. It is covered more in *Melody Maker*, and *NME*, but rarely are women interviewed or analysed in these terms, which reflects the way in which the press has generally treated women (i.e. trivializing them, and dealing with them solely in terms of their physical attractiveness) (see Appendix 1). They are not expected to be able to play an instrument and, if they do, it is not mentioned. For instance, Louise Wener is the driving force and principal songwriter in a band where all the other members are boys, yet journalists have concentrated on her gender and ignored the rest. She says,

> I think the thing that seems to antagonise a lot of the press is that I do most of the writing; that pisses them off in some way. What really cheeses me off is that journalists might ask me about the lyrics but they always ask the guys about the music. It's as though they can't take the idea of a woman with a guitar seriously; they can't believe I'm capable of doing it and so it must be down to the blokes. (*Select* May 1996)

Likewise, Courtney Love told Amy Raphael: 'I get asked about lyrics all the time, but not about the fact that I put a lot of fucking thought into using a Vox AC30 amplifier. . . . But no-one ever asks about the music' (*Guitar World*, November 1995). The exception to this situation is where, rarely, a woman instrumentalist is interviewed in one of the specialist trade magazines such as *Guitar World* or *Making Music*, which are the only sources of information about how women play their instruments. Meanwhile, singing is rarely discussed as a musical skill and female vocalists are not interviewed on how they learnt their technique.

My evidence shows that women are still in a clear minority within all the various (sub)worlds of electric popular music, being outnumbered by men even as vocalists. However, it is when we look at the playing of instruments that women's absence is most notable. Moreover, this pattern has been established for so long that it is taken for granted and rarely commented upon, let alone examined. In the ensuing chapters I shall address my central question: Why have there been so few women playing instruments in bands?

Typical gender distribution of social roles in the popular music world

FEMALE	MALE
singer	instrumentalist
backing vocalist	manager of band
fan	live sound engineer
groupie	technician (guitar tech, drum tech, etc.)
girlfriend	roadie
wife	lighting engineer
mother	driver
dancer	rigger
	road manager
	music press photographer
	buyer for retail chain
	sales rep
	promoter
	plugger
	club DJ
	music press journalist
	radio DJ

RECORD COMPANY	
receptionist	company executive
secretary	A&R director
personal assistant	A&R manager
publicity officer	talent scout
member of sales team	sales executive
member of marketing	team marketing director
packer	
cook	
cleaner	
'tea lady'	
factory worker	

RECORDING STUDIO	
receptionist	studio manager
	producer
	sound engineer
	tape operator
	technician
	programmer

2 Constraints

Subcultural theorists (Hall and Jefferson 1976) took for granted young people's ability to choose what to do in their leisure time, and thus merely addressed the question of how their choices should be interpreted. In contrast, Frith (1983) argued that different leisure patterns are a reflection, not so much of different values, as of the different degrees of opportunity, restriction, and constraint that are afforded to different individuals and social groups. A particular leisure pursuit may be made easy or difficult for an individual according to their social structural position, gender (along with class, 'race', etc.) being one aspect of such societal location. Frith's argument was that, for everyone, leisure, consumption, and style involve a relationship between choice and constraint. I wish to argue that such constraints are crucial to the explanation of women's absence from rock. I shall be considering the degree to which gender operates within the different social classes. One thing which stands out, however, is the extent to which girls and young women in *all* social classes and ethnic groups are restricted in their leisure pursuits compared to boys/young men. It is important to note that there are both material and ideological constraints in operation. In reality, of course, these two are closely interrelated. (For instance, lack of access to equipment is an important material constraint, but one of the reasons for its denial is ideological.) However, for the sake of analytical clarity I shall endeavour to separate them.

Material Constraints

A rock band needs equipment, transport, money, time, and a practice space. Women, compared to men, have less access to each one of these material factors and are therefore at a serious disadvantage in getting a foothold on the first stage of the rock music career.

MONEY

Despite widespread myths, the gender gap in average earnings has stayed fairly constant in real terms since 1971. Because of the persisting sex segregation of occupations and 'deskilling', equal pay legislation has made little difference so that, in the 1990s, women in both manual and non-manual occupations earn, on average, about half as much 'independent' gross income as men and in most heterosexual couples the male partner earns more than the female (*Social Trends* 26, 1996). In 1992, the gross monthly earnings of female non-manual workers were on average only 54 per cent of a man's, compared to nearly 70 per cent in Germany and 66 per cent in France. There is a larger proportion of women at the lower end of the pay range than men, and far more women than men live in poverty, including large numbers of separated women living with their children. Whilst at school, adolescents have three sources of money: pocket money from parents; wages from part-time jobs; and gifts from family and friends. Children spend far less money on themselves than their parents spend on their behalf and a parent is less likely to purchase a drumkit for a daughter than a son. Under 18, earnings do not vary much between girls and boys, but after 18 there is a marked gender differential (Department of Employment, *New Earnings Survey*, 1988). Moreover, market researchers Fisher and Holder (1981) found that in their large and statistically representative sample twice as many boys as girls had a part-time job and that, therefore, the boys were better off. Schoolgirls had to rely mainly on pocket money—to buy clothes, make-up, bus and train fares, club and disco entrance fees, and drinks—which left little for a set of strings, let alone a guitar. Playing in a rock band is a fairly expensive hobby. Costs include: the purchase of instruments and ancillary equipment, strings, drumheads, repair bills, transportation, hire of rehearsal space, etc. and the more you get into playing the more aspirations rise and the more costs escalate. My argument is that women are less able to afford these outgoings.

EQUIPMENT

AIMEE STEVENS (of Frances Belle): I always had ideas of being in a band, but I never had the opportunity of doing anything about it, really. In the back of my mind I'd always wanted to do something like that. But where would you get electric guitars from, and things like that?

Young women typically lack access to rock equipment because parents and schools do not provide it and girls lack the money to purchase their own. Moreover, where equipment is, sometimes, provided (for example, at youth clubs) boys tend to take it over. The reason for this is that instruments are gender stereotyped. Studies show that both musicians and non-musicians share a sexual classification scheme, in which, for example, drums and most horns are seen as men's instruments, whilst flute, violin, and clarinet are seen as women's instruments (Dahl 1984; Green 1997). This was also Hannah Collett's experience: 'I think boys are more into brass, to be honest. Yeah, and girls are more into violins and cellos.' This stereotype is confirmed by children's books in which boys, but not girls, are often seen playing the trumpet. Indeed, instruments have often been portrayed anthropomorphically as 'Felicity the flute', 'Tubby the tuba', and so on. Because they are classified as 'male', parents, teachers, and male peer groups deny girls access to rock instruments.

> **TERRI BONHAM** (Frances Belle): That's another thing about parents. They think that you're going to be 'hard' as well. They want you to be girly. They think as soon as you say 'electric guitar', 'No, that's for boys'. They think you're going to change, as well. . . . I think my mum would just prefer me to play the violin because it's feminine and she says, 'You've had all these classical chances, we've paid for you to do this, and now you go and play that noisy instrument.' Things like that.

The following quotation is taken from an interview which I conducted after a music workshop.

> **'CHRISTINE'** : The girls had tambourines and did all the singing and the boys played the drums. Girls played the glockenspiel. It was a jingly sound and they thought that was feminine. I would have liked to have a go [at the drums] but I didn't, because girls don't do those things. . . . Girls don't have a chance. We're not introduced to these things.

TRANSPORT

Because young women are less likely to own a car than are men they will be dependent on someone else (often parents) for their physical mobility. This is particularly the case for girls living in rural areas: 'Parents. That's how we'd get around. . . . It was the only way we could, because there are no buses at nights' (Terri Bonham). Frances Belle were lucky. Adolescents rely greatly on their parents transporting them to and from their various leisure activities but parents are less likely to approve of their daughter's involvement in a rock band than in dancing classes or a swimming club. Lack of money and transport forces many women to rely on men, boyfriends being used for lifts and the loan of equipment, a dependency which gives considerable power to the men in such relationships. Here we have in microcosm the situation in the wider society: women's lack of material resources creates their lack of social power.

SPACE

In general, in our society, women (especially working-class ones) have less access to space than men. They take up a smaller physical area by the way they sit and use their bodies and there are fewer 'female' spaces.

Lack of Private Space

Schoolgirls, or young women living at home, are unlikely to have much space, yet they often cannot afford to move out. Louise Hartley (Kid Candy): 'When we do gigs I have to borrow amps, because I haven't got room in the house for any. At home, I can't make a lot of noise. My parents like silence and I really don't have the space.' Working-class girls are allowed less space than their brothers within the home (Leonard 1980), which makes parents' attitudes crucial. How far will they allow the living room to be taken over by the noise and clutter of rock? Once married, the husband may have a study or workshop, but the wife's space is often defined as 'public'—the kitchen, the bedroom—and invaded by husband and children. Women with pre-school children are most tied to the home. How would such women meet others with whom to organize a band? And if they did meet them, how would they be able to arrange their lives in order to be able to rehearse and do gigs?

Exclusion from Public Space

Provision and use of public spaces reflects the inequality of leisure between men and women. So-called 'public' space is actually dominated by men, as is first learnt at school, where the boisterous activities of boys monopolize the playground and force girls to the edges, in a similar way to which they marginalize girls within the classroom and claim the greater part of the teachers' time. Likewise, boys dominate parks, sports facilities, and open spaces. Thus, it is no surprise that when music-making facilities are on offer at schools and youth clubs these are also controlled by young males. Girls are hesitant, embarrassed, feel out of their depth, and need positive encouragement from a committed teacher or youth worker who understands these gender dynamics, as was stressed to me by a number of women who have been involved in running music workshops and projects. (Lucy Green's (1997) research shows that music teachers still typically perceive girls to be musically inferior to boys, a fact which must surely translate itself into expectations and create a self-fulfilling prophecy.) It is not that girls are generally less confident in their lives. For instance, girls are more confident about singing and dancing than are boys. Playing supposedly masculine instruments works to undermine their femininity and this is why they feel unsure of themselves. Rosemary Schonfeld who has taught many music workshops over the years said, 'Women tend to be far less confident musically. . . . The first thing men want to do is impress. They want to bash the drums. It doesn't matter if they make a terrible sound. They've got the confidence and they just make a racket and prove themselves.' Leila, working at the West London Women's Music Project, told me, 'Music facilities in youth clubs are nearly always dominated by boys. There's a lot of facilities available in community halls, community centres, that's supposedly available to mixed groups but it's dominated by men. It just doesn't work.' Likewise, the space in which rock music is situated is male-dominated, music shops affording a particularly interesting example. Although some male musicians have told me that they feel anxious trying out equipment, the fact that both customers and assistants are overwhelmingly male means that music shops are their preserve, and, therefore, boys are more at home than girls. In any of these shops you can observe the assertive way in which young males try out the equipment, playing the beginning of a few well-known songs time and again, loudly and confidently, even though this may be the sum total of their musical knowledge. Young women, however, typically find trying out equipment a severe trial. Because they are scared of showing themselves up and being patronized or 'put down' by the assistants, they are inhibited in what they perceive to be a 'male' arena. Nearly all of my interviewees, in both the 1980s and the 1990s, had these feelings:

LOUISE HARTLEY (Kid Candy): I always think they're gonna laugh at me for some reason. I hate them. . . . There's a massive guitar shop in Birmingham called Music Exchange and the guys who work in there just love themselves. They strut around. And if you walk in and try and buy something, they'll ignore you and you have to beg for their help. . . . There's no women work there, either. It's all male guitarists with long hair and tight trousers.

AIMEE STEVENS (Frances Belle): I feel very intimidated. Especially going to ask—they're all stood behind the counter, these massive metal blokes. Well, that's what they look like, judging by their image. I go up and go, 'Can I have a top E string?' because I don't know the proper names or anything, so it's even worse. And they go, 'What gauge? What sort?' And I'm like, 'I don't know'. So I don't like going in and looking at guitars or anything in music shops. . . . When you're trying they're just staring at you. If you don't know much as well—and then they pick it up and go [imitates complicated guitar playing] and you're going, 'Oh no, I'll just take that.'

Whilst experienced players related tales of condescension and patronization.

FRAN (Sub Rosa): You go in and all the blokes are sitting in one corner talking about some riff that they came up with last night, totally ignoring you. They are very patronizing. They see that you're a woman and they think, 'How did you dare come in our music shop?'

More than one interviewee told me that, if a woman guitarist goes into a shop with a man, the assistants tend to talk to the man not the woman, even if the man is not actually a guitarist. Whilst Delia (of Mambo Taxi) confessed that she adopts the strategy of pretending to know less than she does because then the assistants are more helpful.

Frith (1983) argued that leisure in general is perceived to be a male preserve, the 'private' realm of the home being a female domain. He argued that girls, especially in the working class, spend far more time inside the home than do boys, and that they are more closely integrated into family life. Whereas boys, encouraged to model themselves on their fathers, spend more time outside the home. This means that girls are less likely than boys to go to gigs, and even less likely to become members of rock bands.

However, the main way in which women's leisure is controlled by men is through the fear of violence. Empirical research since the late 1970s has shown the prevalence of actual physical and sexual violence, harassment, and verbal abuse.[1] Sexual violence is an omnipresent possibility that affects all women, regardless of class, age, or ethnic group, because more than actual attacks, fear of

---

[1] Dobash and Dobash 1980; Binney, Harkell, and Nixon 1981; Hanmer and Saunders 1983, 1984; Hall 1985; rhodes and McNeill 1985; Stanko 1985; Hanmer and Maynard 1987; Hanmer and Saunders 1993; Hester, Kelly, and Radford 1996.

violence is a crucial constraint on women's freedom, limiting what they can do, where they can go, when, and who with. Research shows that although, in fact, men are more likely to be the victim of (other men's) violence, women *fear* attack far more than men do (Stanko 1987) and teenage girls experience greater fear in public places and specifically of men than teenage boys do (Goodey 1995). Male violence is the number one fear of women today in both the UK and USA (Segal 1990). Over 50 per cent of women feel unsafe when walking home at night compared to only 16 per cent of men and rape is the crime which most worries women in their teens and twenties in England and Wales (British Crime Survey 1994, reported in *Social Trends* 26, 1996).

Although, in reality, women are far more likely to be attacked in their home and by someone they know, research has shown that large numbers of women are afraid to go out alone at night. Indeed, concern about violence determines the leisure patterns of women, especially after dark and where transport is poor (Green, Hebron, and Woodward 1987 and 1990). Public space—the streets, the bus, the tube, the train—are viewed as alien, hostile (male) space. A 'continuum of violence' (Kelly 1988) ranges from the rare (murder) to the routine and common (flashing, the muttering of obscenities, kerb crawling, etc.) and the less serious acts, such as jokes and unwanted touching, can be a powerful reminder of the most serious (Halson 1989; Benokraitis 1997). Even when driving a car the majority of women fear being attacked and more than a quarter of women will not drive alone at night on motorway or country roads (survey by car rental firm Cowrie, quoted in *Everywoman*, March 1996). Many women become totally dependent on men (husbands, boyfriends) for lifts or protective company (Hanmer and Saunders 1983, 1984; Radford 1987), which in turn becomes another form of social control. In Hanmer and Saunders' study, for instance, one-third of urban women aged 16 to 30 never went out alone at night. Furthermore, police advice is often, effectively, a curfew for women, and the whole of West Yorkshire was declared to be unsafe for women for a period of six years while the Yorkshire Ripper was at large. Public space belongs largely to men and women require male approval in order to inhabit it (Radford and Russell 1992).

Women have to invest thought and energy into making themselves feel safe when out at night: walking a certain way, avoiding catching strange men's eyes, crossing over the street to check if they are being followed, making sure they are not alone with a strange man in a railway carriage, carrying keys in their hands before reaching house or car, not parking in underground or multi-storey car-parks. Avoidance procedures are learnt from early adolescence. As women also have to be careful what they wear (for fear of 'provocation'), many female musicians feel that they have to change clothes to get to and from the venue. Sixteen-year-old Charlotte Clark usually travels to and from the gig by bus in her stage clothes (a see-through lace dress) and this has been a very scary experience. Thus, women live under a partial curfew that men find very difficult to understand as, although they are more at risk from violence than women, men are rarely killed simply because they are men. The fact that *some* men sexually attack women means that public spaces *become* male terrain:

Nearly all aspects of the everyday lives of women and girls are affected by the fear, the reality of men's sexual violence . . . Experience of being assaulted or reading about women being assaulted can keep women locked in their homes in the evening, which effectively imposes a curfew on women. . . . The minimum effect of all this experience—from some of which no woman is immune—is to undermine our confidence and restrict our movements. It is a substantial reason why women are apparently cautious about strange territory and new experience. (rhodes and McNeill 1985: 6)

If the world of leisure poses threats for women, that is particularly true of pubs. This phenomenon has been most fully explored by Valerie Hey, who states that public houses have never actually been public for women, but are 'male "play-grounds" to which women are "invited" on special terms' (Hey 1986: 3). Women who go to pubs alone risk being the subject of endless sexist joking, intrusive staring, and being pejoratively labelled. In her study of rural Herefordshire, Whitehead argued that women are objectified and used as cultural counters in an ongoing competition between men to prove their masculinity and virility. Men aggressively defend pubs as their own terrain and attempt to control women who enter them, using tactics ranging from sexual innuendo to physical attack: 'The situations range from quite gentle reciprocal teasing between individuals, to more hostile and boisterous teasing between gender groups, and even more overtly hostile and physically abusive attacks on individual women by groups of men. These more overtly hostile elements should not be separated from the ambivalence being more generally signalled by joking' (Whitehead 1976: 179). Abuse, overt and covert, has been documented in a wide range of male-dominated institutions such as work organizations (Hearn and Parkin 1986; Cockburn 1991) schools (Jones and Mahoney 1989; Walkerdine 1990), and youth centres (Nava 1984).

Sexism appears to be an important feature of male bonding, where denigration of girls and women is a crucial ingredient of camaraderie in male circles. The masculine tradition of drinking and making coarse jokes usually focuses on the 'dumb sex object', the 'nagging wife' or, more derogatively, 'horny dogs' and 'filthy whores'. Learning to be masculine invariably entails learning to be sexist: being a bit of a lad and being contemptuous of women just go 'naturally' together (Lees 1993: 31).

In general, then, it can be argued that male domination of leisure space, coupled with the dual standard of sexual morality, operates to exclude women from the world of rock. In particular, male control of drinking places has particular relevance for young women and rock, for pubs are the most common venue for gigs.

TIME

Women typically have to choose between motherhood and a career. This holds true for women in all types of work but is, I would argue, particularly problematical in the world of rock where the long and unsociable hours and the incessant touring militate against an easy combination of career and personal life. It is difficult for a woman to combine a career in rock with domestic labour, unless the partner is also a musician and in the same band.

Women have less free time than men because of their domestic role. Those working full-time in Great Britain spend eight hours more per week than their male counterparts on cooking, shopping, and housework (*Social Trends* 26, 1996). At weekends, men in full-time employment have around two hours a day more free time than their female counterparts. If there are children, the load of housework carried out increases. There is also childcare itself, as distinct from the extra amount of washing, cleaning, and cooking which children create, so that, typically, in our society, the woman has total (or major) responsibility for childcare and associated domestic labour which reduces women's free time by twice as much as men (*Social Trends* 26, 1996). She may also have a full-time or part-time job. Given the inestimable number of hours tied up in this way, it is apparent why large numbers of women are not in rock bands.

Young women, living at home with their parents, are expected to do house-work. McRobbie (1991), Leonard (1980), Kitwood (1980), Fisher and Holder (1981), and Lees (1986) found that working-class girls did far more housework than their brothers. Although some recent research indicates that boys are be-ginning to do some housework (Reay 1990), it is clear that the activity is still seen as 'feminine' in our society and that girls still do more of it than boys (Gaskell 1992; Jowell 1992; Sharpe 1994). If there are younger brothers and sisters in the family (and especially if it is a single-parent household), the girl will have a crucial role to play in childcare and babysitting whilst her mother is out at work (Sharpe 1994). Girls in such a position are tied to the house, particularly in the evenings, when gigs and practices are scheduled. The greater numbers of mothers working in the 1990s and increasing number of single-parent house-holds means that more girls are trapped in this situation. Research for the Health Education Authority found girls in all social classes complaining that they were expected to do housework whilst their brothers were not (Brown 1995). This came out in my research, too. Hannah Collett (of Frances Belle) told me that she did 'loads' of housework: 'I hoover a lot and have to wash up all the time.' But her brother was treated differently: 'Like, my mum has actually paid him sometimes to do it, which I found distressing.'

Kitwood (1980) argued that middle-class youth experience more leisure con-straints than do the working class. Far more middle-class young people stay on at school to do 'A' levels, many with the intention of going on to higher educa-tion. Middle-class girls (and boys) worry about their exams, and much of their time and energy goes into their school work so that they cannot invest as much of themselves into hobbies. Middle-class parents expect their children to do a lot of homework and therefore restrict the amount of time they are allowed out of the house. They are expected to get back early at night so as to get a good night's sleep to prepare them for school. Kitwood points out that economic dependency makes these young people more likely to conform to their parents' expectations that they engage in 'suitable' leisure activities such as school societies and classical music. The same arguments apply to those working-class girls who manage to stay on into the sixth form. Indeed, the pressures on this group tend to be greater, for many working-class parents expect on their daughters to leave school at 16 (Kitwood 1980; Leonard 1980). Additionally, because working-class parents are making a greater economic sacrifice, in allowing their daughters to stay on at school, they expect their offspring to make the sacrifice worthwhile —by coming home early at night, by getting a part-time job, and so forth. Thus, for many middle-class and working-class parents, rock bands are seen as a threat to their children's educational careers.

> **AIMEE STEVENS** (Frances Belle): We had to split up because we were doing our GCSEs.

> **TERRI BONHAM** (Frances Belle): It's the first thing my Dad said: 'You're not playing that guitar in the months up to your exams.'

> **LOUISE HARTLEY** (Kid Candy): The band's quite temporary, because we're all going to university.

And on top of all this daughters are expected to do housework and often also have part-time jobs, which they do before and after school and on the weekends:

> **AIMEE STEVENS** : All of us seem to work. That's another problem. Terri works on Sunday, so we could never practise on a Sunday. And Sunday was a good day, wasn't it, because we could have had all day?

Being a band member is a very time-consuming leisure pursuit. I am arguing that boys typically have more time available than girls, and that this is an important factor which helps to explain the relative absence of girls from rock bands.

THE REGULATION OF FEMALE PLAY

Parental Restrictions

Girls living at home are under pressure to conform to constraints imposed by parents. Staying in more than boys and getting home earlier at night, they are not allowed out just anywhere and with anyone: companions and destinations are vetted for reputation. Clearly, this higher level of social control is based on the real dangers already discussed. Kitwood (1980) found both working-class and middle-class parents concerned for the physical safety of their daughters and also to 'protect' them from sexual activities. Working-class girls were allowed more freedom with regard to boyfriends than were middle-class girls, who were more heavily protected, especially if they were en route to higher education. They were under more pressure than their brothers to develop 'worthwhile' and 'respectable' leisure pursuits in order to deflect them from sexual relationships. Fisher and Holder (1981) found, in their large mixed class sample, that mothers worried more about their daughters than their sons. Leonard (1980) similarly found that working-class girls had to accept a greater degree of parental control than boys, and had their geographical mobility curtailed. Young women had to be in earlier at night than boys and were not allowed to go out as many times a week. The gap between boys and girls in terms of mobility grew larger as they got older because young women were regarded as needing increasing physical and moral protection. More recently, Sharpe (1994) found similar parental restrictions still applying in the 1990s.

The sort of venues where local gigs are held would be considered unsuitable by many parents, especially middle-class ones who would perceive joining a band as a serious threat because the rock world is peopled mainly by men, associated with sex, drugs, and late hours. Apart from doing gigs, being in a band is inseparable from a shared social life with other band members. If a young woman cannot join in with all this she will not be treated as a full and equal member of the band and her commitment will be questioned.

These kinds of restrictions were mentioned by a number of my interviewees. 'Kassandra''s (upper-middle-class) parents used to lock her in the house to prevent her from going out to rock venues. Annette was a black working-class 20-year-old living at home, whose mother considered playing percussion to be degrading, whereas it was seen as alright for Annette's brother to be in a band. This gender-specific protective attitude is laid on top of a general concern which parents have for their children to get well-paid, secure jobs. This was true of my 1990s school students, as well as my 1980s interviewees.

LOUISE HARTLEY (Kid Candy): I'm not such a bad case, because my parents are pretty free: I can do what I want. But, when I compare the boys I know to the girls, the boys can basically go out and do what they want, whereas with girls the parents tend to say, 'No, you can't do this and that and you've got to be home by this time.' So boys do have more freedom.

MIRIAM COHEN (Kid Candy): I just think parents are more inclined to give sons freedom, because if you have a daughter she can't wander round on the streets at night. I mean, it's still daring for boys to do that anyway, but it doesn't seem that way. I think parents are more protective over their little girl than their little boy.

However, as parental constraints are also to do with getting girls to conform to gender-appropriate behaviour, the range of activities and hobbies considered 'suitable' for girls is considerably narrower than for boys (Leonard 1980). Since rock music-making is seen as a 'male' domain and rock musician a 'male' role, parents discourage their daughters from getting involved in it.

Boyfriends' and Husbands' Constraints

Boyfriends are much more significant in the lives of girls than vice versa and constitute an actual or potential constraint on young women's music-making. A young woman already in a band may acquire a new boyfriend who, whilst admiring her musicianship, may still encourage her to leave. I encountered women who had experienced this. Many young women are dissuaded by their boyfriends from band participation right from the start. Why is this? First, the boyfriend may think it inappropriate that his girlfriend should be seen as more important than himself in the eyes of others. Many males in this situation feel that they are only seen as so-and-so's boyfriend—the 'I'm with the band' syndrome. Men may resent the perceived 'femininity' of such a role. Second, many men feel that being able to cope with all the knocks and strains, both physical and mental, which it entails is 'masculine', whereas a 'real' woman needs a man to shield her from such situations. Third, men often think that they can or could do it better than women which explains the phenomenon of men jumping up on stage at the beginning, middle, or end of gigs and trying to take over the equipment, mostly ones with negligible skills, their misplaced confidence coming merely from being male (and usually drunk). Fourth, a man may feel threatened sexually by his girlfriend's public exposure to other men's eyes. Marion Asch's first husband, tormented by jealousy and possessiveness, tried to prevent her going abroad on tour with the Mission Belles.

Married women have to negotiate for the right to go out by themselves and engage in leisure activities, and out-of-the-home activities are usually an extension of the wife/mother role. Indeed, many women are made to feel so guilty that they should even want any time for themselves that they relinquish the idea of independence in their leisure simply to avoid argument (Green, Hebron, and Woodward 1987). Cowie and Lees (1981) found that having a job was the only legitimate way for working-class wives to spend time outside the home. Whilst Dobash and Dobash concluded from their study: 'The dictum that a woman's place is in the home doesn't so much mean that she shall not go out to work, but that she should not go out to play' (Dobash and Dobash 1980: 91).

A number of the married women I interviewed said that being in a band (and earning money from it) was the only way they were allowed to get out of the house, conjugal norms which may also be reinforced by the wider family and local community.

TERRY HUNT (Jam Today): 'Do you go on tour? Oh. How does your boyfriend feel about that?' I've never [heard] them ask that question of male musicians. It's accepted. But they find it really freaky, the idea of women going of and touring on their own.

The media also reinforce these norms:

ENID WILLIAMS (Girlschool): I remember reading some double-page spread with the Bangles, after they'd just had about three records in the Top 10. And the headline was something along the lines of, 'Why the Bangles have Lonely Nights Alone'. And the whole two pages was about how none of them had boyfriends because it was so difficult when you were travelling around all the time. . . . You always get asked these questions about boyfriends. And I think if a young girl reads something like that she's gonna think, 'I've got the choice between either a career or a boyfriend. And I want a satisfying personal life. I want a boyfriend and I want kids. And no man's gonna want me if I'm travelling around all the time.'

Many other women musicians I interviewed made similar comments.

'KASSANDRA' (of 1980s new wave band): Women who've got relations with men tend to wrap themselves around men, tend to live their lives around men, so that they've got less space to develop themselves. So, [to become a female musician] you either need a gay woman, or a woman who has come to the conclusion in her life that she's going to dedicate her energy to something, no matter what.

Exclusion by Male Musicians

Rock is associated with youth, and research shows that a major preoccupation of young men is establishing their 'masculinity', which exaggerates these so-called masculine traits (Fisher and Holder 1981.) Moreover, masculinity and femininity are relational, each only making sense in terms of its opposite. The very 'masculinity' of activities can only be maintained by the exclusion of girls: 'In order to develop a masculine identity a boy needs to dissociate himself from all that is feminine. He needs to denigrate girls in order to dominate them' (Lees 1993: 301). It is in their younger teens that most male rock musicians start playing in bands so that it is hardly surprising that girls are excluded, since to have one on drums would undermine rock's latent function of conferring masculine identity on its participants. It is precisely because of the fragility of adolescent gender identity that so much 'work' is invested in patrolling the ideological boundaries (by name-calling, boasting, and so on). Girls fulfil the role of 'outsiders'.

If a young woman does acquire a rock instrument and express an interest in joining a band, she may find that no one wants to play with her, which is what happened to Alison Rayner (of Jam Today), who had wanted to play in a band since the age of 12 years: 'I couldn't think who I could play with. The boys at home . . . wouldn't play with me, because they wouldn't have a girl in their band. I was too young to approach older people about it. I had the electric guitar for about two or three years and didn't actually have anybody to play with.' All-women bands may be formed for a number of reasons, from feminist politics to an opportunist strategy for commercial success, but some women who started playing in their teens set up all-women bands simply because male bands would not accept them. For instance, Enid Williams (of Girlschool) started playing with other women when she was 14 years old, although not for ideological reasons: 'I've played in a lot of all-women bands. It was always an all-women band at that time. And that came about because the men we knew who played in bands weren't interested in playing with us.'

As teenage boys tend to take music far more seriously than do girls (Fisher and Holder 1981), they might question the commitment of young women who ask to join their bands. Kim McAuliffe (Girlschool): 'At that time, the guys we knew who could play didn't want to know at all about us. Females playing in a band, at that time, was totally unheard of. They thought, "Oh, girls. They won't be serious and they won't carry on. And they wouldn't be any good, anyway." '

Because there are few institutional settings in which to learn to play rock, informal peer groups are of crucial importance as learning environments. However, teenage girls are typically excluded from these and are thus not privy to the insider information and tips which are routinely traded within them since male musicians tend to be possessive about such technical information.

JACKIE CREW (Jam Today): **Quite often the musicians you come into contact with when you first start are men. I've found it's very hard to get them to show you things. They're very reluctant to part with their bits of information and knowledge. And they'll show you it all fast and say, 'That's how it goes'. And you say, 'Could you show me it a bit slower?' and they go, 'Oh!' As often as not they can't play it slower. They only know that little bit and that's how they do it. Then you try it a couple of times. And when you can't do it, they say, 'Oh, well. You can't do it yet.'**

Sara Cohen (1991) provides further evidence of the way in which bands function as vehicles for male bonding, and how male musicians actively exclude women from participation. She also shows how wives and girlfriends are often kept away from rehearsals, recording sessions, and even gigs. In Cohen's study, male musicians viewed women as a serious potential threat to the continuing existence of their bands, someone's girlfriend often being blamed when tensions arose and bands split up. (See also Fornas, Lindberg, and Sernhede 1995.)

MUSICAL STYLES

Musical style constitutes another sort of constraint. It could be argued that women are least likely to get involved in heavy rock or metal, which embodies the apotheosis of 'masculinist' values (Weinstein 1991). I have come across few women musicians within this musical genre, whereas a lot of women play within the, lighter, 'pop' category of music.

As a new musical style becomes fashionable it can affect the number of women musicians. In the early 1960s there were, in America, a large number of all-female singing groups which faded with the 'British Invasion' of beat music. However, there were few female beat groups, either in the UK or in America (Leigh and Frame 1984), which is all the more surprising since many of these beat groups, and most notably the Beatles themselves, performed quite a lot of covers of American all-girl singing groups. Young women were not performing this eminently suitable material in the new beat group format because singing groups did not have instruments. They could rehearse their harmonies at home and in the school playground but beat music made guitars, bass, and drumkit essential and for these you needed money, transport, and space. Lastly, as electric guitars were relatively new, it would have been surprising if many women had started using them, given the gendered nature of technology. Thus, the development and application of a new form of technology led, both directly and indirectly, to the exclusion of women from groups.

The Ideology of Teen Femininity

THE MASCULINITY OF ROCK

It is not simply material factors which lead to women's absence from rock, for many young women have no desire whatsoever to play in a band because, in terms of gender ideology, rock bands and rock instruments are masculine. The ideology of sexual differences permeates our society. The last two decades have seen the documentation of gender construction processes operating through language, children's toys, clothing, hairstyles, books and comics, television, and magazines. Gender differences become apparent to children even before they reach their first birthday and it has been shown that 5-year-olds already categorize occupations and activities in terms of gender appropriateness (Smithers and Zientek 1991). In particular there is now a substantial body of research in the sociology of education which shows gender differentiation to be an important part of the 'hidden curriculum' of schools (for instance, Sharpe 1976; Wolpe 1977 and 1988; Byrne 1978; Clarricoates 1978; Stanworth 1981; Spender 1982; Mahoney 1985; Whyte *et al*. 1985; McNeill 1987; Weiner and Arnot 1987; Arnot and Weiner 1997; Askew and Ross 1988; Walkerdine 1990; Mac An Ghaill 1994) and in youth training schemes (Cockburn 1987). Delamont (1990) summarizes the various ways in which schools differentiate in terms of gender:

> the organization of the school; the teacher's strategies for controlling and motivating pupils; the organization and content of lessons; the informal conversations between pupils and their teachers; and leaving unchallenged the pupils' own stereotyping and self-segregating of activities. In Britain's schools the sexes are still being segregated; the differences between males and females highlighted and exaggerated . . . (Delamont 1990: 3)

This ongoing differentiation operates to stabilize gender identities which, in reality, are relative, contingent, and fragile: 'this administration, regulation and reification of sex/gender boundaries is institutionalized through the interrelated material, social and discursive practices of the staffroom, classroom and playground microcultures' (Mac An Ghaill 1994: 9).

But why is rock defined as masculine? First, it has always been dominated by men, and, as there are few female role models easily available, this sets up a self-fulfilling prophecy. Second, it is believed that in order to play rock music/ instruments certain physical and mental characteristics are required, such as aggression, power, and physical strength. It must be conceded that there is in reality no one uniform straightforward masculinity: it is fragmented by social differentiation (class, ethnicity, sexuality, etc.) into a variety of masculinities which are also subject to ongoing change (Segal 1990; Connell 1995; Mac An Ghaill 1996). However, aggression, power, and physical strength have been traditionally associated with hegemonic, mainstream masculinity. This comes out clearly in the music press, especially the trade magazines, which rarely show women playing instruments but use their bodies for the titillation of their male readership (see Appendix 1). Because rock instruments and amplifiers are cultural artefacts with sexist values and 'masculine' power embedded within them, girls are not drawn towards them since women who play rock are considered to be putting their femininity at risk. From earliest childhood noisiness and rowdiness are proscribed for girls, although the actual boundaries of what is allowed vary somewhat with social structural location. A certain degree of toleration may come into play before puberty, but such indulgence rarely escapes the onslaught of the 'femininity' project associated with adolescence. 'The physiological and psychological changes experienced by all adolescents . . . require them to reappraise their self-images, and at this stage it is important for these self-images to be reinforced by peers' (Hendry 1992: 81).

Third, rock is associated with technology, which is itself symbolically interwoven with masculinity. Boys get given technical toys; girls do not. Boys' informal learning, in the home and amongst their peers, breeds a familiarity with, and confidence in, all things mechanical, technical, and scientific. Research in the field of gender and science education has indicated that girls' exclusion from technology renders them 'technophobic', lacking confidence and experiencing anxiety when dealing with technical problems and more easily discouraged, whereas boys are not, since the image of science and everything associated with it is seen as 'male' (Kelly 1981; Stanworth 1981; Deem 1978; Spender 1980 and 1982; Byrne 1978; Birke *et al.* 1980; Weiner 1985; Mahoney 1985; Kramarae 1988). At the same time, however, the technical has been traditionally *defined* in a way that excludes women's actual involvement and therefore the link between gender and technology is clearly ideological (Wajcman 1991; Grint and Gill 1995). Technology is culturally constructed as masculine, whilst masculinity is itself partially shaped by technology (Cockburn and Ormrod 1993) in a mutually reinforcing circle which excludes women. Thus a lack of technological competence becomes part of women's identity, just as technical expertise becomes part of men's. Change is slow. It is well known that since the 1980s girls have begun to significantly outperform boys in most subjects in National Curriculum tests, GCSEs, and A level examinations (*Social Trends* 26, 1996). On the other hand, boys still perform better in science and technology and, after 16, fewer girls opt for physics and chemistry as A level subjects. Currently in Britain there are twice as many male as female science undergraduates. Therefore science (particularly physics) is still largely a 'male' arena.

Thus, it could be that girls are drawn towards rock instruments but put off by the multitude of electronic and electrical components, which are a basic requirement for a rock performance.[2] Many of my interviewees mentioned this. Afraid or not, these things are strongly defined as masculine and must therefore be eschewed by the young woman who wishes to preserve her femininity, particularly during adolescence when she is under great pressure to establish her gender in the eyes of her peers. Girls, then, tend to stay 'unplugged'.

---

[2] For evidence concerning the different orientation of boys and girls towards music technology in education, see Green (1997), and Hargreaves and Colley (1986).

FEMALE WORKING-CLASS PEER GROUPS

For working-class young women, 'femininity' is enforced through the female peer group. McRobbie (1978) argued that working-class girls create their own culture, one of both resistance and negotiated acquiescence towards the established order. They rejected official school ideology and replaced it with an anti-school culture of exaggerated femininity: obstructive obsession with boys, appearance, and sexual flaunting. This was both an exciting escape from drab reality and the means by which the girls were ultimately trapped into an early marriage and motherhood. Thus, like Willis's 'lads' (1977), the girls created a culture which then acted upon them as a powerful form of social control. Having limited occupational choice, marriage was seen as as an economic necessity, the only way to gain independence from the family, and also made inevitable by the local gossip networks which enforced a powerful double standard of sexual morality. Further evidence of the latter came from research done by Deidre Wilson (1978), Leslie Smith (1978), Celia Cowie and Sue Lees (1981), and Sue Lees (1986), who found that the behaviour of working-class girls is effectively policed by the vague and shifting nature of terms such as 'slag'. Any girl was at risk of being labelled, either by appearance or behaviour. Abusive sexual terms were taken for granted, largely unquestioned, and even used by girls themselves against others. One way to minimize such labelling was to be 'in love', but marriage/cohabitation was the only really safe place.

Despite all the behavioural and attitudinal changes during the last decade, the sexual double standard is still very much alive and kicking in the 1990s. (See, for instance, the research carried out by Jenny Kitzinger (1995) with both working-class and undergraduate young women.) Furthermore, as Cockburn (1987) has described, the term 'lezzie' has been added to the battery of sexist insults which police young women's behaviour, undermining close friendships between girls. The dual standard of sexual morality underpins both marriage and the ideology of love and romance, restricting the behaviour of young women just as much as sexual attack. Thus, physical and social risks operate to drive young working-class women into apparently protective heterosexual attachments. Empirical research in the UK has shown that a working-class young woman typically gets involved in a serious relationship earlier than her male equivalent and, in contrast to him, is then likely to sever her relationships with her female friends, often at her boyfriend's insistence (Lees 1986; Griffin 1985; and Stafford 1991). Leonard (1980) found that the courtship 'career' commenced earlier for girls (at age 12–14). Similarly, Kitwood (1980) found that working-class girls were often married by the age of 18. To gain any kind of status the working-class girl will make many sacrifices for a stable relationship whereas the boys, under less pressure to get a girlfriend, engage in shared male hobbies.

Fisher and Holder (1981) highlighted the pressure towards conformity which young women's peer groups exert. Striving for femininity to confirm their shaky sexual identities, girls learn to be deferential in order to please the boys, 'quieten down', give up sports, and become ladylike. Afraid of being 'left on the shelf', they thought about boys all the time, while boys did not worry much about girls and it was considered 'soft' to enthuse over them. The pursuit of good looks and a boyfriend takes a surprising amount of time and, once one is achieved, a girl's social life revolves around him since girls tend to take courtship as seriously as boys do rock music. My own research furnished further evidence. Miriam Cohen (of Kid Candy) told me that her female schoolfriends thought that she was weird to be playing in a band: 'Some of them seem to look upon us as if we're a bit strange. People did say things to us like because we're girls we shouldn't be playing guitar and bass guitar. I think some of them didn't see it as normal; the ones that were all old-fashioned. . . . They'll say, "Why are you in a band?" They think it's really odd that I'm not very feminine.' In contrast to boys, then, whose masculine identity is confirmed by playing rock instruments, girls jeopardize their feminine identity.

In the 1990s, the average age for first marriage has been increasing, but women still tend to marry at a younger age than men (*Social Trends* 26, 1996) since, although attitudes have changed and girls' expectations are higher, their real opportunities have not kept pace. More young women are challenging traditional sex roles than in the past yet, Jane Gaskell (1992) has shown, they cannot easily break free as, despite 'liberal' attitudes, young women assess the world as relatively unchangeable and adjust accordingly. Sue Sharpe found that her 1990s schoolgirls placed far more emphasis on educational achievement and less on the goal of marriage. However, boyfriends, love, and romance were still very important and time-consuming. Moreover, a girl is still in an 'ambivalent and contradictory position':

> she must modify or disguise her success in relation to that of the boys (and sometimes girls) with whom she wishes to be popular. She should ideally confine her 'success' to acceptable 'feminine' pursuits which don't involve male competition. . . . Many men still do not like to compete with or be beaten by a woman. This is as true in the nineties as it was in the seventies. (Sharpe 1994: 19)

Of course, both the ideology of romance and the ideology of 'slag' are simply that —ideology: they are normative and do not determine—or preclude alternative— behaviour. Nevertheless, I would argue that, in terms of becoming a musician in a band, these ideological processes do represent as important a set of obstacles as do the material factors which I have already discussed. First, for a working-class girl to get involved in a rock band she would probably have to be involved already in a group of girls who decide to do this together. A girl attempting such a project alone would be rejected by her peers. Second, by adolescence, the pressure to get a boyfriend leads to hobbies and activities being dropped as either 'childish' or 'unfeminine'. Characteristically, girls give up sport at this time, often under pressure from female friends. 'Young women spectate; they do not expect to participate' (Hendry 1992). If a girl learnt to play an instrument in childhood she would be likely, then, to cease playing at this time and, instead, devote herself to activities which allow the possibility of meeting boys. Those young women who do join bands find that they have to allow music-making to become their number one priority. Third, a working-class girl with a boyfriend is expected to traipse around after him, which restricts her autonomy considerably. At gigs there is often a special table for the musicians' girlfriends. Fourth, the expectation that girls will 'settle down' at an earlier age than boys means that if a young woman does get involved in a band she is openly renouncing her marriage chances as far as the local working-class community is concerned. Fifth, some of the artefacts seen as essential for achieving femininity pose an obstacle to playing rock instruments. Although long, carefully painted nails might be a girl's proud possession, they make guitar playing very difficult. Also, you cannot maintain a neat and tidy appearance when you are humping equipment about. All of this clashes with the norms of femininity, which dictate that a girl should hang around and wait for a man to do it for her. In a mixed band the boys might do it all, whereas in an all-women band you do it. Feminine characteristics are a hindrance: 'You find you have to keep up your feminine girly thing and that doesn't particularly go with being in a hard, sloggy job, which is what music's all about' (Terry Hunt of Jam Today). It is difficult to preserve femininity in these circumstances precisely because it is an artifice and gender a 'performance' (Butler 1990). It is assumed that women do not sweat, that their noses do not go red and shiny, and that their hair stays in place so that, while involvement in a rock band can only enhance a boy's status, it jeopardizes a girl's femininity. Lastly, involvement with the rock music world cuts working-class girls off from potential boyfriends outside that world, while if a young woman is already engaged or married and wishes to join a band, her husband or fiancé would be likely to object. As Lees (1986) found that girls could lose their sexual reputation simply by looking 'weird', being in a band may place a girl beyond the bounds of local 'normality'.

All of the above reflects an ongoing set of power relations between the sexes, in which it is men who define and redefine the world.

MIDDLE-CLASS GIRLS

The moral imperatives of the 'dual standard' exert a weaker grip on middle-class girls who are more mobile and their actions less visible to the local community. Although the dual standard runs right through society, the female student can lead a life at university quite separate from that at home. Since the middle class tend to have more widely dispersed networks, the girls know that they are going to move out of the locality (to college, at marriage, or through their job), and therefore their local reputation does not matter that much. As less holds a young woman back from taking chances, playing in a rock band might be seen as one of these.

However, middle-class young women do encounter the *commercial* culture of femininity and can become obsessed with romance. Hobbies and friends may be offered up on the altar of 'the relationship'. Nowhere is this more apparent than in girls' magazines, which focus on romance (McRobbie 1991), and where most things that a girl does are seen as instrumental to getting a boyfriend. Such magazines—massively popular—set up normative patterns which influence the actual behaviour of girls. An adolescent crisis seems to affect women in all social classes. Sue Sharpe (1976) found it to be one of the factors which help to explain the marked fall-off in academic performance among girls during the third year onwards in secondary schools, when a lack of academic achievement encourages young women to redirect their energies into the culture of femininity. On the other hand, the academically successful suddenly feel that it is no longer enough, since having a boyfriend is both an end in itself and, perhaps more importantly, a status symbol. Sue Lees (1993) argued that the reason why girls lose confidence in their early teenage years is because their identity rests heavily on the maintenance of their precarious sexual reputation. Recent research (Brown 1995) confirms that young teenage girls are still less self-confident than boys, worry more, and are very concerned about their appearance. In early adolescence, girls' self-esteem tends to fall and they become self-conscious, as is shown by the autobiographies of middle-class women (McCrindle and Rowbotham 1977; Oakley 1984; Spender and Sarah 1980) and my own interviews. For example,

'SYLVIA' (of 1980s all-female Yorkshire pop band): I think puberty is really traumatic, especially reading this diary from when I was 13. I can remember how low my self-confidence was then. . . . That was the year I started menstruating. But things started happening before that and it was to do with girlfriends and boyfriends, having boys for social status. . . . I think it was sexuality and the social implications of that. I remember thinking, 'I can't stand all of this!' If someone had said, 'Don't worry, you don't have to have a boyfriend. It doesn't matter. You don't need that status', it would have made such a difference.

Sue Sharpe's Ealing schoolgirls (in both the 1980s and 1990s) agreed that boys dislike girls who surpass them in their schoolwork. My interviews furnished similar evidence:

'BRENDA' (of professional 1980s new wave band): I used to be very good at school. I used to do all my work and be top of the class in everything. Then, when I reached adolescence—it's weird—I just gave it all up. I stopped working. I'm sure it happens to girls more than boys. You're not supposed to be brainy as a girl or you're not attractive. I had a lot of trouble getting boyfriends. So I'm sure it had that effect. [So] I started going out, wearing make-up, having a good time.

For many middle-class (and some working-class) young women, higher education provides an escape route from the ideology of femininity and even in secondary school some girls avoid the competitive pressure of peer group ideology by becoming 'blue-stockings'. This may be necessary for middle-class girls, as British autobiographies (Oakley 1984; Heron 1985) have shown that many parents have expect their daughters to put marriage first, whether they went on to university or not. A recent American study showed that even female undergraduates prioritized the search for a boyfriend over their female friendships (Holland and Eisenhart 1990).

What I have been describing here is a set of ideological constraints which young women have to contend with as they grow up in our society as gender is mediated through social class. These pressures affect women of all social classes, although in different ways, because they are not simply passive slaves to this ideology since, as culture is about how people make sense of the world and their situation within it, it is actively constructed and always changing. The material circumstances in which particular groups of girls are situated affect their reading of femininity and the way in which they construct it in their everyday lives. Precisely because culture is a way of handling these circumstances, the daughters of manual workers, white-collar workers, and professionals interpret femininity differently and develop various responses to it. For the working-class girl, as I have discussed, restricted material circumstances and limited hopes for the future push her towards an early marriage and the ideology of romance functions to transform into fun the work of finding her future spouse.

On the other hand, given that the teen culture of working-class girls is not monolithic, why, if working-class young men use music to express a particular form of resistance, do their sisters not also use music in this way? The answer is that female working-class resistance to authority takes the form of ultra-femininity and this is not conducive, as I have shown, to becoming a rock musician. Nevertheless, I found some evidence of a working-class subcultural form of resistance to *femininity*: the 1980s East End renees. 'Renee', meaning girl and short for Irene, was a term the mods developed for girls who wore short hair, monkey boots, and denim jackets. 'Kath': 'You do things that girls don't usually do, like smoke roll-ups or ride a motorbike, that sort of thing. So I suppose anyone that does anything like that is slightly unfeminine.'

If working-class girls do get involved in music they are more likely to treat it as a career than middle-class girls who, having more choices and a more open future, may see it merely as a hobby. Rock offers a dream of money, a life of travel and glamour which few other jobs can supply. Working-class parents may be initially worried about rock's reputation but, once reassured, are likely to back their daughters all the way and even make considerable financial sacrifices. I found this to be the case with the working-class musicians I interviewed.

KIM MCAULIFFE (Girlschool): I was going to do 'A' levels and go on to do commercial art at college. And then, one day I just thought, 'I don't want to do this'. Equipment's very expensive and my parents couldn't afford to buy me any. So the only way I could afford to buy equipment was to get a job. And so I said to my mum and dad, 'Look, what do you reckon? I wanna leave school. I wanna go for the music thing.' And they said okay and that was it. . . . My mum and dad kept us. We couldn't have done it without them. They bought a van and we hijacked it and ran it into the ground for them! So they helped us a lot.

In contrast, middle-class parents, unless musicians themselves, are likely to see rock music as an unsuitable occupation for their daughters (and sons) and do all they can to dissuade them.

Lastly, moving into a so-called male occupation requires an unusual degree of bravery, determination, and strength of character (Brown 1995; Spencer and Taylor 1994; Sharpe 1994):

> It takes self-confidence and courage for girls to break through the prejudice that surrounds entry into male-dominated careers. Throughout their school life, they have experienced many counter positionings of sexes and subjects, they have absorbed the siting of male and female as opposite, and have moved towards the safer 'feminine' areas of interest. They have learned that much of the work men do is associated with so-called 'male' characteristics such as aggression, strength, stamina, competitiveness, ambition, and a technical or analytical mind, which are qualities that conflict with the myth of 'femininity', and probably where they have positioned themselves in relation to this . . . [Moreover] it is not appealing to forge a path into areas that may be hostile or competitive. (Sharpe 1994: 193)

I have presented a whole range of factors which, I believe, explain the relative absence of women from bands. I have not attempted to prioritize them, because they are interrelated in subtle and complex ways and, typically, more than one is in operation at the same time in the life of an individual woman. In the next chapter, I shall draw extensively on my empirical research in examining the specific ways in which these barriers or obstacles have been circumvented or offset in the lives of those exceptional women who *have* become rock music-makers.

3 Routes into Rock

There are many factors which make it possible for women to become rock musicians, despite all the obstacles so far described. For any one person often more than one factor is at work and no one variable is, by itself, a necessary or sufficient explanation: there is no single 'typical' female route into rock music-making. Moreover, the relationship between these variables in the lives of women musicians will probably be as inextricably complex as in the analysis of educational achievement or delinquency. Why should it be otherwise? Bearing this in mind, I shall now outline the few variables which stand out as enabling women to evade or overcome the social and cultural constraints which I have already described. Other writers have held up youth subcultures as the major source of resistance to cultural tramlines (Hall and Jefferson 1976; Willis 1978), but, once the question of gender is raised, it is obvious that women are just as marginal and subordinate in subcultures as elsewhere (McRobbie 1980; Frith 1983; Thornton 1995). The relevant point, here, is that most musicians (male or female) do not come out of youth subcultures. From my own empirical research, I have concluded that the only youth subculture which provided a route was punk, since it offered young women more cultural space than previous youth groups. In contrast to subcultural theory, I have found that the following are the significant routes into music-making: a musical family, a classical music training, an art education, involvement in drama, gender-rebellion, musician boyfriends/husbands, higher education, accessible female role models, feminism, and lesbianism.

Musical Families

The family, being an important agent of gender socialization, inhibits most girls from involvement in rock music, which is usually seen as some sort of rebellion against family life, and so parents have been generally less supportive of their children's involvement in rock and roll than, say, in sport or dancing. However, rock does not necessarily involve anti-family rebellion. Indeed, some musicians follow in their parents' footsteps. From her empirical research in Milton Keynes, Ruth Finnegan (1989) concluded that musical families were far more important than social class in leading to musical involvement. My own research indicates that, where one or more parents have been in bands, the musical aspirations of daughters are both encouraged and materially supported. Thus, family background turns out to be significant. Margaret Thompson and Bunty Murtagh (of the Mission Belles) each came from the same working-class family with a tradition of musical entertainment, both parents and grandparents making a livelihood from performing. From a similar family, Ali and Sue Smith had a father known as 'Banjo', who was a pub entertainer, while their mother sang and all seven children were encouraged to sing and do 'party pieces'. As a result Ali and Sue are multi-instrumentalists and singers and their sister Liz plays the harmonica. In these cases, family background was the main factor leading to a musical career.[1]

In all, about one-third of all the women interviewed had a musician in their immediate family whilst growing up. Parents who are, or have been, rock/pop musicians, understand the world of popular music, have connections in the music business, and tend to encourage their children to play music as a hobby and pursue it as a professional career. These parents typically offset the material constraints by buying their daughters instruments, paying for lessons, and providing transport. They may also function as role models: 'Kath''s father had played trumpet, banjo, and guitar in various contexts, including a skiffle group. When she was 9 he offered to teach her the guitar, but she decided on drums and, although most parents would not relish their daughter learning drums, 'Kath''s father bought her a cassette and book to help her learn, and paid for her first drumkit. She was allowed to practise at home, and later her whole rock band was provided with rehearsal space in the family's small terrace house.

In a few cases, a daughter was clearly being encouraged to fulfil a parent's frustrated musical ambitions. Teresa Hooker, guitarist in Oxford's all-female indie bands 'Death By Crimpers' and 'Beaker', started piano lessons at 5 or 6:

'I was always surrounded by musical vibes from my mum and she was very keen to make sure that I had all the resources that she never had. She put me through the piano lessons so that I could read music. . . . She said, "You'll thank me for it later" and I did.' For some women, such as Jennifer Bishop (16-year-old bass player in all-girl punk band, Tampasm), a musical parent has clearly been the main influence in getting them into a band: 'I used to sit there with my dad and listen to him play the guitar and I decided I wanted to play the guitar as well. . . . I think that if he hadn't encouraged me to play the guitar and said "bands are good fun and if you want to do that you should", then I don't think I would have been in a band.' However, some parents who, although music lovers, were not musicians themselves also encouraged their daughters, going to extraordinary

---

[1] In the past, the tradition of 'family bands' was the means by which a large proportion of women became musicians. Martha Vicinus (1979) has documented this tradition for the interwar years in Britain. In America, many jazzwomen were introduced to playing and trained by their families, as Sally Placksin (1985) and Linda Dahl (1984) have demonstrated.

lengths in their support. Enid Williams (Girlschool): 'Our parents lent us quite a lot of money. We all had very working-class backgrounds, and we were very lucky that we had parents that helped us out in that way. My dad mortgaged the house so that we could buy a PA.' Sara and Kate Watts's music-loving parents' lives and livelihoods changed radically as they became increasingly involved in their daughters' hobby—Treacle. With their father as chauffeur and protector, the girls were able to sing in clubs in their early teens. Later, he bought instruments, paid for van hire, helped write lyrics, and became their manager. He did a sound engineering course at Red Tape studios and built a sixteen-track studio in the basement of their house. He now acts as an agent for other bands and venues, while their mother became their publicist.

The age at which some of these women started was very young. Claire's father, who had not been allowed to play the instruments of his choice as a child, decided that if she wanted to play something, she could and at the tender age of 5 she said, 'I want a drum kit'.

CLAIRE (Atomic Candy): It was a proper drum kit. I loved it—it was fab. It was a Premier kit, wooden shells and real skins. My dad was very encouraging. So I went on from drums to violin. After the violin, I played brass.

In sum, supportive parents, especially musical ones, are an important factor in offsetting many of the material and cultural constraints on young women and thus enabling them to develop careers in rock. In fact, many famous women musicians and singers have a musical parent or two: Carleen Anderson, Dolores O'Riodan, Suzi Quatro, Kate Bush, Neneh Cherry, Janet Jackson, Whitney Houston, Diamanda Galas, Sinead Lohan, Yoko Ono, Natalie Cole, Rosanne Cash, Melody, Sheryl Crow, Lesley Rankine, Nina Gordon, Kristin Hersch, amongst others.

Classical Music

Many young women have a classical training whilst they are of school age, via lessons at school and/or private tuition,[2] the piano being the most popular instrument. Although this instrument (along with violins and flutes) is typically characterized as feminine and therefore works to affirm hegemonic femininity, girls who are given music lessons are thereby, at least partially, able to escape from the teenage world of romance and boyfriends since the daily discipline of practising takes up much of their free time Another, less 'feminine' way of acquiring a 'good musical training' is by joining a local brass band and a couple of my interviewees had done this.

[2] Ruth Finnegan's (1989) study indicated that at school girls were far more involved in the main choirs, orchestras, and ensembles than boys were. It was thought 'natural' for boys to be sporty but 'cissy' for them to be musical. 'In general . . . apart perhaps from the instruments popularly viewed as "for boys" (brass and percussion), there were far more obstacles to engaging in school music for boy than for girls' (p. 203). Lucy Green's (1997) study confirms this.

The vast majority of classically trained musicians do not join rock bands and so, clearly, rock musicians do not need to be classically trained. On the other hand, it establishes a proven ability to play an instrument and a 'musician' identity and a number of famous female rock/pop performers have been classically trained: Sheryl Crow and Astrid Williamson took music degrees, Bjork was at music school for ten years, and Laurie Anderson studied violin as a child. Over half of the musicians I interviewed, in both the 1980s and in 1995, had received some classical training. However, there are some interesting differences between my 1980s sample and my 1995 sample. Some of the women in the earlier group simply drifted into playing rock instead of classical music while seeking others to play with or because they realized that they were never going to make it professionally. The classically trained women tended to become interested in popular music at a later age than average, sometimes not until they were at university. In particular, girls growing up in the 1960s and 1970s simply did not think of playing rock/pop. In contrast, the 1995 sample tended to have become involved at a much earlier age and the gap between playing classical music and playing rock/pop appears to have been significantly narrower. Whereas women who went to school in the 1960s and 1970s were likely to have only been taught classical music and to have encountered strong prejudices against pop/rock, some of my 1995 interviewees were clearly influenced by teachers who saw pop/rock/jazz as perfectly legitimate.[3] One result of these educational changes is that some of my 1995 interviewees, at an early age, formed bands inside school. Katherine Garrett (The Mystics): 'When I was at school, I did my A level [in music] with one older girl and we started a little band together when we were 15 . . . that was my first live performance and I loved it.' Sometimes, a music teacher made all the difference. Caroline Scallon (of Soul Devotion) told me that her involvement in bands was due to an 'inspirational' teacher, a jazz musician who encouraged her to play at his gigs when she was only 14. The school also had a four-track soundproofed studio. Meanwhile, Claire Lemmon started playing at the age of 9 because her primary school teacher formed a guitar group.

In fact, a classical training can be both advantageous and disadvantageous for the rock/pop musician. It is an advantage to be able to read music if you want to play lead guitar. A classical training can enable a musician to help novice instrumentalists within an all-women band and also provide a struggling professional with a means of subsidizing their band activities by teaching. On the minus side, some women told me that they had had to forget their training in order to play pop/rock and a strict classical training can lead to an inability to improvise:

MARY (Atomic Candy): I don't believe in reading music because I know lots of people who are Grade 8 or so who you can't have a jam with because they don't know what you're playing. You take the music away from in front of

---

[3] 'The changes have been formally underwritten and implemented on a national basis, through the music syllabus for the sixteen-plus General Certificate of Secondary Education (GCSE), which started running in 1986, and through the National Curriculum for Music for ages five to fourteen, which began its development in 1992' (Lucy Green 1997: 145).

them and they're completely useless. I'd rather approach it from the point of view of being able to join in and play something because you know your instrument and you know your pitch.

Traditional music teachers do not take kindly to their pupils adapting classical pieces creatively, as Andrea (of Mambo Taxi) recollects: 'When I did learn a piece, I'd end up altering it and then I'd completely forget how it was meant to go and turn up and play my version of it. And the piano teacher would completely lose his temper and say "Do you think you're better than Beethoven?!" I never even got to grade 1 and I got thrown off my GCSE music course.' There is often a kind of rock'n'roll rebellion against the very nature and taken-for-granted norms of the classical training itself.

'ANNE' (keyboard player in 1980s all-female bands in York): I was at university studying music, and I was really pissed off with the whole thing of formal music training. It's to do with being in control. When you're in an orchestra you just play your part and do what you're told, and that's that. You've got nothing of your own coming out. I decided I wanted to learn an instrument that hadn't got any of those connections with concerts [an accordion] . . . I started a real reaction in the music department. I couldn't really relate to it and I wanted to disrupt a lot. And I had this great friend who also wanted to. We were both rebels, and we both left after the first year.

However, whilst 'Anne' may have rebelled against the confines of classical music, she went on to form no less than three all-women bands in her home town: a street band, a rock band, and a big band.

On the other hand, it is also true that since most of the girls who study music, including guitar, at school do not go on to join bands, there are other important factors at stake which discourage some women from carrying on:

CAROLINE APPLEYARD (Treacle): Most of them just pack it in and stick it under the bed. 'Cause I know loads and loads that did that. When we did it at school, there weren't many lads at all [that] did it, which was weird [given that] there tend to be more male musicians about than female musicians. But I think a lot of it is you get pressure from your friends who take the mickey out of you a bit. At that age . . . I think women are more scared of showing themselves up than men. They don't want to take the risk . . . and go on stage . . . and, [not] worry about what people say . . . I think they've sort of got boyfriends and things like that, instead and [they're] sort of more interested in that.

Art and Bohemianism

Frith and Horne's book, *Art into Pop* (1987), starts with the observation that 'a significant number of British pop musicians from the 1960s to the present were educated and first started performing in art schools'. The authors point out that from the 1960s the art school and rock worlds drew closer together, so that if a woman sees herself as 'artistic' she will probably find herself mixing with musicians and be more likely to become one. Indeed, the following well-known female musicians were artists: Yoko Ono, Sade, Nina Ramsby, Sarah Blackwood (of Dubstar), Gail Greenwood (of Belly), Liz Phair, Kim Gordon, Lesley Rankine, Gina Birch and Ana da Silva (of the Raincoats), Polly Harvey, Patti Smith, Laurie Anderson; and the members of Canadian band Jade all met at art school. My own research indicates that in many all-women bands one, or even two, women have undergone an art education. Thus, 'Suke' (of a commercially successful 1980s all-female pop band) spent six years at art college and had two art degrees, her interest in music and desire for a guitar coinciding with a conception of herself as an art student. She listed her interests: 'Arty people and things people were doing at art school. . . . But then art is connected to music. . . . That's when it started—as soon as I went to my first art college.' Similarly for 'Deb' (of Brighton), becoming a singer in a band (and also a sound engineer) was tied in with her art school experience, since she approached music in an analytical way, applying the theories she discovered at art school. She saw music-making very much as an art form and was more concerned with making aesthetic statements than entertaining people: 'I see it as an extension of art. . . . I'm interested in music as part and parcel of cultural activity . . . I've spent seven years thinking about the position of the creative artist.'

In my research sample there were a number of women who felt they had to choose either art or music for a career, or who fluctuated between the two, like Fran (of Sub Rosa): 'I got into music college and I got into art college. I flipped a coin, because I couldn't decide which I wanted to do, and I ended up going to art college.' Art schools provide an important institutional base for people who have sought to define themselves as 'creative' or 'non-conformist', but you did not necessarily have to actually attend an art school to lay claim to this sort of identity. Although some women musicians I interviewed had never been art students they still saw themselves as essentially 'artistic', this being tied in with an image of themselves as 'individuals' and as crucially 'different' from the archetypal 'teenage girl'. This was true in the 1970s:

'SANDRA' (drummer in 1980s all-female Yorkshire band): I was a hippie. . . . I had long hair and beads and used to walk around in bare feet . . . It's being different. I mean, I felt different all the time. I never fitted in and couldn't conform, so I might as well make the most of being different. I always think that [my] feminism comes from that as well.

And it was still true in the 1980s, as Caroline Appleyard (of Treacle) recalled in 1995:

I always was one of the weird ones. There was a group of us girls who were all a bit different, like. Goths and punks and rockers and stuff. There was about seven of us all hung about together. I didn't do it to be different. I just sort of didn't fit in with the way that the other ones thought. They'd spend all dinner time doing their make-up in the toilets, but I'd have a pair of ripped-up jeans and baseball boots. I couldn't understand their way of thinking and they couldn't understand my way of thinking.

Since the 1950s varying versions of the bohemian/artist identity have offered successive generations of young people an escape from the narrow conventions of suburb and small town. From the 1940s on bohemianism has provided an alternative self-image and the promise of a future beyond locally available options which did not depend on being a member of a large group. You could be a bohemian by yourself, drawing on films, records, and books, and, as both the literature and reality of bohemianism circumscribed women into limited roles such as 'chick', 'earth mother', and so forth, women have often identified with the male bohemian role (Rowbotham 1973), precisely because bohemianism is an individualistic fantasy, which liberated the imagination from gender and other constraints.

Drama

Drama, like art and classical music, is an outlet for girls' creativity and one which can prefigure performance on the rock stage. My research suggests that, for female musicians, drama is more important than art. In both the 1980s sample and that for 1995, about half of those I interviewed mentioned drama as being an important activity in their schooldays when they performed in school plays and belonged to dramatic societies. Most of these women had also been extroverts and informal entertainers, who put energy into making people laugh. Indeed, a number of my interviewees had wanted to do acting as a professional career and one had studied drama at degree level. In the 1980s sample, some women had started playing music as a direct result of their theatrical experiences.

`'JOY'` (of various 1980s Birmingham bands): I used to do a lot of acting. I was in loads of plays at school. Then I did drama at college. And I did pub theatre for three years in Birmingham . . . What happened was we'd been doing a lot of theatre. I was unemployed for a bit . . . and we just used to go round to a flat and bang on things and make up amusing songs, just by improvising. And then we started taping it. None of us had much to do. We just started picking up guitars. We just drifted into it.

This is how one women's band got together:

`'SYLVIA'` (of 1980s all-female Yorkshire pop band): I started getting involved in music in 1975. There was a theatre group that went to Edinburgh that did a show. And there was music in that. We sang in that. And some of the things, we wrote for it. And then, when the theatre group finished . . . we carried on playing music.

It is probable that these women would never have joined bands without this theatrical experience. In contrast, drama did not figure as such a direct route into rock/pop for many women in 1995, and I think that the reason for this difference is to do with the fact that those who were teenagers in the 1960s or 1970s were less likely to have had the goal of joining a band because there were so few role models available. They therefore tended to get involved in bands at a later age, sometimes via some other activity, such as agitprop political theatre groups, many of these women stating that it had simply never occurred to them to be a musician. On the other hand, although it was still exceptional, those who were teenagers in the 1980s or 1990s were more likely to have had the explicit aim of joining a band, the schooldays interest in acting running parallel with music.

Gender Rebels

For many boys, playing rock music is part and parcel of youth rebellion, often a bohemian one against everyday conventions and, specifically, the norms of domesticity. This is true for many women, too, although their rebellion has an extra dimension. Rock is a man's world, and the conventional guise of a ' "rock'n'roll" gypsy—rootless, free and promiscuous' (Street 1986: 128) is a male image so that, for women, making rock music has often been a subversion of the restrictions imposed by femininity, one which, for many of my interviewees, started in the home from an early age.

> **VI SUBVERSA** (Poison Girls): My mother wanted very much for me to do well: make a good marriage, have a good home, nice children, all that sort of thing. So I just got stroppy all round and started getting into trouble. I was totally disturbed, but it was healthy. I was reaching out. . . . I remember making a decision, about 11: I was gonna be a tearaway and stop being introverted and repressed and get into trouble. I started to want to leave home when I was 13, and got into trouble with the authorities. . . . I got absolutely freaked out by the demands of my mother, and realized I had to leave home to keep sane.

It was many years later on that she discovered rock and took to it with a vengeance: 'There was all this fire and stuff going on in rock music and I loved it.'

The second battleground is school. 'Gina' (1980s sound engineer): 'I hated needlework and I got thrown out of the class. . . . I suppose I was quite disruptive, actually. The boys did metalwork and woodwork, and we did cookery and needlework. When I was thrown out of that I did woodwork for a term. I was doing it just because it was only boys doing it.' One factor common to nearly all of my interviewees (in both the 1980s and in 1995) and therefore, I believe, highly significant, is that in childhood they identified with boys rather than girls, were involved in boys' pastimes and often played in boys' gangs. In particular every single woman who played drums—the most supposedly 'male' instrument—said they had been, for want of a better word, 'tomboys'. 'Hilda' (Noisy Neighbours):

'I always saw myself as being a boy. And when I had fantasies about glorious exploits, I was always a commando or something. Being a brave, courageous, hard toughie—that was what I wanted to be. I never wanted to be a nurse or anything.' A number said that they had frequently been mistaken for boys and some, like 'Heather' (keyboard player in 1980s mixed Oxford band), once wished that they could actually become boys: 'I didn't like the idea of being a teenage girl, and I didn't want to do the things that they did. I wanted a sex change.' On the other hand, most women that I interviewed had not actually wished to *become* boys or masculine, but merely to escape the constrictions of femininity, as I have indicated. A significant number of my interviewees were brought up in an unconventional background in which gender stereotypes did not impinge as much as usual or where parents were described as 'gender-blind'.

> **'BETH'** (sax player in 1980s Birmingham bands): I didn't realize how fortunate I was in my upbringing. I didn't realize how free of all these hang-ups I was until they got imposed by other people. Because I had none of this thing about being female and the restrictions. It was only when I came to college that I began to get the shit thrown at me. I've never had those barriers to break down because, at home, my mother was a very active woman. . . . It would be mum and us who'd build brick walls.

In the 1995 sample, three of the women who said that they had not been tomboys had, however, been brought up by 'feminist' mothers. Others, in both samples, said that either their mother or father or both had made them feel that they could do anything in life, and supported them in any activity which they chose irrespective of the gendered nature of that activity.

Discussion of family backgrounds usually lays emphasis on mothers, fathers often being neglected. However, one striking finding in my research is the importance of fathers as role models. 'Deb' (1980s sound engineer): 'I love technology, but then that's probably come from my dad being an engineer. We used to talk a lot about physics. In fact, he's never been any different to me or my brother. We had really long conversations about all sorts of things. I used to watch him change plugs and do fuses.' In some cases, clearly, the father had wanted a son and the daughter was being reared without the usual feminine restrictions.

> **TERRY HUNT** (Jam Today): I think I was very lucky. My father made me feel I could do anything. Like, I was very ill when I was six, but rather than my mother bringing me dollies, [he] used to bring me broken transistor radios and bits of machinery and a set of tools, and I used to take everything apart and put it all back together again. I used to walk around in a shirt with a screwdriver in my top pocket because that's what [my father] did. . . . I was the surrogate son, definitely. But it wasn't that my father ever treated me like a boy. I never felt like a boy. He just made me feel like anything was possible.

Two musicians I interviewed were sisters and had been brought up in a similar way to Terry:

FRAN RAYNER : My dad, there was no doubt about it, wanted to have a son. And . . . he got three daughters, instead. But, although in terms of his work and how he sees women he's fairly sexist and discriminates against women, he didn't too much at home. He taught us about cars, as much as he knew. He encouraged us to be involved in what he was doing; he liked that. Probably both of us know more about cars than he does now, and he would probably accept that.

Fran's father bought her a motorbike, a purchase which most fathers would not contemplate. These women grew up without fear of technology or the usual assumptions about men being better at technical and mechanical tasks.

My evidence suggests the significance of girls perceiving male roles as available—not being confined to traditional feminine behaviour patterns. Fathers treating their daughters more like sons seems to be the important factor here, regardless of the particular attitudes of the parents towards gender in general.

Often girls from such backgrounds pursued so-called male subjects at school, such as the sciences and mathematics. In the 1980s sample, one woman had been the only girl in her school to take woodwork, whilst another was the lone female in the metalwork class. My interviewees included mathematics, animal psychology, and science graduates, for whom a childhood pursuit of 'male' hobbies continued into adulthood, and they engaged in activities such as carpentry and electronics. Quite a few rode motorbikes. A number had done 'masculine' jobs for a living, including motorcycle messenger, van driver, printer, farmworker, gardener, electrical engineer, civil engineer, piano tuner, bus driver, carpenter, plumber, and designer of spare parts for furnaces. Such women found it easier to enter the male-dominated field of rock music because they already had the confidence to tackle supposedly 'male' tasks. Before becoming a drummer, Judy Parsons (of the Belle Stars) was already a world expert in the field of mud-in-suspension:

I picked up hydraulics quite rapidly. A lot of the blokes used to say, 'You can't do that. That's not women's work! Let me do it.' And I'd say, 'No, no, I'm quite alright'. I was wielding these huge bits of equipment and learning how to move heavy things alone. It was really quite gruelling physical work.

Similarly, many women in the 1995 sample seem to be unusual. Gayl Harrison (of Sidi Bou Said) had been the only one in her year doing technical drawing. Miriam Cohen (of Kid Candy), who was the only girl in her class doing mathematics, was preparing to go on to university to read civil engineering, whilst co-band member Louise Hartley was one of only seven girls in her school studying physics. Both Miriam and Louise were aware of being different from the majority of the girls they knew, who were into pop rather than indie music and were fans rather than musicians.

LOUISE : I've got a brother and I'm very like him and I'm like my dad. I'm not like my mum. I don't like doing girly things. I'm not one to sit in the corner and giggle and talk about girly things. So maybe that's what's made me more into music. . . . I didn't wanna change. All my friends went down

this, 'Well, let's be girls' route and they were into make-up and their hair and everything. And I could never do that because, for one, I felt very ugly at the time. I had a brace and crooked teeth. And I think I was the last out of all the girls to have a boyfriend, because of the fact that I never went out and wanted to change myself and be girly. And I stuck to it. And yet now I have as many boyfriends as any girl of my age.

Resistance to femininity was, for some middle-class girls, aided by schooling, particularly for those, like Emma Anderson from Lush, who went to schools with a strong academic tradition which, rather than steering their upper-middle-class charges into sexually stereotyped dead-end jobs, instilled high aspirations and self-confidence in their pupils. However, middle-class girls did not have a monopoly on resistance to femininity since, in my 1980s sample, more than one working-class women's band had carried the tomboy style over into the band's own discourse, reflected in their clothes, lyrics, and stage posture. Although these particular women were in long-term revolt against the norms of hegemonic femininity, it was not a feminist or lesbian stance, and joining a rock band was not perceived as a feminist act. They just refused to live within the confines of traditional femininity, and thus engaged in music-making much as they would in playing pool.

In conclusion, the 1980s and 1995 samples are very similar. First, nearly all of the women interviewed had been gender rebels as children. Second, families turn out to be important again: many of these women had either a mother or father, or both, who encouraged them to believe that they were capable of doing anything that they wanted to do, regardless of whether it was deemed gender-appropriate by others. I note that this is also true of a number of other well-known musicians, such as Carol Bley, Janis Ian, and Tanita Tikaram, whilst Patti Smith, k. d. lang, Emma Anderson, Kat Bjelland, Kim Gordon, Lesley Rankine, Dolores O'Riordan, and Kim Deal were, to varying degrees, gender rebels. Confidence gained from engaging in so-called masculine activities and hobbies in childhood has enabled women to learn to play 'masculine' instruments and contribute to a 'masculine' musical form. In turn, those women have been contributing towards making the world of rock and roll less masculine so that in the long term gender rebellion may become a less necessary precursor.

Boyfriends/Husbands

It is clear from my 1980s research that one way in which women join rock bands is via their sexual relationships. The musician's wife or girlfriend gets involved in her partner's social world, gaining access thereby to 'insider' knowledge, such as how to get gigs, how to practise, and how the rock world works. She is exposed to key values of the musician's world and, especially, that of playing music. She has role models close at hand, her partner may encourage her to start playing, and there is musical equipment available. A woman's desire to play music may be an attempt to integrate her social life more closely with that of her partner, so that she sees more of him, as, for instance, when she joins the same band. Or, it may be that she is going along to his gigs and wishes to swap the passive role of fan for the more exciting one of performer.

> **JUDY PARSONS** (Belle Stars): That's why I got in a band . . . watching your man play a gig . . . it's a really frustrating experience. . . . He dragged me along. You get there early and you sit there with a pint. You sit there night after night. I remember all the time I was sitting there I was thinking, 'Christ! If I'm gonna be in this place it's much better to be up there on stage.' I was looking at the drummer, thinking, 'It's really easy what he's doing. I'm sure I could do it' . . . And that's a huge motivation for getting in a band. Because, by force of circumstances, I was at gigs but I was in the audience.

This is like the situation where a woman plays golf in order to avoid being a grass widow. Judy was not even particularly interested in rock music until she met her husband: 'I've never really had a burning love for music. . . . [My husband] has always had a huge love for music—it really excites him, he loves it. So now I love music and I love listening to records. And I can talk about it for ages.' If a male musician wishes his wife or girlfriend to become involved, then he is in a very good position to aid her. All of the members of 'Suke''s 1980s commercially successful pop band had got involved via their husbands and boyfriends.

> I was going out with a boyfriend that was in a band. That's how I became interested in being in a band. . . . It never really occurred to me that you could be a female musician, [but then] I saw this advert and thought, 'How marvellous. Girl guitarist wanted for all-girl dance and beat band. That sounds exciting.' He said, 'Why don't you answer it?' So I did. I applied for it with just a hobby in mind, and he pushed me along, and gave me his guitar, and showed me how to do a bar chord.

One Yorkshire pop band I interviewed was composed of four mothers, none of whom would have been playing had they not married musicians:

> **'SANDRA'** : Our husbands had always played in bands. We used to meet that way . . . so we thought, 'Why don't we have a band? Then we can get out three evenings a week as well!' If you've got it every day of the week from your husband . . . a bit gets rubbed off. . . . It's been an escape from being a boring housewife. . . . We were all at the same stage—with kids and housework. We were sat at home with nothing to do, while . . . our husbands were out.

On the other hand, only a minority of women got into bands via this route and in my 1995 sample there was just one women's band where knowing male musicians had been an important factor. The female members of Kid Candy were all school students going out with members of a male band and it was clear that their boyfriends had encouraged them to take the initial plunge in joining a band (at only 15 years of age) and proudly supported them thereafter: 'That's how we got introduced to the world of bands basically', said Miriam Cohen.

> LOUISE HARTLEY : It's always my boyfriend that gets me into bands. I've only ever been out with musicians. It used to be guitarists; I'm onto drummers now.

But, importantly, (guitarist) Louise had always wanted to be a pop star and had already taught herself to play. Similarly, although (bassist) Miriam had been helped by her boyfriends, she had always wanted to be in a band and was a classically trained pianist. They had the motivation but lacked the confidence which was what their boyfriends helped them to achieve. Miriam: 'It'd never dawned on me that I could play anything other than classical music on the piano until we got in this band. I got a bass and I thought, 'Wow! it's not that hard.' It just seemed like a really big step. It seemed like [only] these famous people could do this.' It seems that many young women who are always going out with male musicians are candidates for becoming musicians in bands themselves if only they are encouraged. As well as Miriam and Louise, this was true of Ali:

> ALI SMITH (Diatribe): My boyfriend was a saxophone player and I always found myself going for saxophone players. I couldn't work out why I fancied them, 'cause most saxophone players I knew weren't that exciting. I was the instrument that was exciting. So I decided I would get that instrument and then I could become that exciting.

Sometimes, male musicians do not want the competition, although if they do not feel threatened, there is much that they can do to help and support their girlfriends' or wives' musical ambitions. This support could also come from lesbian partners, of course, but, although many women were much influenced by seeing women they knew perform, none of my lesbian interviewees seem to have got involved in playing in bands because of their girlfriends.

Educational Institutions

For young women, going to university provides freedom from parental restrictions and considerably more control over their own lives. It is also a period of time when women are removed from the obligations of earning a living[4], housework, and raising a family. Student culture allows involvement in many activities which are difficult to fit into a nine-to-five routine so that it is easier to get band members together in the same place at the same time, hours being more flexible than in ordinary working life. Thus higher education, whether art school or university, is a context in which some of the important constraints which I have already discussed are lifted. Moreover a college environment will often provide material resources: equipment storage facilities, rehearsal space, use of

---

[4] The abolition of grants and the introduction of fees is, of course, changing this situation.

minibuses, and a venue for gigs and sometimes student union funds will help to subsidize costs.

A number of the musicians I interviewed started playing whilst at college, and all-women bands have often developed in university towns. It would appear that the university was an important factor in the emergence of the women's music scene in York where a significant number of the people in the three women's bands (Rash, Contraband, and the York Street Band) were either students or ex-students from the university. Similarly, Brighton's all-women band in the early 1980s—Bright Girls—emerged from among university students, as did Huggy Bear a decade later. In Oxford, the all-female early 1990s band, Death By Crimpers, developed whilst Clare Howard and Teresa Hooker were at university when they had time for one or two gigs a week. However, now Clare is a teacher, 'It's a strain now doing a gig on a Saturday night'.

My 1995 sample included both current school students and a surprising number of women who had set up bands whilst they were at school, which stands in stark contrast to my 1980s interviewees who got into bands at a later age, since those who even considered playing in a band whilst of school-age simply had no one to play with. The 1995 interviewees sometimes started school bands with other girls as there were more around who could already play instruments or were prepared to learn. However, being in a band whilst at school poses particular problems (of homework demands, money, and transport), and is often only successfully achieved with parental support. Tampasm (the Brighton all-girl punk band composed of 16-year-olds) and Kid Candy (the Birmingham girl-majority band of 18-year-olds) had this, although in both bands it was conditional on continued commitment to schoolwork, and not taking risks with personal safety. I have already described the unusual degree of support given to Sheffield's all-girl band, Treacle, by Sara and Kate Watt's father.

Role Models

Role models appear to be crucial.[5] It was not until the punk period that there were many high-profile female instrumentalists to act as role models for female fans to emulate. American guitarist, Shareen of Ms45, recalls:

> When I was a kid I had this huge poster of Keith Richards up on my wall and I'd sit there and go, 'Oh, I wanna be Keith Richards when I grow up', but the closest I could come was like, you know, Anita Pallenberg and that did not look like any fun. And then Chrissie Hynde and Pattie Smith came out and all of a sudden I could envision myself in the picture. And before that, call it a

---

[5] This has been confirmed by the experimental research of Rosemary Bruce (Bruce and Kemp 1993) who demonstrated that primary school children's choice of instruments to play could be strongly influenced by the sex of a live role model (quoted in Green 1997).

lack of vision or whatever, I could not place myself in the frame. I couldn't place myself as subject.

Some women told me that they had first become motivated to play music, or join a band, by seeing other women playing in a rock context. 'Brenda' (of a 1980s professional New Wave band) remembers seeing women play in an electric band when she was 13 or 14: 'Amazing women. Very good, they were. Very strong women. It definitely had an influence on me. There's no doubt about it . . . I never thought a woman could do it.' In the following case it was not actually seeing a women's band performing but, rather, hearing a record (by the Runaways) which inspired 'Sophie' (of a 1980s rock band) to play:

When I was 16 I heard this record on the radio. . . . So I went out and bought it. I thought, 'It can't be girls playing this. It can't be!' I thought, 'Oh, God! I can't believe it.' I bought their albums and I went mad on them. And that's when I wanted to join an all-girl band, from then on. That's before I even started playing.

Many of the women I interviewed were highly aware that they, in turn, were serving as role models for other women.

VI SUBVERSA : **I saw a 3-year-old girl at Hebden Bridge. She was sat . . . looking while we did our soundcheck. And I thought, 'Great! She's watching my daughter [playing]', and she'd seen me on stage. And I'd never seen anybody like that before I started. I didn't know that there were women doing it at all. Knowing that that little kid saw me play, and that my daughter found it natural to play bass guitar—I just think that's wonderful. I feel really privileged to be part of that.**

In fact, a decade later, one of my 1995 interviewees mentioned Vi Subversa specifically as an influence in getting her into playing electric guitar. Likewise, in the 1990s, Oxford indie band of twenty-somethings, Twist, had served as a local role model for the 16-year-olds in Frances Belle.

4 Punks, Feminists, Lesbians, and Riot Grrrls

The single largest surge of women into rock music-making in the UK was in the late 1970s and early 1980s as a result of two phenomena: the 'moment' of punk rock and 1970s second wave feminism (then known as the Women's Liberation Movement). This sudden increase in the number of women playing in rock bands was recognized by the media at the time in a flurry of articles about 'women in rock'. Similar media excitement greeted the Riot Grrrl phenomenon of 1993 but, in Britain unlike America, Riot Grrrl remained little more than a label lazily applied by journalists to any and every young women's rock band and rejected by all but a handful. Insofar as Riot Grrrl did exist beyond its media fabrication, it can be seen as the boisterous youthful offspring of punk and feminism which I shall discuss after dealing with its far more significant parents.

Punks

In the late 1970s and early 1980s there was a marked increase in the number of women in bands; the number of women playing instruments in bands; the number of women-only bands; and the general visibility and importance of women within popular music. Punk and its aftermath, new wave, played a significant role in bringing about this situation by changing a whole range of existing rock coventions, which opened up a space in which women could play. Apart from enabling women punks (like Siouxsie Sioux and Poly Styrene) to become musicians, punk made it easier for *all* women to get on stage, irrespective of whether they played punk music. As a result, a wave of all-women bands emerged playing music in many styles: pop, power-pop, ska, R'n'B, reggae, rock, heavy metal, and electronic music. Although punk proper was short-lived (1976–7), its after-effects were important, since increasing numbers of women were getting into bands in 1978 and 1979, so much so that as the decade turned the media recognized a new phenomenon called 'women in rock'. Thus, in spite of the male domination of punk and the misogynism of its lyrics, it was an important catalyst for women's entry into music-making, enhancing career chances of all women musicians by the early 1980s, compared to the preceding period. I shall briefly analyse why that was the case.

In the 'progressive' rock period, which immediately preceded punk, instrumental virtuosity was required since numbers tended to be lengthy with long, elaborate, instrumental solos. Punk simplified music, in terms of structure and rhythm, making spirit more important than expertise so that, for a while, amateurishness and mistakes were in fashion. For this reason alone, many women who had previously lacked the confidence even to consider joining a band started performing since if boys could play knowing only one or two chords, then so could women. It was punk which got Vi Subversa (of Poison Girls) playing for the first time in her life: 'We emerged in 1976/77 when the punk thing happened. Punk was very important, because until then I felt alienated from music. . . . The ethos of punk was that anybody can get on stage and do it. And if punk had not happened I don't think we would have been allowed on stage.' Women started bands and gigged right away, learning en route because audience expectations changed and such absolute beginners were accepted, even at prestigious venues.

'SOPHIE' (of a 1980s rock band): **Everybody could play in bands who couldn't really play. You could do gigs. There was a lot of gigs at that time. Like, the Marquee used to be a very select type of place, and then in '77 everyone was playing there. . . . The feeling was good; everyone was so friendly. . . . [Without punk] we wouldn't have formed a band 'cause we would have thought we was terrible. We all learnt from scratch—all of us together. . . . We done our first gig after we'd done only one rehearsal. We was absolutely abysmal. . . . We weren't serious about it. We just used to do it for a laugh, really. It was good fun.**

'Kassandra' and 'Becky' told me how, in 1979, their new wave band was touring English universities within one month of forming. Becky did not know how to play bass, but she was able to manage by just playing one (root) note per song on the bass throughout her first gig. 'When we started we were terrible and we went down really well everywhere!' ('Kassandra')

Bands like this were a breath of fresh air on a basically stale rock scene. The sheer nerve of the women, in getting up on stage and trying, was appreciated and added to the novelty.[1] Punk also reversed the trend towards increasingly expensive equipment and proclaimed that 'cheapest will do', which meant a smaller financial outlay to set a band up, and so the earnings differential between young

---

[1] But the liberating effect of amateurism and poverty was inevitably short-lived. They became more skilled and desired better equipment. Moreover, whilst virtually all the male punk bands made a fairly fast transition to professional status, few female bands survived into the mid-1980s. This suggests that the transition from amateur to professional status is easier for male bands.

women and men was (temporarily) irrelevant. This factor probably encouraged more women to join bands. My band started off with a trifling total outlay of £100 for all the amps, microphones, and stands. The bass player's instrument cost a mere £20 and she did not get a better one for two years.

The established gender conventions of performance, image, and appearance were undermined by punk since, in common with women's movement bands (and many female punks were explicitly or implicitly feminist), the traditional emphasis on attractiveness and glamour was challenged, rejected, or playfully undermined. Punk women, like Poly Styrene and Laura Logic, refused to be defined by conventions, breaking all the existing rules of feminine clothing in ways that were striking at the time, although taken for granted now: skirts too short, slits too high, etc. As new female images were possible, a woman could be childish, eccentric, butch, or tarty. Conventional notions of femininity were attacked and parodied by taking fetishized items of clothing and pornographic images and flaunting them back at society. This, at the time, brazen attack on the 'double standard' was reinforced by the bands' names, such as the Slits, Strumpet, the Streetwalkers, the Harpies, and the Snatch. In contrast, other women were determinedly asexual, trying to avoid all existing sexual codes: 'I was an anti-front person. I used to wear this big mac and hang onto the mike and hardly move' ('Deb', sound engineer).

Ugliness was celebrated and, in contrast to the beauty advice in magazines, punks, male and female, deliberately uglified themselves by applying make-up in garish ways and by dyeing their hair shocking colours. In this way the whole emphasis on the creation of 'natural' beauty was undercut so that women performers could also be fat, tall, and even middle-aged. Candy Ballantyne (Jane Goes Shopping): 'Punk was a great equalizer. I was struck by the fact that punk girls didn't think they had to live up to any kind of standard woman image. You could be any shape or size and you'd be quite acceptable.' As new female vocal styles emerged, a far wider range of women's voices found expression. Frith (1981) points out: 'The legacy of punk to women's rock was that in making ugliness an aspect of authenticity, it opened up to female singers sounds that had previously been regarded as unfeminine and therefore unmusical. In punk, "strident", "grating", "screeching", "squawking" (once applied dismissively, for example, to Yoko Ono) were terms of praise.' You did not have to sing 'properly' or even sing at all: you could just engage in semi-talk, a style which Patti Smith popularized initially. Your voice did not have to sound sweet or warm or sexy, which encouraged a lot more women to start performing. 'There have always been women singing, but not that I could identify with. 'Cause I was told that I was not pretty enough to go on the stage and be one of those. I didn't have a pretty voice, or pretty looks' (Vi Subversa). Vi was in her forties, but she did not try to disguise her age. Indeed, she drew attention to it via her lyrics about the menopause.

Because playing 'standards' and copying other bands was out of style, women felt encouraged to write songs, for DIY was the norm. Male punk bands often wrote aggressive and insulting lyrics, some of which were directed at women. As

Laing stated, 'the lifting of the taboo on the unsayable in rock discourse ended in a new way of saying something quite old: a celebration of male sexuality as essentially aggressive and phallocentric' (Laing 1985: 46). Undeniably, the lyrics of some punk bands, such as the Stranglers, were as misogynist and sexist as those of the Rolling Stones (Reynolds and Press 1995). Yet, at the same time, punk allowed women to voice their anger and frustration with the sexual status quo, by singing about hate, writing angry songs or specifically anti-romance lyrics. A wide range of new topics entered the musical discourse, ones which spoke of aspects of women's experience, previously considered inappropriately unsexy or taboo: housework, motherhood, menstruation, contraception, rape, anorexia, female masturbation, cunnilingus, and faking orgasm. The insertion of the female body into musical discourse was reflected by a rash of gynaecological-sounding band names, such as Bleeding Women, Ova, Anna Rexic, Bodyfunctions, PMT. Moreover, these new themes were covered by bands playing a diversity of musical styles so that the results could be direct and aggressive or subtle and ironic. My own band, the Mistakes, played power-pop dance music with (often) deceptively happy sounding lyrics about things like bisexuality, female economic exploitation, and nuclear death.

Furthermore, as punk fragmented into new wave, experimentation was rife as musicians deconstructed the grammar of rock: the convention of verse-chorus-verse-middle eight-verse-chorus was undermined and unusual time signatures replaced the traditional four-four. The vanguard experimental band the Raincoats unpredictably speeded up and slowed down within songs and appeared, at times, deliberately to be singing out of tune. Gender-specific notions of rock were questioned as part of this overall process of deconstruction, and by how they held their instruments and related to audiences, female punk and post-punk performers went further in challenging the sexist connotations of established performing styles than did their male equivalents: I would agree with Laing (1985) who argues that:

> **Most punk bands shared with earlier groups the guitar-based line-up and the 'spontaneous' adoption of a narrow range of guitar-playing and parading genres. . . . the performance of male artists generally showed an uncritical adherence to standard styles which emphasised macho postures. In complete contrast, most of the best-known female punk musicians set themselves up to undo the conventional performing roles provided as models by mainstream music. (Laing 1985: 87, 98)**

Because non-rock instruments became fashionable, it was possible for classically trained women to play, say, the violin or the flute in a popular music context, since a band did not necessarily have to include the classic rock instrumental components. If no female bass player could be found in the locality then a band might compensate for the lack of a bass with the use of a percussionist or an extra keyboard-player. As punk undermined the 'male-guitar-hero' pose, a lead guitar was no longer necessary since solos were out of fashion. (This anti-elitism resonated with the democratic principle in the women's movement which insisted that nobody should take up too much 'space'.) In many women's bands instruments were often swapped around, as Vicky Aspinall of the Raincoats told me, 'We're not so concerned with being a good guitarist or a good singer, which is why we all play several instruments and why we all sing . . . in order to "deconstruct" it a bit. It's not the one person at the front.' I would argue the greater questioning of established norms and conventions of both music and social behaviour reflected the effects of 1970s feminism.

As the punk phenomenon spread throughout the UK, adopting its own commercial dynamic, it soon solidified into a far narrower (and sexually stereotyped) stylistic range, which marginalized female punks. However, because female performers maintained the freedom to experiment with sexual imagery and resist gender stereotyping, their influence has been great. Thus the musical experimentation of the Raincoats influenced grunge and the ethos and spirit of punk infused the Riot Grrrl bands of the early 1990s.

I did not expect my 1995 interviewees to have been much influenced by punk and post-punk, yet some did mention it as being an important inspiration for them as teenagers. For instance, Mandy (of Ms45) told me that if it had not been for punk she would never have started playing and Debbie of Echobelly was, as a 13–14-year-old, inspired by a tape of the Au Pairs, the Slits, and Vi Subversa. Others, like Katherine Garrett (of the Mystics), said they had been influenced by punk's echo: 'I realise that a lot of it has sunk into my generation without people even knowing where it's come from.' The importance of punk as a female route into bands persisted into the late 1980s and early 1990s. Caroline Appleyard (in 1995 a highly accomplished 26-year-old bass player) mentioned two reasons why she started out her musical career playing in punk bands in the mid-1980s:

> I discovered punk when I was about 17. . . . So I started playing in local punk bands. . . . I think I ended up playing punk because I couldn't play anything else. . . . I think there's a lot less sexism in punk. . . . I was playing bass in quite a few male bands and I never, you know, I never got any sexism off 'em at all or the audience. And they didn't have you in the band like, say, to look nice, they had me in the band 'cause [I] played bass. It didn't matter what sex you were. So that was great with punk. . . . Whereas in your heavy metal . . . I've had so much crap off some of them.

It was significant that, in 1995, Brighton's only all-girl band was punk: Tampasm, who described their music as 'Courtney Love meets the Sex Pistols', played their first gig in 1993 when they were only 14 years of age with a drummer they had only had for two weeks. This would have been less possible in other genres; but with punk music, said Jennifer Bishop, you 'didn't have to be brilliant'.

In considering the overall impact of punk, my evaluation differs from pre-existing (journalistic) texts (such as L. O'Brien 1995; K. O'Brien 1995; Reynolds and Press 1995; Steward and Garratt 1984; Gaar 1992; Evans 1994) because the latter are focused solely or mainly on the well-known professional bands. Whilst it is true that 'potential long-term acts such as the Slits and the Raincoats disappeared after all-too-brief careers, damaged by the need to have male approval within the business' (L. O'Brien 1995), I disagree with Lucy O'Brien's argument that punk had little effect at the grassroots level. Indeed, my own research (focused as much on the local level as the national) shows that punk had profound local effects as well as national. A remarkable number of women set up bands in towns and cities around the UK during the late 1970s and early 1980s, ones which do not feature in journalistic accounts simply because they stayed local, amateur, usually unrecorded and invisible to the national music press.

Feminists

ALISON RAYNER (Jam Today): I don't think I would have started playing in bands if I hadn't become involved in the women's movement.

Like punk, the history of 1970s and early 1980s feminist musical initiatives has largely been hidden or ignored. Steward and Garratt (1984) document some of this important history and Gill (1995) contributes a useful chapter on lesbian musicians, whilst most recent texts seem to have forgotten it completely. It is to be expected that journalistic books on women in rock only discuss high-profile professional musicians; much interesting music never gets written about because of the accidental nature of success. Confronting this absence is crucial for academic knowledge and for women musicians and would-be-musicians.

In the 1970s and 1980s, feminism was a major route into music-making and all-women bands sprang up in numerous towns and cities for the first time. Some feminists got involved in rock for political reasons, since being in an all-women band was a means of communicating a feminist world-view: it was a chance to write lyrics which challenged ideological hegemony. Many others had long-held musical aspirations but lacked the confidence to approach a male band with a view to joining. Early 1970s 'equality feminism' emphasized the importance of women entering male terrain, doing things which only men were supposed to be able to do, so that, regardless of the lyrics and the music, being in a band was a political statement in itself, and it was recognized as such at all-women gigs. When I first heard that some feminist women in my locality were trying to get an all-women band together I was down there immediately despite my very limited playing abilities. Many women, who would not otherwise have ever considered joining a rock band, have been encouraged to make music by the separate playing context which the 1970s women's movement created. Indeed, some started playing an instrument for the very first time simply because there was a need for all-women bands to supply live music at women-only socials.

Feeling excluded from the mainstream (male) rock world, feminists created a musical world of their own, in which they could play solely with, and for, other women. Having the chance to rewrite the 'rules' of the lyrics, of band membership, of the gig, of the stage, and even of the music itself, women established a different, and alternative, group culture to that of the 'straight' rock world. (I shall discuss this later in the book.) The women's movement converted many women from non-musicians to music-makers, via providing a sympathetic 'space' for their early endeavours since feminist audiences were very forgiving: however badly a novice band played they would be clapped and supported. It was enough, at first, that they were playing at all. Women-only gigs were also safe since there was no verbal abuse or sexual harassment. The British press made a big fuss about the handful of women-only Riot Grrrl gigs in 1993, seemingly oblivious to the thousands of these events that had become routine on the women's scene in the 1970s and 1980s, ones which were never covered in the main music papers because there were hardly any female journalists—besides which the press were not courted. Nevertheless these gigs did exist and not just in London; I personally attended around 200. Thus, feminist fledgling musicians had the benefit of emerging in a sort of protected environment whilst they honed their musical skills. Some, like the radical separatist Harpies, had no intention of ever playing at mixed gigs.

Both punk and feminism were against complex instrumental solos: guitar virtuosos were deeply unfashionable because they were seen as masculine and simplicity was favoured. Since it was up to women to create a more modest, non-competitive, collective, and democratic alternative, feminist musicians in the 1970s and early 1980s positioned themselves in direct opposition to 'cock rock': 'mikes and guitars are phallic symbols (or else caressed like female bodies), the music is loud, rhythmically insistent, built around techniques of arousal and release' (Frith 1983). For this reason feminists tended not to play metal or heavy rock but, rather, reggae, pop, jazz, latin, and improvisational/experimental music (like the Feminist Improvisational Group). Some feminists (as in the early position of Ova) would only play acoustic instruments. However, this was a minority position and, for many, a temporary one, although female guitarists in feminist bands in the 1970s and early 1980s tended to stick to rhythm guitar, with the instrument not assigned any more prominence or status than any other instrument. Quite a few bands included keyboards in their line-ups, which capitalized on the number of women with classical piano training.

Both punk/new wave and feminism opened up a space for a wider variety of image and presentation of self. In terms of voice, women could sing like choir girls, talk like rappers, shriek, scream, bellow, roar, and more, ignoring the traditional rules of feminine stage glamour, the norm for feminist bands tending to be no make-up, flat shoes/boots, and jeans/trousers. You could be any shape or size; you certainly did not have to look attractive in terms of conventional femininity. All of these factors made it much easier for women to take the stage.

Feminist songs reflected the politics of the personal, which provided the confidence for any woman in a feminist band to try her hand at songwriting. Love songs became heavily politicized and women wrote anti-romance songs. Unprecedented topics emerged: periods, puberty crises, housework, and so on (as I have already listed under punk above). Writing your own lyrics and music, and thus expressing your own creativity, was conceptualized as 'feminist' or even 'female' and held in contrast to male bands churning out faithful copies of (male) standards. If covers were performed, the lyrics were invariably altered.

Figure 2: Clothes and image.

Above: Tampasm, do tongues Club, The Lift, Brighton 1995. Charlotte Clarke on vocals.

Below top: Sam Battle of Beaker, The Elm Tree, Oxford, 1995.

Below bottom: Clare Howard of Beaker, The Elm Tree, Oxford 1995.

Early British feminist pioneer bands (with prosaic names), like the London Women's Rock Band and the Northern Women's Rock Band served as important role models for a whole clutch of new women's bands which emerged in the late 1970s. 'Anne' (of 1980s York women's bands): 'I got into the women's movement and I saw the Stepney Sisters play and that was the first women's/feminist band I'd seen. And I thought, "Oh, I've got to get into a band." ' In turn, these bands have served as role models for more women. I was in a feminist band which gigged around the country for a number of years, and I have been told by a whole succession of women that it was seeing the Mistakes perform which inspired them to start learning to play an instrument.

Because the earliest bands to spring out of the contemporary women's liberation movement were often a sort of musical variant of a 'women's group', the politics was sometimes as important as the music. Terry Hunt (of Jam Today) recalls her first women's band:

> We met once a week and we used to talk after every rehearsal. We were all really eager to talk to each other. We just used to talk and talk and talk. We just used to sit around the table and it was amazing. . . . We used to take turns. It became more like a consciousness-raising thing as well as a band. We were really close. We decided we were only going to have people in the band who were exactly politically right. We used to audition them, but not for their playing—for their politics.

Moreover, the network of women's music workshops which feminists developed around the country (without any funding at all, state or otherwise) was an important source of inspiration for many women, and a chance to try out rock instruments.

'SYLVIA' (of Yorkshire pop band): I went to two 'Women and Music' workshops in Liverpool that summer of '76. And there were women from Stepney Sisters and the Northern Women's Rock Band and all that. And I picked up a bass there. That was the first time I laid hands on a bass, [and yet] there had been a bass guitar in my house for a whole year and I'd never touched it. And I came back from those workshops thinking, 'I've got to play an instrument', and I thought, 'Right, I'm going to learn the bass.' So I did.

Places which had a strong feminist movement in the 1970s developed all-women bands. First, having a lot of feminists in the area meant that there was a reasonable-sized 'pool' of potential women musicians; that is, women who would be willing to learn to play in a feminist context. Secondly, regular women-only bops provided the opportunity for novice bands to debut in a supportive environment. All-women socials created a demand for women-only bands. Brighton used to have a regular event called the 'Women's Monthly' which provided the local band with at least one gig per month.

Feminist musicians often helped other women with equipment and musical instruction. For example,

'ANNETTE' (of 1980s reggae band): I'd seen pictures in the [local paper] and it said 'All girl band'. And I was really into being in a band at the time. I'd seen [the bass player] on the street, and I spoke to her and asked her about the band. I went round to her house and played the bass. She showed me the notes and how to put my fingers. She gave me lessons for about a year—free. She wouldn't take any money. I asked her. She wouldn't take nothing.

As Annette was unemployed and could not afford a bass or amplifier, another local woman came to her aid: 'She said I could have [the bass] for £50. She was going to Leeds . . . She left, and I'd only paid her £10. And she said I could have it free after that. So I didn't bother paying the rest. It was really good luck. Then she sent a message and said I could have an amp, free, to go with the bass.'

Sometimes equipment has been passed on from band to band within feminist circles, particularly in areas with a strong local women's movement (like London, Nottingham, Oxford, and York). The 1970s London Women's Rock Band lent a bass to the Stepney Sisters on the understanding that it would always get passed on. In turn, this bass and a piano were lent to Jam Today. Feminist politics underlie the practice of sharing/lending/giving equipment, offering women opportunities they would not otherwise have had. Similarly, a strong local women's movement has also developed communal strategies for space which has helped with rehearsals. Fran (Sub Rosa): 'Because nobody's got any money, we all have to share. This is a co-op house, so we're all used to the co-op ideal that if somebody's got it then you share it around. If somebody's got a gig then things will be lent out.' Feminists, committed to collectivism, even had a political policy on roadying and setting-up that everyone should do it equally. This was immensely encouraging for women joining bands. On the other hand, no one could have a free ride; singers had to cart equipment around like other band members.

Lesbians

Lesbianism is also important and overlaps considerably with feminism. The 1990s women's scene in Nottingham is virtually synonymous with the lesbian scene, and in the late 1970s and early 1980s, in Oxford, the central core of the feminist alternative scene was lesbian. A significant proportion of women-only bands have been lesbian, partly because the women's movement of the 1960s and 1970s contained a large number of lesbians, who preferred to create music with other women rather than men. As separatist politics became increasingly important during the 1970s, it was argued that lesbianism was not merely an individual sexual preference but a political commitment. Eisenstein summarizes the argument:

it was lesbians who were most likely to focus personal attention and energy on women rather than on men. A woman who sought and received validation from other women was not hostage to male approval. If the personal was the

political, then the choice to give primacy to a woman in one's personal relationships was of great political significance. (Eisenstein 1984: 48)

Many feminists thus became lesbians, in terms of their identity, if not necessarily their sexuality, and lesbians became politicized as feminists. This was how Alison Rayner got involved in Jam Today:

Becoming a lesbian and then getting involved in Gay Liberation . . . a lot of the politics of Gay Liberation fitted in with certain aspects of feminism. And it was almost without really being aware of it, because I'd started going to women's things. I went to one or two conferences. I went probably because . . . there was going to be a social. I gradually got drawn into it. . . . I was involved in the collective for a while. I helped organize a Women's Day march and a social in the evening . . . and we had the Stepney Sisters playing at it . . . . Then I got into music and that was where my energy went into the women's movement.

Lesbians had the most need of women's bands, to provide live music at women-only events, such as bops after Gay Pride marches.[2] They were also in need of musician role models, many lesbian musicians being firmly in the closet.

Although nowhere near as large and significant as the American women's alternative musical industry, during the 1970s British lesbians developed a coherent subculture with its own norms, values, and institutions, which represented a more radical alternative to dominant culture than any of the formations studied by subculturalists.[3] Many women who became involved in this world got drawn into music-making, and the music they created reflected their subcultural perspective. Joining an all-women band gave lesbians a chance to break the heterosexist discourse of rock and pop by, for instance, writing and performing love songs addressed to women. Moreover, lesbians had liberated themselves from the need to prove their femininity and conform to heterosexist expectations— the role of wife or girlfriend, and so on. Without these commitments lesbians were (and still are) freer than the average woman to engage in rock music-making if desired.

`VANESSA'` (Fabulous Jam Tarts): I think a lot of female musicians are lesbians. Because to be out there doing something, you've got to be strong; you've not got to have a guy telling you you can't do this. You've got to be a lot of things that, if you're heterosexual and married or with a male partner . . . you know, there are women who are told what they can drink by their men!

By the 1980s there was a significant core of talented, experienced professional female musicians, at the centre of a changing landscape of (often jazz-orientated)

---

[2] This was a pressing problem as quite a few 'straight' non-feminist bands would not play at all-women events. Moreover, lesbians wanted 'woman-identified women' to perform: bands who would sing love songs for and to the women in the audience, and whose lyrics would reflect a lesbian consciousness.

[3] Lesbian and feminist subcultures have proved just the sort of subcultural experience which McRobbie (1980) said was needed as an alternative to male-dominated youth subcultures.

all-women bands in London with an overlapping membership: Jam Today, the Guest Stars, the Sisterhood of Spit, Lydia D'Ustebyn's Swing Orchestra, and Hi-Jinx. In particular the big bands formed a training ground for a further generation of women musicians.

However, feminism and lesbianism are no longer a major route into rock music-making in the apolitical 1990s, when being gay has become a fashionable lifestyle and commercially exploited. The triple emergence in the 1990s of American lesbian performers k. d. lang, Janis Ian, and Melissa Etheridge offered lesbians some mainstream role models. Yet, although Debbie from Echobelly and the bisexual Skin from Skunk Anansie have an increasingly high profile (both within mixed heterosexual bands), British lesbian musicians have still to achieve such commercial success and, as Gill (1995) points out, some lesbian performers in the mainstream remain in the closet because it is simply too risky to come out. Nevertheless, there are plenty of lesbians playing in bands. Yolande (bassist with Marcella Detroit) told me, in 1996, that 50 per cent of the female musicians that she meets are lesbian. Similarly, there has been a continuous stream of lesbian bands from the 1970s until the 1990s (such as Well-Oiled Sisters and Atomic Candy), their success remaining largely within the lesbian community.

DEBBIE SMITH (Echobelly): It could be just purism or fear of breaking out into the main arena, or it could be the music press just refusing to acknowledge you, as happened with 'The Brendas'. They got maybe two or three write-ups in the *Melody Maker* in a six-year career. All the journalists that go out and see groups, they're mainly men, or they used to be, and they wouldn't go to a women's day at the Hackney Empire or an Aids benefit and most of the lesbian bands I knew were playing in those arenas, so they wouldn't get noticed.

Lesbianism's public persona has been subject to considerable political dilution and today has no necessary connection with feminism, so that it is no longer the *political* route into women's music-making that it once was. Some lesbian women whom I interviewed in 1995–6 felt that their sexuality was irrelevant or of negligible importance to their music-making and a few were still 'in the closet'.

Riot Grrrls

In 1993, exactly a decade after the post-punk British media wave of 'women in rock', another media fanfare announced the arrival of 'Riot Grrrl' and women in bands became newsworthy again. As Riot Grrrl was essentially an American import and this book is about music-making in the UK, I shall concentrate on the movement's fate in Britain. However, it is necessary to give a résumé of the American scene.

Riot Grrrl (a term coined by Bratmobile) was the chosen label for a political movement of young feminist women in the American 'indie' or underground music scene, originating in grunge and hardcore. Frightwig, an all-female grunge band formed in the early 1980s, was the original inspiration for the new wave of strong female underground bands later in that decade: Hole, Babes in Toyland, L7, and the Lunachicks. Courtney Love (of Hole) with her 'kinderwhore' image and her talk of killing off 'boy rock', in turn inspired Kathleen Hanna to set up Bikini Kill. Apart from their confrontational lyrics, these women bared their breasts and grabbed their crotches on stage and elsewhere. (On British television Donita Sparks of L7 dropped her pants and while at Reading Festival she removed her tampon and threw it into the audience.) Terms such as 'angry women' and then the derogatory 'foxcore' were initial attempts by the media to label what appeared to be a new phenomenon, but the name chosen eventually by some of the bands themselves was Riot Grrrl. As the press then applied the label to a wider number of bands, it is important to note that not all bands of young feminist women accepted it. Hole, and L7, for instance, despite inspiring the movement and although similar in attitudes and behaviour, distanced themselves from 'Riot Grrrl' for fear of being trivialized. Insofar as there was a specific origin of the self-conscious Riot Grrrl movement, it seems to be Olympia (Wa.) and Washington DC in 1991. A political agenda was formulated and an attempt was made to create an organized network amongst all-girl bands, via fanzines so that the Riot Grrrl movement was a genuine female youth subculture with the explicit aim of encouraging women to move into all areas of the rock world. Political action included coast-to-coast networking via the DIY production of feminist fanzines.

Emerging from a historical context changed by two decades of feminism, Riot Grrrl was feminist to the core and yet it was also a generational revolt as, by style and language, Riot Grrrls disassociated themselves from the 1960s/70s generation. They celebrated girlishness by wearing big plastic hairgrips, slides, bunches, and sports tops. The name itself speaks volumes: a recuperation of the term 'girl' against the politically correct (yet now tame) 'woman' of their mothers' feminist generation, but with a new spelling that turned it into a growl of feminist anger. A key feature of Riot Grrrl was a confrontational attitude which challenged not only sexism but also the established political correctness of the 1990s. They dealt in irony, contradiction, and parody. Riot Grrrls wrote 'slut' and 'bitch' on their bare limbs and stomachs, neutralizing sexist terms, provoking apprehension and mystification in generations of older feminists. In the context of the new 'third wave' feminism of young American writers such as Susan Faludi (1992) and Naomi Wolf (1990 and 1994), it was a reaction, first, against what was perceived as the pessimistic 'victim feminism' of an older generation and, secondly, against the anti-feminist backlash of the 1980s. The lyrics were about the concerns of female teenagers in the 1990s: eating disorders, the beauty myth and 'body fascism', bodily mutilation, date rape, oral sex, and incest.

Like punk, the music itself was determinedly lo-fi and committed to amateurishness so that what counted was raw energy and spirit rather than musicianship.

However, unlike punk, it was not that different or distinctive; not *musically* radical. Indeed, Riot Grrrl did not denote a specific style of music: most bands were punk, thrash, grunge, or some kind of combination. (Kathleen Hanna of Bikini Kill sounded strikingly like Poly Styrene, for instance.) What was important was that it was music which could be played from scratch, and, thus, it functioned as a clear route for women into rock. This very simple music, combined with girl-relevant lyrics and an evangelical approach towards getting as many young women into bands as possible, clearly had long-term results in America, its success aided in part by help from a 'mainstream' girls' magazine, *Sassy* (Gottlieb and Wald 1994).

The British Riot Grrrl scene was smaller, less significant, and less well documented than the US movement, so much so that I had difficulty getting first-hand information from anyone who was (or had been) happy to be called a Riot Grrrl. As British Riot Grrrls have been notoriously distrustful of the press and also academics, the main Riot Grrrl band in the UK, Huggy Bear, would not give interviews. The Voodoo Queens, another band commonly called Riot Grrrl, refused the term and also an interview. I did interview Amelia of Heavenly, however, who had been over to Olympia and was instrumental in bringing Riot Grrrl bands over to the UK in 1993. I also interviewed a number of informative women in Mambo Taxi, the Frantic Spiders, Death By Crimpers, bands commonly labelled Riot Grrrl, a name they all resisted. Because Riot Grrrl was not a specific style of music, but a political process/movement, the label became indiscriminately attached by the media to any band composed of young women, usually much to their irritation. Other information I have gleaned is based on reading the music press and books by music journalists: Amy Raphael (1995), Liz Evans (1994), Karen O'Brien (1995), Lucy O'Brien (1995), Simon Reynolds and Joy Press (1995), Evelyn McDonnell and Ann Powers (1995). As there is, so far, little academic literature on the subject, I did use Joanne Gottleib and Gayle Wald (1994), which was solely about the American scene. Lastly, although not Riot Grrrls themselves, a number of interviewees have spoken to me of the impact of reading about the movement's activities and listening to bands such as Huggy Bear and Bikini Kill.

The UK scene started in 1991 when some feminist students from Sussex University formed the punk band Huggy Bear, releasing their first single 'Herjazz' and declaring Year Zero of the boy-girl revolution. In March 1992 they were ejected from the television programme *The Word* for calling the producer a 'woman-hater', which led to a *Melody Maker* front cover for the following week. In 1992 Huggy Bear supported Bikini Kill and Hole, and there was a joint Hole and Huggy Bear women-only gig at London's Subterrania venue in 1993. As Huggy Bear had an explicit feminist agenda, they challenged male domination of space by urging girls to invade the male territory of rock bands, rock journalism, and, more controversially, the taken-for-granted gendered spatial configurations of the gig. Normally at punk and indie gigs, the immediate front of stage space ('moshpit') is home for a seething mass of adolescent boys, energetically (and often aggressively) slam-dancing and pogoing in a scrum of male bonding which pushes girls out to the margins, for fear of being injured or groped. On their 1993

UK tour, Huggy Bear encouraged girls to take over the moshpit and requested the boys to move to the back, often sparking trouble. In Wales, no one complied and a riot ended the gig while at another gig, Jo (the bass player) was hit. In fact, hardly any of Huggy Bear's gigs were women-only, but, as the attempt to improve girls' visibility and safety was critically misinterpreted as the exclusion of males, it was strongly resisted, provoking a misogynistic backlash in the *NME* letters page. In fact, some boys attended Huggy Bear gigs just to give them a hard time.

Huggy Bear attempted to radically change the somewhat stale British indie music scene. They turned gigs into political debates, making speeches from the stage, and distributing self-penned pamphlets. They launched a fresh underground information network of fanzines, such as Ablaze, Girlfrenzy, and Reggae Chicken. 'Zines had been important at the time of punk and then declined. In the early 1990s they were revived by clubbers on the rave scene and direct action political activists such as hunt saboteurs, the Anti-Criminal Justice Bill Coalition, and Earth First. Indeed, there were connections between Riot Grrrl and the wider anarchist and deep green movements. For example, the Leeds/Bradford Riot Grrrl group used to meet in the 1-in-12 club in Bradford, an energetic alternative space for anarchists, punks, and DIY activists (Wakefield and Grrrt 1995). The group networked via fanzines, making contact between women musicians easier in the locality, and organized a day of women's music workshops.

Around the UK, other Riot Grrrl bands were formed, such as Linus, the Furbelows, Limpstud, Pussycat Trash, Skinned Teen, and Lollyshop. However, in contrast to the USA, press mediation led to the British movement's premature death and few bands today use the label 'Riot Grrrl'.

ANDREA (Mambo Taxi): **Riot Grrrl was very healthy and going quite well and then the press grabbed it and then everyone fled from it. There were fanzines springing up. There were little clubs springing up. There were hundreds of female bands springing up, really unknown ones, outside London. We used to get passed fanzines and sometimes women used to write and say, 'I'm setting up a club to celebrate women in my town. We want you to support it' and obviously you'd be there. The problem was that half of us didn't know a bloody thing about it. That wasn't why we were doing it. So, to turn around and go, 'Yes, we're Riot Grrrl' and then someone go 'what is it?' Our bass player said, 'If Riot Grrrl is being feminist and being in a band, I've been one since I'm 17'. It was all of a sudden a label stuck on an ongoing thing, anyway. It became a bit ridiculous, 'What is the fuss about?!' It was just very much a media thing.**

In the UK Riot Grrrl was heavily mediated from the start, with the British music press divided into strongly pro and anti camps and their columns bristling with debate.

DELIA (Mambo Taxi): **They got all this rubbish in the press about Huggy Bear inciting women to beat men up at gigs and crap and it made a lot of people hate Huggy Bear without even seeing them or reading them. And we got**

caught up in it. We'd turn up at a gig and if the support band was a boy band, you'd see them quivering in the corner. We'd say hello and they'd say, 'Oh, we thought you'd be really annoyed because we're boys!' And they'd say, 'You're all lesbians, aren't you? We thought you'd be all shouty and sloganny'. . . . Huggy Bear had such bollocks [sic]. They don't trust anyone now and I don't blame them. They've been fucked around. They're fed up with the whole thing. . . . People are always saying to Mambo Taxi, 'Do you have an agenda?' (for taking over the world). We play inane pop music, you know! We must be a Riot Grrrl band because we were this girl band playing with Huggy Bear. We were all anti-sexist, obviously, but we never even thought about it before. I'll say, 'Stop pushing her around' to a bloke from the stage, but it's not 'Let's kill all the blokes at our gigs'.

Consequently, most women musicians did not want to be associated with Riot Grrrl. Even Courtney Love, iconized by Huggy Bear, criticized the movement for promoting a 'teensie, weensie, widdle, cutie' image, lack of musicianship, and of grabbing publicity. Some who criticized it (like P. J. Harvey and Stereolab) found themselves attacked as reactionaries in the Riot Grrrl 'zines. Moreover, sadly, Huggy Bear, feeling that biased media attention had disempowered them, refused to give interviews to potentially supportive UK girls' magazines such as *Select*.

Clearly, there were novel aspects to Riot Grrrl, but there were also many continuities with both British female punks and feminist bands, although these have been neglected by most commentators who presented Riot Grrrl as totally new while the declaration of the Year Zero thereby wiped out the hidden 1970s feminist heritage. However, I perceive Riot Grrrl as the stroppy daughters of 1970s punk and feminism. Names of bands like Snatch, Ovarian Trolley, and Thrush confronted the dual standard of sexual morality and the negative associations attached to the female body, recalling the names of punk bands in the 1970s/early 1980s. Another similarity was the claiming of space for women at gigs. In 1992, women-only gigs were trumpeted by the press as unique, but there were thousands of women-only gigs in the 1970s and 1980s, and there still are such events, routine and unreported in the press. The seemingly novel practice of challenging the male-dominated front-of-stage space was also in line with 1970s feminist practice when many bands routinely invited women down to the front of stage and requested that men make a space for them, which they usually did. Sometimes, microphones would be handed to women in the audience and they were encouraged to come up on stage and sing backing vocals or dance. Riot Grrrls gave out leaflets at their gigs, sold fanzines, and engaged in polemic from the stage. The semi-Riot Grrrl band Mambo Taxi sent out chordsheets of their songs, so that girls could play along with the records. They had numerous letters from girls asking for advice and so Andrea wrote, photocopied, and distributed a twenty-nine-page booklet on how to put on a successful gig. This kind of activity also had antecedents within the feminist women's music scene of the 1970s and early 1980s. For instance, in 1979 the Raincoats (in many ways a prototype Riot Grrrl band) published a booklet setting out their aims. In particular, the organization

Rock Against Sexism promoted anti-sexist gigs, literature, and fanzines. Lastly, feminist musicians ran numerous women's music workshops throughout the 1970s and 1980s.

On the other hand, there are some interesting differences. One dissimilarity is that Riot Grrrl involved boys too and some Riot Grrrl bands (like God Is My Co-Pilot and Huggy Bear) were mixed. In contrast, the 1970s and early 1980s bands on the UK women's scene would not on principle have a man in the band, or even in the building: no male sound engineers, lighting engineers, or road crew; women took pride in total self-reliance. Another contrasting feature is that Riot Grrrls (like other 1990s female musicians) were much more overtly sexual than women in the earlier period. The archetypal image of 1970s feminist bands (excluding punks) was the straightforwardly androgynous or even masculine one of short hair, jeans, and no make-up, the antithesis of the Laura Ashley femininity of the time, a 'one of the boys' kind of look. Since then, various performers, most notably Annie Lennox and Madonna, have made visual image central to musical performance with a succession of recreated personae. The image of Riot Grrrl (and particularly Courtney Love's 'kinderwhore' look) was studied, ambiguous, and polysemic, but it was also open to misinterpretation, employing a supposed irony which could be easily lost on some segments of the audience, most of whom would be only too delighted to give her an ironic fuck.

It is arguable whether Riot Grrrl has had as much effect in the UK as it did in the States. Indeed, it never really took off nationally in the first place, and has remained highly localized in a few cities where the energizing activity of one or two highly committed women inspires others (such as Newcastle, Glasgow, and Leeds/Bradford). My research suggests that it has not had the same long-term impact in the UK as punk. Interviewing women in 1995–6, I discovered that many of them knew little about Riot Grrrl and some had never heard of it. Not one of the women I interviewed would call herself a Riot Grrrl, while some believed that the whole UK Riot Grrrl scene was a media myth beyond the activities of one band: Huggy Bear. Many of the bands described as Riot Grrrl were playing long before the term existed and were annoyed at being so indiscriminately labelled by the press. My interviewees included a variety of styles and political position: Valley of the Dolls, Death By Crimpers, Beaker, Treacle, the Frantic Spiders, and even the acoustic duo Pooka.

SARA WATTS (Treacle): The first gig we ever played and we were not Riot Grrrls in the slightest. We were little and innocent and I'd got my pretty dress on and my hat and we were singing cover songs. And the only cover[age] we ever got in the *NME* was 'all-girl riot band Treacle go down a storm in Sheffield'. . . . I don't know where that came from.

DELIA (Mambo Taxi): We got really tired of the whole Riot Grrrl thing. So we didn't want to do anything that would encourage it.

Death By Crimpers defied considerable pressure to say that they were Riot Grrrls, as it was fashionable at the time. Ironically, Amelia Fletcher and the rest of Heavenly *did* firmly consider themselves to be part of the Riot Grrrl movement in 1993, but were not seen as such because of the band's more gentle sound. On the other hand, some bands (like Sidi Bou Said) benefited from many more live reviews during the Riot Grrrl period simply because they were women. Furthermore, some of the women I interviewed knew a lot about Riot Grrrl and had supported it. Skin (from Skunk Anansie) told me that a lot of young women had picked up guitars because of Riot Grrrl, before the scene 'strangled itself', while Delia said that it encouraged more women to go to gigs. The renaissance of fanzines helped the young DIY indie band Bis build a fanbase in advance of their career move down from Glasgow to London. Amelia Fletcher, who was responsible for bringing Bratmobile over to the UK, argues that the lack of musical skill was essential to Riot Grrrl, as a climate had to be created in which people were willing to listen to bands who were spirited rather than competent, thereby inspiring other girls to think 'I can do that too': 'No band that could play could have done what Huggy Bear did, 'cause they needed to not be able to play to be like they were.' Riot Grrrl, by revamping feminism for the 1990s, made it seem more relevant to teenagers who viewed the feminism of their mothers' generation as too rule-bound. Because there seemed to be a confusing forest of things that you should not do or say unless you wished to be judged 'politically incorrect', they felt dispossessed and so they rewrote the feminist script for the 1990s.[4]

AMELIA FLETCHER (Heavenly): Riot Grrrl was done by a bunch of 16 to 17-year-olds who felt that feminism didn't apply to them in any respect and then suddenly realized it did: date rape, pro-choice, boys being bastards . . .

LAETITIA (Stereolab): I thought it was an interesting moment. Not necessarily in the fact that there was a movement, but in men's reaction and how freaked out they were about it. They were threatened. And that was interesting . . . they felt under attack. And if they had nothing to reproach themselves they wouldn't have reacted. They would have gone 'Bullshit!' But it just proved that there is still lot of work to be done in that field.

What is also interesting is that, unlike the punk period, for the first time the music press itself was under attack, which led to many more female music journalists and, therefore, to women's bands being treated more sympathetically.

[4] According to journalist Emily White, this was also true of American Riot Grrrls: 'It's surprising how many are daughters of seventies women's libbers. For all their anger and violence, many of these girls come from nurturing, healthy mother-daughter relationships, often families where the father was left early on as the mother became politicised' (Emily White, 'Revolution Girl Style Now', in McDonnell and Powers 1995: 404–5).

5 Joining a Band[1]

Typically, a male band starts when a group of friends (usually at the same school, of the same age, and living in the same locality) gradually evolves into a rock group.[2] My research suggests that in the past this has not been true of female bands, none of the bands I researched in the 1980s emerging in this way. Amongst the 1995 sample, a handful did but there were often important mediating factors. Two female school student bands developed in the early 1990s in the unlikely setting of an Oxfordshire village, Eynsham, where a single male youth worker played a pivotal role in encouraging girls to set up bands. He paid for and arranged tuition for them from Oxford band members, provided free rehearsal space and access to equipment, and set up prestigious gigs for them in Oxford. Insofar as there has been a change during the 1990s I think this can be related to changing fashions. Since more female school students see playing in a band as 'cool' there is a slightly larger pool of female musicians. However, because bands arise from friendship groups, the tendency among teenagers is to have boy bands and girl bands rather than mixed ones, and this is borne out by my research. Kathryn (Frantic Spiders): 'It was just doing it with our friends, who were girls. There was an official pop band who used to do . . . covers and they all played their instruments really well and we thought we didn't want to be in it 'cause we didn't play well enough. So we just formed our own band.' Like other school student bands in the late 1980s, the Frantic Spiders, who started when they were 15, were the only female band in their school and were distanced from the boy musicians:

CHARLEY : **When I first got an acoustic guitar, there was a group of people who would every lunchtime all go and play electric guitar in the music room. They were all boys. 'Cause I really wanted to go and do that and I felt completely intimidated because they were so arrogant about it. If you were a girl, the only**

---

[1] An earlier version of this chapter (based on my 1980s research) appeared in Frith and Goodwin (1990).

[2] This conclusion is based on reading the biographies and autobiographies of male rock stars, talking to male musicians in my area when I was in a band, and what little sociological evidence is available: e.g. in America, H. Stith Bennett's study (1980), and in England, Ruth Finnegan's research (1989). Also relevant: *Band of Hope*, a Radio 4 programme produced by Peter Everett, transmitted 6 Apr. 1988.

> way you could join in their little music group was if you were really sexy and
> could sing, 'cause that's all the girls were thought to be good for was being a
> singer in their band. So it was just horrible. I just kept out of the way.

Had this been in the 1960s, 1970s, or early 1980s, my research indicates that
Charley would have been alone in her school and not joined a band until her
twenties.

Many male musicians practise alone for years before joining a band, a pattern
which my research suggests was also rare amongst women.

SHAREEN (Ms45): I think there's a male musician rite of passage where
somewhere around 12 years old you decide that you have zits and you're
never gonna get a girl, so you buy yourself a guitar, lock yourself in your
bedroom for the next five years, and get your technical mastery down. Girls
don't seem to get the rite of passage.

As I have already shown, women get involved in a band via other routes. In setting one up, certain material requirements must be met and until this happens
the first rehearsal will not be reached and 'the band' will remain an aspira-
tion, rather than a reality. A man joining an already established band would be
expected to own the necessary equipment, whereas, because of the shortage
of women instrumentalists, a woman might be welcomed into a women's band
with no instrument whatsoever: 'Harriet' (of 1980s London pop band): 'I think
they would have been severely handicapped if they had wanted to get somebody
who had all their own equipment . . . I didn't have any equipment at all.' Most of
my interviewees, in both the 1980s and 1990s bands, believed that women were
less fussy and less competitive about their instruments and musical equipment
than the male musicians they knew.

FRAN (Sub Rosa): Men like twiddling about with their knobs and fiddling
about with their electronics and what their equipment can do, and how
many pedals they've got, and how many flashing lights they've got on it. Like
they've got six strings on their bass instead of four. And what colour it is and
what make it is. Whereas women just go, 'Oh, I've got an old drumkit, that'll
do.' Women aren't specifically precious about their equipment, even though
they'll try and get the best they can afford and get hold of. They won't be
faffing about with knobs and spending three hours tuning up when you've
only got three hours to practise in and you're trying to write a half-hour set
or something. . . . I think a lot of it is men trying to prove to each other that
they've got bigger and better equipment.

A major problem is finding a suitable and affordable practice space, as most living rooms are too small and financing this is an important limiting factor for the
unwaged. Of the 1990s school student bands, Frances Belle and Treacle would
probably have never got going without free rehearsal space; whilst, for Brighton's
all-girl teenage band, Tampasm, rehearsal room costs meant they simply could
not afford to practise as often as they would have liked. Lack of money led some
women to utilize cheaper rates by rehearsing at night and others, like 'Sandra', to

tolerate highly inhospitable surroundings in order to be able to start practising: 'It was really grotty; right next to the canal, very damp basement and very cold—miserable to play in.' Male bands also face these kinds of problems but less than women, I think, as (having more money) they are more likely to be able to afford reasonable rehearsal space.[3] Andrea (Mambo Taxi): 'We were incredibly lucky in the beginning 'cause we had free rehearsal space. That made so much difference because we were so god-awful that if we'd had to pay to get up to a decent standard I think we would have given up.' Transport also poses problems for the poor and the young. Unable to drive, school student band members, like Miriam Cohen (of Kid Candy), have to persuade their parents to drive them to practices or else drag their instruments around on public transport: 'We have to go all the way to town and back and if you have to get a bus, you're really tired and I never get up the next morning for school.'

Once a band has equipment, and access to both transport and a rehearsal space, it is in the position to start making music.

Initial Issues

Two issues confront the novitiate band:

(*a*) Who will play which instrument?

(*b*) What kind of music shall we play?

The first issue is not one that typically confronts male bands since male musicians are more likely to have some skill before joining, or at least they attend the first practice with some clear idea of which instrument they will learn. Quite a number of women I interviewed had never played any rock instrument before, and the sheer shortage of female musicians means that often the following happens:

'SOPHIE' **(who joined her 1980s rock band as a guitarist): We just couldn't find *any* good female bass players around. There were just none. We advertised and everything. We just couldn't find anyone who was good enough. So I said, 'Oh, why don't I play bass and we'll look for a guitarist?' And they said, 'Yeah, OK'. But then we looked for a rhythm guitarist and we didn't find one. Then we just decided to stay a three-piece. You've got to find the right sort of person to join.**

Although male musicians are usually drawn together to play a certain style of music, this is not necessarily true of female musicians because of the small size of the 'pool' of players. For a lot of those I interviewed, the desire to play in an

---

[3] Stith Bennett found that most (male) rock bands form whilst their members are still living at home with their parents and therefore the main practice space tended to be in the family home—the garage, cellar, or living room. The discrepancy with my own findings (where few bands practised in the parental home) may be due to the difference in housing between America and Britain. On the other hand, most of my interviewees were no longer living at home; besides which parents tend to disapprove of their daughters being involved in rock bands and are unwilling to allocate space in the home to them.

all-women band was initially far more important than the style of the music itself. Some novices had no preferred style, whilst others had to compromise to join a band, leading to problems later.

> **'SUKE'** (in 1980s all-female commercially successful pop band): It would be nice to have more choice, other players to play with. It can be a problem, if you're really set on being a reggae player and you come from Leeds and there's only one girl-band, and they're not really into playing reggae. Then you're stuck. . . . But I didn't know what I wanted to play until I joined the band. I only [recently] discovered that I'm really a sort of 'funky' player . . . and I'd love to be in a heavy funk band.

It is rare for a female band to start out with an agreement on the style of music they are going to perform, their projected audience, and so on.

> **'SUKE'** : It's really difficult, because if you haven't been through that whole thing of playing covers and Jimi Hendrix solos and Eric Clapton things. . . . You have never experienced the whole thing of playing rock, and a bit of this and a bit of that—to have gone through it all and [then] put it aside, to know exactly what you want to play. So, for me, the three years that I've been playing have been an experiment, sorting out what direction I personally, and the band, want to go in. And I think it's really showed. . . . I think it would be good for anybody that was thinking about being in a band to get an electric guitar at 12 and do all those bedroom and garage things, go through all that so that you've got it all sorted out in your head. So you don't have to go through all that experimental period once you're in a band that's trying to be successful. You need to exhaust all that, so that you've got a direction once you're in a band.

Musicians-wanted cards for male bands stress the style of music to be played and include the names of the bands that have influenced them, whilst advertisements for all-female bands typically do not because it would narrow down the female musician population likely to apply. The positive side to this is that a variety of musical styles and experiences can, and often does, converge into something quite original.

Learning to Play Rock

For some the very rudiments of playing their instrument are learnt within the band.

> **'SUKE'** : [Girls have not had] a whole history of having played guitar in garages and things. What girls have been confronted with . . . is being a girl-band in a male-orientated world. How can we do this? How can we go about this? We were all in the same boat together. None of us could play

any better than anybody else. So we helped each other. We listened out on my old record player for the bass line, and all those that could play guitar and bass tried to work it out, until we got it—in the end—and then the bass player played it. We listened to the horns and helped Mary work out the horns. So we helped each other. Right from the word go there was this working-together atmosphere, each one having an equal say in the matter.

Other women who have been classically trained, who are therefore 'musical' and may even define themselves as 'musicians', still have to learn to play rock. An outsider might assume that a trained musician would be easily able to transfer her skills from one musical genre to another. However, being able to read and understand written music is no clear advantage in rock. Some, like 'Anne', even argue that it is a disadvantage: 'That's the thing about being classically trained, you've got to throw it all away and start again.' I shall address this issue in some detail because it applies to many women in bands, especially keyboard players since more girls have piano lessons than boys.

My research clearly indicates that many classically trained female musicians have trouble making the transition, which can be a source of great anxiety as a woman's identity as a musician is threatened, involving a crisis of technical confidence. Many years of classical training—and for some women I interviewed that included degree courses—means internalizing the norms and social structure of the classical world, according to which the (male) composer is exalted, whilst the individual (female) player has low status. It is difficult for women to rid themselves of the effects of this hierarchy, which is part of the hidden curriculum of a course in classical music.

ROS DAVIS (Rash and Contraband): You've got to get rid of all the ideas that you've got to play only the music that's written down, and you're sort of servicing the composer. . . . It did take a while to get the confidence to get away from the written music. . . . That's the transition you have to make: from the theoretical to 'feel'.

Players have to rely on their memories, another new experience for the classically trained, and having been taught to follow a written score, classical musicians find improvisation and jamming problematical. Moreover, playing pop means developing a new style from classical. Thus, as on keyboards the hands are doing different and usually far less complex things, the player can feel redundant.

ALI WEST (the Mistakes): The thing about playing in a band is, each individual doesn't have to do that much for it to sound good. And I didn't realize that at first. And, I think, probably, I just put in too many fat chords, which isn't necessary. You can often play just a single line and it's really effective. . . . It was very halting at first. I didn't know what to do with my left hand. I do feel I have evolved a style for playing pop music now, but I hadn't then and it was just trial and error.

The redundancy of classical skills is even more apparent with synthesizer playing. This woman played a monophonic synth and thus could not play chords:

CANDY BALLANTYNE (Jane Goes Shopping): It just seemed rather a waste. It seemed that here's somebody who is able to be dexterous and yet not doing it, and being more of a technician. I mean, I like the sounds that I produce and it's nice to make them. It's just that, often, on stage I feel totally at a loose end. I think, 'What the hell am I doing here? I'm not really doing anything. I'm only playing one note!'

Nevertheless, Candy still saw the opportunities which pop offered in a very positive light: 'Classical music is pretty well painting by numbers, because somebody is telling you what to do.' Many classical musicians become critical of their training. 'Beth': 'The rules of harmony! The only rule you can possibly use is whether or not it sounds right! Even if you're writing music, surely you hear what you're writing down? But some people write music as a mathematical exercise.' Rock/pop also poses a new problem of audience. 'Harriet': 'Most of the stuff I've played before, I've had dots in front of me. And when you've got to concentrate on that, you can't think about your relations with the audience, because the relationship with the written music is more fundamental to the performance. Whereas, being in a rock band it's not. It's just you and the audience.' Finally, perhaps surprisingly, although used to analysing classical music in depth, 'educated' musicians often do not do the same with rock and pop. 'Harriet': 'It sounds really silly to me to say this, but . . . I haven't been really aware of listening to things closely at all, or analysing—which is a complete contradiction, having been involved in a music degree, done an analysis portfolio, listened to and pulled classical pieces apart, and yet had the attitude to pop music that I enjoyed it, but . . . I think I have listened to pop very lazily.'

Amplification

For many women joining a band is their first experience with amplification which may mean overcoming anxieties about electricity, so that many, like 'Suke', spoke of their initial fear of 'feedback': 'I had to turn up for the audition . . . and I felt, "Oh, God!" 'cause I'd never played electric guitar—and with a plug! Into the wall! . . . I turned up and I was really scared.' Guitarists have to overcome this and to see it as a resource to be tamed and exploited for effect. They have to learn the effects of amp settings; how speakers and speaker positions affect sound; the use of various kinds of effects pedals for sustain, compression, fuzz, delay, echo, etc.

VI SUBVERSA (Poison Girls): I think there is a tendency for us still to be scared of equipment: the 'black-box-with-chrome-knobs' syndrome. . . . I've obviously become very familiar with what I do but I still don't feel physically as at one with my equipment as I think most men do.

Being in a band enables women to learn the tricks of the trade which would otherwise be hidden from them.

JUDY PARSONS **(Belle Stars): I've never really done the record scene—which I think you might find is common to a lot of women, for some reason. Men learn the whole set of Eric Clapton solos . . . and you get Billy Cobham drum solos off. And I listen to a record and I think, 'Oh, that's great!' Then I sit down at a drumkit and nothing happens. And I never go on through that bit, thinking 'I will sit here. I will analyse for four nights exactly what he's doing and work out how he plays those two bars. I will do it' . . . and I think that's a female attitude.**

Most women musicians know that analysing records is a useful method of learning; however (in contrast to the male musicians studied by Bennett 1980) most do not do it,[4] since they lack confidence in their ability, ultimately, to work it out and are therefore not willing to invest the very long hours required. On the other hand, being in a band gives them the necessary incentive as they learn from each other. Because boys usually know other boys who are learning, they can compare work on records and figure sounds out in small groups, but, since electric music is perceived as male terrain, girls tend not to be in rock-music-making peer groups, so that if they do try to learn the electric guitar it is typically a solitary experience (unless they are going out with a musician boyfriend who is willing to help them). Moreover, as they leave their teens, women buy fewer records than men and are far more likely to live without a record or CD player. Indeed, some of the women musicians I interviewed still did not possess one.

Singers

Even singers have to deal with new techniques such as learning to sing through a mike, which is quite different from acoustic singing:

ALI WEST **: I found . . . that I had to project my voice far more. And I don't think I sing very well through a microphone. . . . It's just a completely different style, really. I feel I tend to shout a bit when I'm singing through a mike, because I'm worried about it being heard. In fact, the more singing I've done the better I've got, obviously.**

Since most female school students sing in a choir-type 'pure' voice which has been traditionally ruled out for rock and most pop, they often lack confidence in their singing ability. Given that more girls sing than boys, it was highly ironic that Sheffield's Treacle was initially an all-female rock band with a male vocalist:

[4] H. Stith Bennett (1980) emphasizes the importance of record-copying. He assumes that all bands start off by copying records together. In contrast to Bennett, both Ruth Finnegan in her Milton Keynes study (1989) and Deena Weinstein in her study of heavy metal (1991) found that all the bands (apart from 'copy bands') played a high proportion of original material.

SARA WATTS : It seemed to add a bit more meat to it. I mean, the singer we've got now is brilliant because she's got a really strong powerful voice. I think at 13, 14, 15 all the girls' voices that we knew were quite [demonstrates in a 'whiny' voice] high. I don't think it fitted in with the sort of music we wanted to do. But as we've got older there are obviously more mature female voices coming out.

Brighton's Tampasm adopted the Riot Grrrl screaming style:

TERRI BONHAM : There aren't enough girl bands that are, like . . . well, there are some that are really feminine and drippy, singers like Eternal, or there are the really hard people like Hole. And I think people don't want to be like Eternal but they don't want to be like Hole and stuff. There just aren't enough bands in between to show that you can do this. You turn on *Top of the Pops* and it's just one or the other or it's male bands. There aren't enough people showing that . . . you don't have to be hard rock with guitars. . . . We were quite timid. Songs with 'la la la' in them. That's another thing we got criticized for. For being girls, having 'la la la's.

Because the voice is taken to be 'natural', even in women's bands vocalists can feel insecure 'just singing', as if they are not contributing (or learning) as much as the instrumentalists, and are therefore more easily replaceable. Women singers thus often learn to play an instrument as well, even if it is just some form of percussion to be played occasionally, like the tambourine or a scraper. This can be a gesture too against the limited 'chick singer' role prescribed for women in rock bands in the past, who would 'sit out' on instrumental numbers and was not seen as an integral member of the (male) band. My research shows that this attitude was widely held by feminists in the 1980s. Vi Subversa: 'When we were just beginning to make music, I felt excluded from that because I was singing. Sylvia and I both started fiddling around with the bass guitar. But she got to it before I did. So I thought, "Alright. I don't want to be left out of this. I'll try the rhythm guitar." '

As so many women sang, many feminists felt that they had to earn their place in the band by learning to play an instrument and by being fully involved in the 'equipment' side of things. There was also commitment to the democratic sharing of vocals, to give all women who wished to a chance to sing.

ANDREA (Mambo Taxi): It was meant to be a collective input, completely democratic. The lead guitarist wasn't meant to be the lead guitarist. There wasn't meant to be a lead singer. This is why we had line-up problems 'cause, obviously, that's a very difficult thing to maintain. We wanted to give everyone the feeling that they had an equal input. That was a conscious decision. The people that stayed in Mambo Taxi continued to work like that, but the two girls that left and formed Voodoo Queens did it with Anjali being the leader and focus of the band.

Learning to Play Together

There is a subtle and complex web of skills and norms involved in playing together. Band members must be able to listen to each other, and they must also be able to hear separate instruments—whether on a tape, record, or live. Some band members have always been able to pick out individual sounds whilst listening to a piece of music, whilst others (more) learn this from being in a band, and all members improve this skill by practising together. Many of the women I interviewed, like Ali West, mentioned that they became more analytical in their listening habits when they first joined a band: 'This has changed my whole way of listening to music. Because I can no longer listen to it as a whole. I have to analyse it down to whatever everyone's doing.' Norms regulate tempo, volume, and tone, as well as what to play and when to play it. Because some learners play too loud and/or too much and have to give others 'space', this activity can be more or less competitive, which is one problem women musicians have had in male bands, both in the 1980s and 1990s.

> 'HILARY' (in 1980s all-female Yorkshire rock band): It was really awful—who was going to do the biggest and longest and loudest solo? The drummer was into playing Led Zeppelin. The guitarist was into playing something totally different. There was no communication. . . . [The drummer] was always playing very loud drums and not listening. That was the one thing they didn't do. They didn't listen to each other. There was no feeling of sharing in the music . . . like, you know, it goes backwards and forwards between people, this feeling. Whatever it is, it never happened at all. It was just 'Get in there and play as loud as you can'.

> DELIA (Mambo Taxi): We'd all had bad experiences in the past with boys, with them being quite domineering and impatient and kind of macho. Though we hadn't had all bad experiences. It wasn't like 'We'll never play with boys again'. It was just, 'Let's try it like this. It'll be fun. It'll be a laugh.'

Because, for all musicians, male and female, what matters most about group music is that individuals are sensitive to what everyone else is playing, the novice must develop an overview of the whole sound, rather than a concern with her own role within it. This point was mentioned often by my interviewees, many of whom did believe that it was easier to learn these skills, at least initially, in the context of an all-women group. Ali West (the Mistakes): 'I think probably we encouraged each other far more, or allowed each other to progress at our own rates, far more than men would. And I think a lot of men are quite wanky about how they play.' On the other hand, several women felt that some constructive (and necessary) criticism was missing in the carefully democratic atmosphere:

> 'JOY' (in 1980s female pop band, London): I kept thinking, 'God, they must think this sounds awful and nobody's telling me!' It felt very much like I was

working in a bit of a vacuum. . . . It's almost as if there are sort of sacred areas—you don't tell anybody that what they're playing on the guitar is crap. . . . People can do what they want, even if it's not particularly good.

In contrast,

'BECKY' (1990s new wave band): **Nobody gets upset about it. Like, if you say, 'Oh, I don't like that bit'. You work it out one way or another, so nobody gets upset about it. [And when conflict does threaten it is resolved.] It mainly happens at the end of rehearsing . . . you know what you're like after four hours playing. You're not fresh. So we just say, 'Oh, let's not work on this because it's all loose . . . so let's leave it till next time.' I think that's one of the reasons why we don't beat each other up!**

For the band to develop, some compromise between an easy tolerance and mutual criticism has eventually to be worked out, although even when this is accepted problems remain to do with authority. The 1980s musicians I interviewed were all committed to notions of group equality because leaders were unfashionable and, reflecting feminist politics, ideologically unsound. In 1995, again, as nearly all of my interviewees were committed to democracy, many believed that female bands were less autocratic than male bands. Fran (Sub Rosa): 'Women tend to work together more, or maybe that's just the women I've met. But I have worked with straight women before and they also tend to work as a group rather than one individual ego dominating.'

Rehearsal

All the bands in my research had norms of mutual help and tried to share out rehearsal tasks like loading and unloading the equipment and setting up. When deviance occurred it was recognized as such and was often referred to within the band, since people who do not pull their weight create ill-feeling. What's equally important, though, is that in order that discontent may be expressed and resolved privately, people other than band members are excluded from the practice space so that the band can concentrate on its tasks and come to see itself as a special kind of social unit. If they have to deal with 'outsiders' intruding on their space, bands quickly learn for themselves that privacy is necessary for reasons of both efficiency and morale. In the 1990s, Frances Belle used to have boys hanging around outside their practice space all evening, banging on the windows: 'And then we'd come out and tell them to bugger off, and they'd say "you sound really shit" or something' (Hannah Collett, of Frances Belle). If a women's band is to survive, male outsiders must be excluded in its early stages, especially boyfriends or husbands, while it is particularly necessary that male musicians are excluded because they can be threatening and judgemental.

'KATH' (in 1980s London rock band): There was one girl . . . who was in our group whose boyfriend played guitar. And he was teaching her. And, at rehearsal, she'd say, 'Oh, I can only stay for half an hour'. And we used to get really fed up with her 'cause she didn't learn the songs. And her boyfriend was always with her, dragging her along. They used to sit there together all the time. And we got really fed up with her in the end. So my brother just said, 'Let's play a twelve-bar'. 'Cause that's the first thing that everyone learns. He said, 'You can play that, can't you?' And she was sitting next to her boyfriend and she goes, 'Oh, I dunno. Mick, can I play a twelve-bar?' So after that we decided to get rid of her and she hasn't done nothing since.

If this had been a women's band the boyfriend would probably not have been tolerated in the first place, since it is important that women are seen to be learning to play for themselves and not endlessly dependent on a man's direction.

Ancillary Skills

Musicians have to learn other skills. Even packing the vehicle efficiently is a learnt task, and, because strength is assumed to be a prerequisite for such 'humping', women need to discover that skill is just as necessary.

ALISON RAYNER (Jam Today): Equipment can be heavy but I don't think that's really a problem. Because women may not be as strong as men in terms of their physical force, but you don't need brute strength to carry equipment, even heavy stuff. You need to know how to do it. You need to lift it carefully and the right way. . . . There's been lots of times when we've had people come up to us at gigs—maybe it's a student union and there's three or four students delegated to help carry the PA out. And, like, you get two guys who pick up a bin [i.e. speaker] and drop it half way down the steps, because they don't know what they're doing. And they're probably twice as strong as we are. And then Beatrice and Joan will come along and they can barely see over the top, and they'll pick it up and carry it to the van. It's how to do it. Women carry plenty of heavy objects. Women carry babies around. Lifting things is like a knack. If you do it the right way you don't strain yourself.[5]

If the band is ever to be able to gig, musicians must also learn how to repair equipment and do routine maintenance tasks. Mending jack plugs, for example, means soldering (typically the first time that women have done this), while drummers must learn how to change drumheads. In time the keyboard player is able to change the guitarist's strings, and the guitarist to organize the keyboards.

[5] I think that at least some of the equipment could be made in a smaller and lighter form, and certainly trolleys could be used much more than they usually are. As Cockburn (1981) has argued, work equipment reflects the pre-existing pattern of gender inequality, because, by being designed for men it automatically excludes women.

Everyone discovers how to set up all the equipment and, when some fails to work, each band member must be willing to address the problem. Women are at a disadvantage here because girls are not taught skills such as soldering. Furthermore, technical manuals assume all kinds of technical knowledge unfamiliar to women.

JACKIE CREW (Jam Today): **Once it sounds like it's getting technical, I immediately think, 'I don't understand that' and I turn off. In a way, I deliberately don't understand it because I think I can't cope with it. I personally find PAs quite unfathomable, because I'm not electrically-minded, I'm not mathematically-minded, and I think I get put off. . . . It's like I can't comprehend it as a whole. . . . I can't get into my head what can do what.**

Language

Many women begin to play quite ignorant of the technical terms, phrases, and abbreviations characteristic of the languages for artefacts and sounds used in bands. 'Hilda' (Noisy Neighbours): 'Kate had done this Grade 17 piano [joke!] and knew all about musical theory. Miriam knew what the names of the notes were and also had some experience of arranging songs. And I didn't have a clue what they were on about most of the time.' Once again, men are at an advantage since 'masculinity' demands technical literacy and so, when men start playing rock, they pick up the jargon fast because they are concerned to be seen to know what they are doing, whether they actually do or not. Young women, however, are typically wary of such terms and reluctant to familiarize themselves with them, especially as boys often use these terms deliberately to exclude outsiders, particularly girls.

A shared language is necessary simply to be able to communicate with other band members and, eventually, sound crews and the recording studio. A band member must obviously get to know what is meant by a 'bar', 'middle eight', 'riff', 'phrase', 'bass line', and so on. A lot of miscommunication occurs at early practices because people mean different things by these terms and, if self-taught, often make up their own original names for things, yet in time everybody is able to name each other's equipment parts and effects—'snare', 'hi-hat', 'toms'. This is professional jargon which sounds pretentious but it implies that you are a fully-fledged rock player who understands the way the world of a band operates. Learning the language, in short, means taking on a new identity, making a new distinction between 'insiders' and 'outsiders'. Such knowledge functions as a form of 'cultural capital' (Bourdieu 1984) or, perhaps, 'subcultural capital' (Thornton 1995).[6] It gives power, which I think men typically use in a less self-conscious way than women do since it is clearly associated with the masculinist

---

[6] Sarah Thornton, 'I've come to conceive of "hipness" as a form of subcultural capital . . . subcultural capital is embodied in the form of being "in the know"' (1995: 11).

rock world. This has certainly been so in my own experience and, regardless of musical style, has come out in my interviews with other women musicians who are often reluctant to 'talk shop' on makes of guitar or new amplifiers, and are hesitant about being too 'technical' even among themselves.

Getting some Numbers Together

In order to perform in front of an audience a band must be prepared to conform to the norms of the gig, which, at most, means presenting a 'set' of carefully constructed numbers which takes a lot of time and effort to work out. It is more enjoyable, for beginners, just to play together as the mood takes them, although this immediate gratification has to be sacrificed if the band is to perform live. Some interviewees recalled their shock at this need for hard work, which was the greater if they had no experience of arranging.

'BECKY' (of 1980s London new wave band): **Before Maxine and Jane they were just jamming. They weren't into sitting down and working out the song for hours and hours. I think that was the only difference between me and Kassandra, and Cathie and Karen. 'Cause they were more into just playing free. And next time you can't remember *any* of it. I love doing that too but I like writing songs as well, working hard on them. It does you a lot of good—sweat!**

'HILDA' (Noisy Neighbours): **It took a long time, because we weren't very musically capable, to work out what notes everybody ought to be playing . . . and how to arrange a song. We'd five numbers and it had taken about four or five months to work all that out. People like me, who didn't know what was going on, used to get bored and pissed off because it took such a long time to do the arrangements, though I recognize that it was very important.**

Most of the bands in my research wrote most, if not all, their own material. However, in some bands the composition of a finished article was a rare occurrence, first because not many members are capable of doing this, particularly at the beginning of the band's career and, second, the norm of creative space for everyone would lead to resentment if a member was continually told exactly what to do. (The same is true of some male bands.[7]) Nearly all the women's bands I researched in both the 1980s and 1990s subscribed to the unspoken convention that everyone contributes to the arranging of the songs and the working out of one's individual parts. Thus the person who initiates the song has to get across her own ideas without stifling other people's creative input which can be

---

[7] However, all the bands Bennett (1980) researched had official leaders: there was one main organizer and all the other members were 'joiners' and it became the organizer's band. The bands I studied may have been initiated by one or two people but that did not mean they held more power. The pattern of intra-band power was one of shifting alliances, varying over the band's lifetime.

difficult. If a woman cannot play the notes she might hum or sing it, although even this can be problematic. 'Beth': 'You hear it in your head and yet you can't necessarily grab hold of it quickly enough to sing it. . . . You can hear this riff and you can hear the rest of it in your head that's supposed to be going with it, and it's wonderful. But when you just hear that by itself you've lost the rest of it.' The most typical case is of someone (or sometimes two people) presenting the band with a number which was partly written.

> **'VANESSA'** : Usually a part of it is written and there are various ideas, either a few words or there's some chord or some such thing and then we all put stuff into it. 'Cause Suzanne will say 'Can you do this on the bass?' and I will say 'No, I don't really want to do that. Can I do this on the bass?' and Carol will, sort of, do the chords and Suzanne might show her what the chords are and then she'll say 'Well, I want to do it this way'. So we all, basically, we get the idea and we do our own things with it.

All kinds of variation on this pattern existed. A prerequisite of composition is that the nature of what is conventionally meant by a 'song' or 'number' has to be learnt. A pop song is usually not much more than three minutes long; it has verses and choruses and often a 'middle eight'; it needs some kind of 'intro' and some kind of ending; it has 'lyrics' and not just a set of words. Likewise, there are compositional norms for other genres.

A band is therefore both a context and an opportunity for writing so that many women found themselves coming up with songs quite unexpectedly.

> **ALI WEST** : I never wrote a song until I joined the band. It was only joining the band that encouraged me to write anything. And I didn't know that I could before I did it. I quite surprised myself. It was a good feeling to write songs that we played. . . . I don't really write songs now, now that I'm not playing in a band. Because it's stupid writing them, 'cause I know they're not going to get played.

If the band needs songs then at least one woman has to step into the breach. The imminence of the first gig reveals songwriting talents, which can lead to resentment and conflict, particularly if they have not already arisen. At the start of a band's career, members are wary of upsetting each other's feelings and doubt they are competent to criticize anyone else's material, especially if they have not themselves written anything yet. No group style or standard has yet emerged since the band is typically still experimenting and most things are given a try-out. Anyway, as there is a shortage of material, all songs are gratefully received. Later, however, as regular songwriters emerge from within the band, there can be too much material and choices have to be made, and the longer the band has been playing the more likely this is to be the case. Then conflict occurs between the goal of doing the best songs possible for the group and the value of self-expression for its individual members, which can easily lead to arguments and to hurt feelings.

ALI WEST : That was partly because we were so collective and everyone had to come to some kind of consensus, but also because it's a very intense kind of thing to be doing, playing music with other people. And then especially as we wrote our own stuff. I'm sure that had a lot to do with it. Because if you do cover versions, then you're not likely to argue so much about the arrangement and what different people are playing. Whereas, when people did their own songs it mattered so much more what everyone did.

Feminist bands have often felt that the original material they play must be written by women (usually from the band themselves); non-feminist bands, too, are often unhappy about featuring new songs by 'outsiders', particularly males. Whereas male bands, in the 1970s and 1980s, tended to start by doing covers and only later attempted to write their own material, most women's bands mixed originals and 'standards' from the start.

'HILARY' (in 1980s Yorkshire rock band): The main difference was that they [the men] hadn't got as much originality as the women I've played with. Or they wouldn't use it. They wanted to just do cover versions of things and be the same as other bands have been. And they just hadn't got the creative energy that women have got. They wouldn't use their own creativity or they were cut off from it . . . The guitarist in this band was technically really good. But he was just shit scared or couldn't find his own style. And he'd just copy things. . . . They'd play the record and you were supposed to [copy it]. Having played with women before . . . I was really glad that I had done, because if that had been my first experience of trying to play it might have put me off for ever.

In the 1970s and 1980s, women's 'creativity' was as much a matter of politics as inspiration. Some feminists in my research, for example, argued that women's bands should not do 'covers' because the majority of existing songs have been written by men and it was about time women's voices were heard, the implicit suggestion being that women write different sorts of songs than men, in terms of both lyric and sound. For these women, songwriting was an ideological duty which was also fun. In the 1990s, although none of the bands I interviewed had an explicitly feminist political agenda, many interviewees still stressed the importance of women writing their own lyrics. Sam and Teresa (of indie band Beaker) believed that it was important that everyone should know that women were *capable* of writing their own material, as did the 16-year-old members of Frances Belle: 'Because otherwise they get classed and labelled as stupid—"girls can't write their own music" ' (Hannah Collett).

TERESA HOOKER (Beaker): I think, possibly, people expect it of you, being an all-female band, that you won't be able to write your own stuff. People always used to say to us 'Do you write your own stuff?' and we'd go 'Yeah' and they'd go 'Oh, wow!', like it was really unusual.

However, there have been 'non-feminist' factors here too. As already emphasized, many women join bands as complete novices who, if they play 'covers',
run the risk of being compared, unfavourably, with the originals.

'SANDRA' (drummer with 1980s pop group): We did lots to start with—badly,
as well. Well, to start off with, you see, we didn't have any songs and we just
fancied playing together as a band. So we thought, 'Right, what songs do we
like?' And we tried playing those. 'Hold On I'm Coming', 'Keep On Running'—
sixties kind of stuff. . . . We just played it to the best of our abilities—which
wasn't very much at the time.

This group quickly changed to writing its own material, and even when women's
bands continue to perform standards they often adapt the lyrics to a new gender
persona. Indeed, feminist bands in the 1970s and 1980s changed the words
as a matter of political subversion (though sometimes *not* changing the words
was equally subversive, as when lesbian bands sang love songs addressed to
women).

'SYLVIA' : We did 'I Saw Her Standing There'. . . . A woman saying, 'I saw *her*
standing there' just gives a different twist to it. And we did 'Da Doo Ron Ron',
with 'I met her on a Monday and her name was Jill', changing the sex of it so
that you had whole lesbian undertones to it. I think that is fun. As well as
finding those ones which were about how men were not to be trusted—which
are there.

'Arranging' (deciding on the structure of songs) can lead to friction and, although
it does tend to be a collective process in women's bands, not everyone contributes equally, even if the underlying principle is agreed: however much the
various individuals contribute, arranging means treating as primary the overall
sound.

VI SUBVERSA : There's discussion and compromise. A sort of refining process.
What usually happens is, in the beginning when you're working on a song
there's too much. And so we thin it out. So, I might play only half the original
riff I thought of, because the rest of it's being compensated by the bass
guitar, or a drum pattern. And I think that's what's exciting about working
with the band: that is, working with other people, nobody's actually playing
the whole thing. It's only the little bits that we're doing and the way they
connect to form a [whole]. I think that's wonderful. I love that.

Bands develop a variety of strategies for resolving disagreements about songs.
Often things are discussed at length until a consensus or compromise is reached,
and sometimes a vote may be taken. Beaker, a band committed to present fun
rather than future commercial success, simply agreed at the start that if anyone
disliked any part of any song it would be immediately dropped.

Identity and Commitment

Most women starting out in groups do not define themselves as musicians. Largely because musician is defined as male, women do not symbolically internalize 'musician' into their identity. This is similar to the situation in art: 'Creativity has been appropriated as an ideological component of masculinity while femininity has been constructed as a man's and, therefore, the artist's negative' (Pollock 1988: 21). Those rock 'beginners' in my sample who did see themselves as musicians tended to be the ones who had been classically trained, but that was certainly no guarantee of such self-definition—one woman I interviewed did not think of herself as a musician despite years of classical training, Grade 8 on the piano, and a few years experience in a rock band.

> **'SANDRA'** (of 1980s Yorkshire pop band): At first, when people used to say, 'What are you?' I wouldn't say a drummer. 'Cause even now I don't think of myself as a drummer. I just say, 'Well, I sort of play the drums'. I can't say, 'Oh, I'm a drummer' 'cause it used to sound really odd. I suppose I am, but . . .

This lack of confidence makes women susceptible to criticism, especially from male musicians.

> **'SANDRA'** : We're a bit sort of hesitant. We aren't confident enough. We're just hopeless. We sit there going, 'oh . . .'. In everything else we're quite good at what we do—which is looking after kids. We're confident in that way.

Once a woman does start to see herself as a 'musician', or even as a band member, this new identity affects the whole of her life. She will listen to music in new ways, discuss it differently, and engage in technical talk with other musicians. Band members go to gigs together to watch other bands and pick up ideas, and so other people's gigs too come to be experienced differently—musicians tend to stand at the front and watch exactly what various members of the band are playing. Going out to hear live music ceases to be simply a social event, becoming yet another part of (hidden) band 'work', and in this setting the role of musician provides women with a shield against the strictures of the double standard, since it is suddenly legitimate to go up and talk to the musicians during the break or after the gig. So long as her identity as musician is known or made apparent at the start of the conversation, she will not be placed in the 'groupie' category.

> **'HILDA'** (Noisy Neighbours): When I was playing in that band, I found it much easier to talk on more equal terms with blokes that I had known vaguely around the music scene in Coventry for a year or something—musicians. Once I was playing in a band—and word gets round, you know—and gradually they realize that you're actually playing in a band. And I was able to talk to them on a much more equal basis.

Because you have a clear purpose and now look purposive it is easier to be at a gig, which gives you confidence and a new place in the music world.

In doing my research I've interviewed women in bands which variously play the whole gamut of popular music. They also have a wide range of experiences: from the local band which has played only a few gigs to the commercially success-ful band with records in the Top Ten; from women who have only been playing one month to women who have been together for more than decade. Whatever the differences, they faced the same problems of commitment in becoming musicians in the first place. It is undoubtedly true that women find it hard to commit them-selves to music in the way Bennett (1980) shows that male musicians do since, typically, they do not have that *total* dedication. Bennett argues that the musician has got to be involved in his music to the exclusion of everything else. He has to be able to 'get out of himself' at practices, so that he is unaware of the rest of his environment. We can assume that the male musician who is a father will certainly not have the major responsibility for childcare. Male musicians do not take their babies along to band practices; indeed many would find the idea unthinkable. However, some women do have to do this, and clearly, in this situation, they cannot forget they are mothers.

'JANE' (of 1980s Yorkshire pop band): When we first started I used to take Sam with me up to Janice's and he just used to play with the toys. [But] you couldn't get into it. You couldn't relax. My mind was always, 'Oh, God! What's he doing?' . . . You've got to have children to understand that, I think. When they're around, you're just totally involved in them. I find I get them to bed and, if I'm going to a practice, it takes a while to readjust . . . to get into that other state of mind.

Having children affects the choice of practice place, what time of day or night practices can be held, duration, and frequency.

TERRY HUNT (Jam Today): We were going to Leyton, but since Linda's had her baby we need to have a place that has two rooms. In fact, this place is rather good. It doubles as a recording studio and has glass panels. So we can sit and peer at the baby through the panels.

ALI SMITH (Diatribe): We have this place we go and play all night. You start at eleven o'clock at night and you finish at six o'clock in the morning, which means I can take my baby with me and she will sleep in the studio 'cause she's still portable, and my boyfriend will stay with the other two children.

'KASSANDRA' (of 1980s new wave band): Sometimes we had to wrap up practices earlier because we didn't have a babysitter and the child wanted to go to bed. We had to stop. Or, she wanted to go and pick him up from school, or whatever.

Getting a babysitter can be a problem and it is costly. If one is hired for rehearsals, then it seems a luxury to do so in order to go to other people's gigs too, and so women musicians who have children go out to gigs far less often than other musicians, if at all.

'JANICE' (of 1980s Yorkshire pop band): We undoubtedly get on differently because we're all women and it works differently. We've got sympathy with each other, with our respective problems, with fitting everything in. And someone says, 'Well, look, I can't do this because I've got to take this little child to the doctor', or, 'He's ill and I can't . . .', we'd all sympathize. Whereas, if you were in a male band and you said, 'Oh, I'm sorry, I can't . . .' they'd say, 'Oh, crikey, her and her kids!'

Musicians schedule their lives around music as mothers do around their children. Only highly successful—and rich—musician mothers can resolve this contradiction satisfactorily. Men who are musicians are more likely than other male workers to understand the importance of being in a band and to accept the complex arrangements this necessitates. However, it is also apparent that they see their own role in music as being much more important than that of their wives. (The women I interviewed who had young children were either single parents, or married to musicians.)

ALISON RAYNER : The baby comes with her. . . . Her husband is a guitarist, and he is the breadwinner and brings in the money to pay the mortgage. And she has the baby. So the baby comes to rehearsals. . . . She's in this nuclear family set-up and, of course, the way it's set up doesn't work around a woman being a sax player in a band. That's a big disadvantage in terms of work. So we all have to pull to help things work. Sometimes, I don't like it if I feel we're supporting this nuclear family set-up but, on the other hand, why shouldn't we support her and be as helpful as we can to her. . . . He just goes off to his gig. I mean, can you imagine him turning up to his gig with a baby? I mean, what a joke, you know! . . . If Janice's husband turned up at a gig with a baby I should think they'd be shocked out of their brains! He wouldn't do it though.

Women are, then, expected to be most 'committed' to their families, to their children and partners. Before this, a girl's search for a boyfriend may be one reason why girls' bands break up or, indeed, never get off the ground in the first place: boyfriends resent the amount of time band practices take up and put pressure on girls to leave (and research makes clear that similar pressure is put on older women musicians by their partners).

However, if women musicians aren't (can't be) committed as exclusively to their music as men, friendship was a far more important aspect of musical life in the bands I studied than it seems to be in accounts of male bands. There was less of a split between practice sessions and 'normal' life; one could argue (as male musicians do) that there was less 'professionalism' (Bennett 1980). This was certainly true of bands just starting out.

'HILARY' : I think the difference is that if somebody has had a row with somebody, or somebody isn't feeling too good, they don't come into practice and pretend nothing's happened. It's real. Whatever's been going on in people's lives comes to the practice. And with guys it's not like that.

'SANDRA' : You get to the practice and somebody's in a bad mood or pissed off
or something. And it always affects it. And in the four of us, with kids and
everything, somebody's bound to turn up at a practice each time feeling
rotten. . . . Some practices we'd play one number and spend the rest of the
time talking. 'Cause it was an excuse for all of us to get out and go to the pub
and have a drink and moan about this and that and the other. So, even if we
didn't practice, it was nice just to get together as a group to chat. [Whereas,
when she played with men] we didn't talk about bloody kids or anything.
With them it was go there and you'd play. You don't piss around. You're
playing for two hours and you make good use of it. So I wouldn't go along
there and say, 'Oh, I'm pissed off with Tom, and Judy keeps wetting the bed'.
I knew I was there for one reason only and that was 'cause they needed a
drummer.

Practices were social events for Sandra's band, a chance to get together and talk
since the band was a friendship group and not just a unit which produced music
together. 'Chats' seem to be important in all-women bands, especially in their
early stages. There is usually a lot of getting together apart from practices, lots of
phone-calls and general contact, and the friendships built up within bands were
often as important as the music itself. This aspect of 'being in a band' seems often
to outweigh the lack of money, the frustrations, the hard work, and the scant
chance of commercial success. For women—and this may be the paradoxical
twist in the explanation of why they don't 'make it' in rock as often as men—the
immediate experience of playing together is a source of strength and pleasure
and purpose far more important than individual commercial success.

'KASSANDRA' : We're all in love with each other, in a way, but it's platonic.
We do admire each other a lot and it feels like we're one person when we
play. . . . It's like a family. We are very close and it's given me all these extra
people that I care about and they care about me. It's more than just working
together. . . . It's adventurous, exciting. It's like a gang. You're mates. You're
up there together.

'BETH' : We have a good time when we play. We have a good time and a laugh
when we rehearse. And we enjoy it. We're not striving for anything in
particular. . . . I've always enjoyed the gigs. Even bad gigs I've enjoyed on
stage, because you get a good feeling going together. We know what's
happening and we're all laughing at each other . . .

6 Going Public

The First Gig

TERESA HOOKER (Beaker): Nothing will ever frighten me as much as doing that first gig. That is the most scary thing I've ever done. Driving test? No problem. Exams? No problem. Everything since that first gig, I just thought about how frightened I was then. It's a big confidence thing.

As the first gig marks the band's 'coming out', band members will be seen and judged as musicians, whether they apply that label to themselves or not, which makes it a crucial learning experience in which factual information, norms, values, attitudes, and expectations will be absorbed. There will be more than one 'audience' at this first gig. Strangers, lovers, friends, relatives, the promoter, the sound crew, and local musicians form discrete audiences, about whom the band may feel very differently. The first gig, therefore, is chosen with care. If it is perceived as a disaster it could be the last. There is often a fear of other musicians being in the audience since novices may not wish to be 'judged' by their 'peers' at this stage. However, when a new band launches itself onto the local scene, members of other bands are usually present out of curiosity, particularly if it is a women's band. Feminist bands have often chosen to emerge at an all-women gig, where they will not be exposed to male scrutiny and criticism.

'HILDA' (Noisy Neighbours): Because it was a women-only audience they were very pleased that it was women who were playing and there was tremendous enthusiasm because of that. And I thought that whatever we did they would have liked [it]. They didn't give a shit whether we were good or bad. . . . They were just thinking, 'How nice it is that these women are playing'.

In stark contrast, these 14-year-old school students were confronted by male violence:

CHARLOTTE CLARK (Tampasm): This bloke was just being really lippy. . . . We went up on stage and he was just taking the piss because we were girls. And he goes, 'Get on with it!' while we were setting up. And I turned round and I said, 'We'll be on in a fucking minute, you cunt!' and the next thing I knew he's smashed a Newckie Brown all over his head. There was blood dripping all over the floor and he was lurching towards the stage and I was terrified. I was standing there, my first gig, going [whimpers] 'Help!'

How soon the band does its first gig depends on a number of factors. Novices might take longer before daring to go public, but one who joins an existing band may have no choice about plunging in, as Juliet Bowerman discovered: 'When I found out that I had a gig in three weeks I thought, "Phew, but I'll get on with it and if I can't manage it I'll flee the city! Or if after the first gig I'm terrible, I'll leave".' Experienced musicians in a new band may feel that they have reputations to live up to and may choose to delay their arrival onto the gig circuit. The 'moment' is of some significance, too. For instance, at the time of punk, bands were able to gig almost immediately. Similarly, in the 1980s, many feminist bands gigged soon after forming because of the demand for women-only entertainment by both lesbians and the women's movement. However, the intervention of 'outsiders' such as musician husbands or boyfriends may force the pace:

'SUKE' (in 1980s all-female commercially successful pop band): Both Josie's boyfriend and mine were dead keen about the whole thing and thought it was great and helped us enormously. They were doing the whole of the London circuit, both of them . . . and Joe decided that we weren't gonna go anywhere . . . so he booked us a gig to give us a goal to work towards.

Gigging raises new transport problems. Those bands which emerge with the help of musical boyfriends typically have access to their vehicles and this is a distinct advantage. In other bands the existence of one or two women with cars is crucial since, initially, gigs tend to be poorly paid (if at all) and if a band has to hire a van it will find itself out of pocket at the end of the evening. The 1990s schoolgirl bands, with little money and unable to drive, were the most disadvantaged. Charlotte Clark (of Tampasm): 'We usually get buses and we've been known to walk miles with the drumkit in a shopping trolley, as well. We were actually going to steal one and paint it pink and make it the official Tampasm one!' Gigging usually necessitates further equipment purchase as well as the borrowing or hire of items, although, if there is more than one band on the bill, sharing a 'backline' (amplifiers) might be negotiated. In this way a novice band may be able to do a number of gigs before they are forced to purchase their own equipment. Once again, those women who got into a band via the help of boyfriends tended to borrow equipment from those same male musicians, although this tends to put the woman in a dependent situation, which can be exploited by the man concerned. Equipment becomes part of the interpersonal politics of the relationship—not a desirable situation. Likewise, married women with young children are often totally dependent on their husbands for cash: 'I'm tied to Paul, hook, line and sinker! He's not been too bad but it's always *his* decision what we spend on what and where we go' ('Janice'). Borrowing of equipment cannot continue for long as gigs start to clash and band members begin to be more fussy about getting their own particular sound right. This inevitably necessitates an increase in members' financial investment in music.

Gigging also leads to a substantial increase in the amount of time a band takes up. The performance itself may last only one hour, but the (unglamorous) work underpinning that exciting 'moment' might last the equivalent of a day, and it may come as a shock. What follows is a typical outline.

Before the gig there is usually advertising to be done: ringing the local papers and radio, flyposting, and so on. The venue will have to be inspected, PA hired. Musicians must check their equipment to make sure that it is in top working order. The question of what to wear must be discussed and clothes got ready. Some members may have to arrange for time off work, depending on how far away the gig is. Mothers will have to arrange for babysitters. A van must be hired, or car borrowed, and a provisional 'setlist' worked out. On the day of the gig, each band member must collect their equipment and load it onto the vehicle which must be driven to the venue. On arrival, it has to be unloaded and carried up stairs, round corridors, in and out of lifts and, eventually, onto the stage, where it is 'set up'. Instruments must then be tuned. Next, there is the 'soundcheck' in which instruments will first be individually checked for 'sound' (volume and tone) and adjustments made to the PA and individual amps. Then the band will run through one or two numbers so that the overall sound can be adjusted and set. After this, if there is more than one band playing, the women may have to move all their equipment off the stage to make room for the other band's equipment for their soundcheck. At this point, during the lull before performance, the band will devise a 'setlist' or alter the existing one. Some members might decide to do warm-up exercises on their instruments in the dressing room. After performing, the whole procedure has to be carried out in reverse:

MARY (Atomic Candy): So you drive all the way down from Nottingham, get there, rig the PA up, wait for the rhythm section to arrive, soundcheck yourself, go out and try and find something to eat, get changed, play, come off stage, sell lots of tapes, talk to lots of people, not have a beer because you're driving, and then have to drive all the way back to Nottingham again. That's how glamorous it is. Oh yeah, and unload the car when you get home. Carry your trusty seventy-five watt combo through the door.

It is frustrating having to hang about until the other bands finish playing in order to be able to get the equipment off the stage and the hour or so spent packing up is not usually perceived as fun. For those women's bands which get going with the aid of musician boyfriends, help in 'roadying', driving, and setting up is usually available. A couple of younger bands unabashedly admitted to exploiting their femininity to get help:

LOUISE HARTLEY (Kid Candy): The boys do it. They get to lug everything around. We always make sure we play with boy bands so they can lift the heavy stuff. We don't really do a lot of loading.

MIRIAM COHEN (Kid Candy): It's 'Quick, help me carry this!' They love it.

In contrast, self-consciously feminist bands have taken pride in doing without male assistance.

The gigging stage is marked, then, by a considerable increase in commitment—of money, time, and hard work—and, as band members weigh up the effort and costs involved against the returns, the first gig is a critical point for the band's survival. Enjoyment shared and relived afterwards will boost morale and auger well for the band's future. On the other hand, a negative first experience of gigging will cause some band members to leave, and the future will be uncertain. A few women realize that they do not actually enjoy performing live; others become 'hooked' overnight, while some find that their enjoyment from gigs increases gradually. Whichever way, it is a learned experience: the lucky ones learn to enjoy performing in public and, once learnt, they are reluctant to relinquish such pleasure, the 'high' from the gig outweighing weeks of hard work, frustration, aggravation, and arguments, which can come, at first, as a surprise:

CANDY BALLANTYNE (Jane Goes Shopping): One of the positive feelings, which I never thought I'd feel, is the amazing high you get from performing. I think the first time was the most amazing, because you built yourself up to this incredible event and there it was. I suppose it's like a drug. As soon as it was finished you just wanted to do it again. I felt very depressed the next day.

Many women performers used the drug metaphor to explain why, despite all the hard work and obstacles, they continued to gig.

MARY (Atomic Candy): If it's a huge gig and you're playing to, like, several thousand people, you get that rush of almost uncontrollable adrenalin. It doesn't make you shake, but it's like when you smoke a really strong grass joint and it goes just like that, and you're just holding onto the chair because you think you're going to go whoosh out of the chair. It's that sort of feeling. Nothing can substitute. It's amazing.

Learning

All gigs are learning experiences, but particularly the first, when the culture of the gig is absorbed. One obvious lesson is the work involved in being in a band, which includes what happens at a gig, the kinds of contingencies that may arise (technical, social, emotional) and how to deal with them. Thus, the more control a woman can exercise over the gig environment the better, and in particular bands learn to keep a wary eye on both promoters and other bands. Vi Subversa (Poison Girls): 'A very ambitious band . . . abused us, put our guitars out of tune before going on stage, ripped off our equipment. Because they were very competitive and they wanted to blow us off the stage. That's happened a lot'. They learn to deal with the sound crew:

JUDY PARSONS (Belle Stars): We did our first gig. There was a PA there that was not a PA—no mike on my drumkit or on the main band's. A PA [that] sounded worse than any cheap record player. And he wanted £10. We said, 'We'll give you £10 if you mike up the saxes, and do this, that and the other'. And he said, 'No way, grumble, grumble . . .' and didn't know what he was talking about. So we took all our equipment off stage . . . and we put it all out the window. . . . We didn't pay him.

Band members have to become familiar with the material environment of the gig. They must learn how to set up their own equipment on stage, to understand the acoustics of the room and how it might affect the sound, how PA systems work, the optimum time to tune up their instruments before playing, and how room temperature affects them. There are also many tricks of the trade to be picked up—from other musicians, and technicians. Charley (of the Frantic Spiders) recalls her first gig: 'I loved it but my biggest memory was turning up and thinking, "what's this?" It was only a little vocal PA and I'd not even thought about if you play a gig then you have something that the microphones go through. And there were big amps there and it was all so confusing. And it was about six months before I finally worked out what exactly happened with this PA thing.' If women become singers, or play the sax, they may manage to avoid full immersion in this sea of technicality, although to participate fully in a rock band even a vocalist should understand the technical aspects for they dramatically affect the sound. To withdraw from the process of collective decision-making is to lose influence over the final performance. Yet, in my research, some women who had been playing in rock bands for years, said that they still had not completely overcome their 'technophobia'.

JUDY PARSONS (Belle Stars): A lot of my problems are to do with a mental attitude. . . . There's a huge thing in my brain that just shouts out, 'Practical? Not me, not me!' And I have to fight that: 'You can do it. You've got a brain, you have ability. If a man can work out how to do this, you can do it.'

As such blocks are overcome they are replaced by confidence and pride in one's new skills:

CHARLEY (Frantic Spiders): I remember after we'd done about ten gigs we went somewhere and there were monitors and we'd never had monitors before. . . . I remember saying, 'Look. These are monitors. These are what the vocals come through on stage' and feeling really chuffed because I'd worked out what they do.

Fluency in this technical language is important for women's self-definition as a musician or bona fide band member as well as for gaining respect from other (usually male) musicians and, thus, being accepted into 'the club'. Even one's status with audiences can be affected: for example, if a woman appears unable to adjust her microphone stand, then she is diminished. Clearly, one's standing with the crew is crucially affected by one's competence and confidence in the technical field, so that women have to prove theirs by being articulate about technology as only this will give them influence over such crucial matters as the off-stage and on-stage sound. This is important as soundchecks can become battlegrounds between bands and sound engineers, in which various power strategies are used, including deliberate mystification. Language is thus crucial.

VI SUBVERSA : All of technology is dominated by men . . . but I'm fucked if I'm going to say it belongs to them. It's ours! Right? Every single wire that's been put together was made by a man who was fed, nurtured, supported by women somewhere. I think we've got to reclaim the lot. It's to do with how you talk with the PA, how much they understand what you're doing and so on.

One needs to know the terms used in mixing: 'gain', 'graphic', etc.; those terms which describe the various pieces of PA equipment: 'monitor', 'tweeter', 'woofer', 'jack-to-jack' . . . the list is long; and general terms used in the gig situation: 'setlist', 'support', 'soundcheck', and so on. Once this technical language is learnt, it distances the musician from 'outsiders'—the audience, the non-initiated, non-musicians.

Another important part of gig culture is the normative structure. Some of these norms may be fairly manifest, while others are subtle and may never have been anticipated until the situation arises. For example, who is going to introduce the numbers ('front'): 'It's something we never thought of and when we went on stage, suddenly we were thinking, "Who's gonna say something?"' ('Joy'). Likewise, what do you do when you cease playing? 'We all stood there at the end. Instead of saying "thank you" and getting off, we just stood there, just froze to the spot. Didn't know what to do' ('Sandra'). Similarly, how does one 'do' a sound-check? Band members learn that they are expected to stay within earshot to be ready to be called on stage to soundcheck their instruments, listening out for each other as each instrument is checked. They learn how to devise a setlist, how to communicate with each other whilst playing and with the audience.

Bennett (1980) refers to the ritual scene of 'getting up for the gig' in the band van before the (male) rock band goes on stage. Deena Weinstein (1991) discusses the same phenomenon in relation to heavy metal bands. Women's bands also devise their own rituals: they spend time together before performing, although it is less likely to be in a van and more likely to be in the dressing room or toilet. 'Getting changed' is a significant point in the evening, marking the transition from the everyday self (in the old clothes typically worn for setting up) to the new self of rock performer. Donning stage-clothes is an enjoyable pre-gig ritual which women share as it signifies the end of the hard slog of preparation and the beginning of the really pleasurable part of the evening. Delia (Mambo Taxi): 'Getting ready for a gig, you'd feel like you were about to play. . . . It also makes it a special thing. . . . If we played in normal clothes we'd never put so much into it. A costume and getting ready was like a little ritual and putting on too much make-up and making your hair go higher and seeing if you could get any more rings on.' It is also usual for the band to get together immediately after their performance, reaffirming group solidarity, especially if the gig was a difficult one or, conversely, highly successful:

JUDY PARSONS : After that gig we came back to the dressing room and we
all screamed, which I'm sure only a girl band would do. For about twenty
minutes we just screamed in high-pitched voices, all of us. . . . Whenever
the band enjoy themselves they scream like that, which I think is something
that male bands never do . . . It was as good as doing the gig, the screaming
afterwards. When we have a good gig we do it. And sometimes before we go
on, if we want to, we have a bloody good scream.

Body, Gender, Image, and Performance

It is often only immediately before the first gig that a woman becomes conscious
of the kind of decisions that have to be made about image. 'What shall I wear?'
might very well be a last minute question, surprising her by its sudden importance, after the more practical problems have been dealt with. A band might not
even discuss the question collectively yet, ultimately, a group decision always
has to be taken on this issue, even if the decision is simply to have no policy at
all. The nature and amount of compromise between the individual and the group
varies considerably from band to band but, certainly, performers are forced to
become self-conscious about their clothes and general appearance, and there is
always an ideological aspect to this. 'What shall I wear?' is inevitably linked to
'what am I expected to wear?', even if these expectations are deliberately not met.
Dressing for the stage cannot be completely 'innocent' or spontaneous since it
always involves some deliberation. Even the decision to look 'natural' is a choice
and indeed a sartorial strategy in itself.

Although all rock musicians have to address such questions, because of the
greater pressure on women (in general in society) to conform to gendered stereotypes of attractiveness, they assume greater importance for women's bands.
Certainly this is the perception of my interviewees in the 1980s and 1990s. The
expectation that women look 'attractive' is both a constraint and a pressure, and
women who deviate can expect censure.

ALISON RAYNER (Jam Today): There's that great emphasis on women's looks.
If we were all incredibly attractive and wearing masses of make-up and
looked very sexy for men, probably that would be just fine. It wouldn't
matter whether we could play or not. They would just look at you. But we're
obviously not into that at all, so you get a certain amount of criticism on that
level. . . . They have a certain expectation of women on stage: that they
would usually be singers and look quite good.

Although all women must tackle these questions, a particular set of thorny problems have confronted feminists, who as performers have been highly concerned
about the political implications of their appearance, which is not merely an aesthetic issue, but an ideological and political one. Indeed, in the 1980s women
musicians seemed more worried about their appearance than about their playing.

'VERONICA' (in 1980s Oxford pop band): I feel confident about singing and I feel confident about the band, in that I know that we can all play moderately well and practices are good, and therefore gigs should be good. The things I feel shy about are how I look, the clothes I wear, if people are commenting on them or not, and feeling bad because I don't move. That's what bothers me more than ability.

Even explicitly non- or anti-feminist bands voiced concern over these issues since, for any woman, being on stage *in itself* connotes sexuality to the audience:

'SUKE' (in 1980s all-female commercially successful pop band): I quite like sex appeal [but] I think there's an extent I would be careful not to go [beyond] . . . because seven women on stage is a very heavy thing. And I think it could come across as very heavily sexual if people weren't careful. . . . I quite like sexy corsets and things like that, but I don't think I would wear them on stage because it is so openly, blatantly sexual.

Women musicians typically want to look attractive but do not want to be seen as 'sex objects'. 'Harriet' (in 1980s London pop band): I do think about what I'm going to wear and usually get paranoid about it. . . . I wouldn't wear anything that was specifically designed to be sexy, because that's not how I want to present myself. I don't want to present myself as a sex object; I want to present myself as a musician.' The view held by many feminists in the 1970s and 1980s was that one should be as 'normal' or 'natural' as possible on stage: for example, one should only wear the sort of clothes that one would be wearing in everyday life rather than 'stage clothes'.

TERRY HUNT (Jam Today): You can see who is and who isn't a feminist, because when they get up on stage they tart themselves up and they pose and pout. . . . We get up and we play and we are ourselves. We're not trying to project an image. We're not being false. What you see is what we're like all the rest of the time. I don't wear stage clothes.

'JOY' (of 1980s pop band): I don't think you should look too different on stage, 'cause I think there are people in the audience who think, 'God, they are so different. I could never be like that'. I think it's important that the audience recognizes that you're just ordinary people, like they are.

However, 'normal' for some meant jeans or dungarees (the stereotype of feminist dressing in the 1970s), whilst for others it meant miniskirts. 'Natural' is meaningless in a social discourse, besides which the stage is an extraordinary situation where strong expectations exist of how women should appear and such norms regulate their appearance. The 'natural' response of some has been, simply, fright: they dressed down for fear of drawing attention to themselves. The idea of wearing 'normal' clothes on stage is an attempt to break down the performer-audience gulf, to demystify and deromanticize, but, however the performer dresses, she is making some sort of statement:

VI SUBVERSA : You're making a total statement. You're asking for attention. You're asking people to look at you and hear you. And you're throwing away an opportunity if you don't work with that. You're saying something whether you like it or not. So if you're going up in ordinary clothes you're saying, 'Here I am in ordinary clothes'.

Many women's bands have effected a compromise between stage clothes and 'ordinary' clothes, making comfort and practicality the determining factors in their choice. Sheer practicality means that drummers cannot wear tight skirts, while, for guitarists, it can be dangerous wearing high heels on stage amongst all the electric cables and difficult to operate foot pedals.

'VERONICA' : I never wear high heels, especially not on stage. I always wear shoes that I can move about in. I think that's really important—a lot of the problem with women's clothes stems from shoes, in that women wear high heels that they just could not walk normally in. Therefore you do make yourself a fragile little thing that totters around.

Vi Subversa's choice of clothes developed out of her experience of rough gigs:

I've got two sets of stage clothes now: one for a gig which I think is either going to be cold or hassley, which is very tough and is made out of very strong, heavy, black cotton drill—trousers, because if you're bending down doing fuzz boxes and things you don't want to have a skirt on . . . And I've got another version which I use in a safer venue, which is thinner and has got a very shimmery top. . . . If you're going on tour it's got to be hard-wearing and washable.

Another practical reason for getting changed was that pre-gig work inevitably meant getting sweaty and dirty. Similarly, many women changed again after performing. Many varied what they wore according to their prior evaluation of the gig, some not bothering to change if the audience turnout was sparse or the gig looked unlikely to be a success. Some 1980s lesbians would only get dressed up for women's gigs because they wished to avoid fulfilling men's expectations, whereas, with women, they felt free to wear 'feminine' clothes as these would take on different meanings within the all-women (and predominantly lesbian) context. Often a number of reasons were combined: the refusal to get 'dressed up' for men; the wish to avoid conforming to sexist stereotypes; the need to avoid sexual approaches from men; and safety.

'SARAH' (of 1980s Brighton pop band): I'm not interested in dressing up for men. I don't see any point, reason, or function to it. I feel more vulnerable at a mixed gig and clothes are a vulnerable area for me, being large, and, partly, I'm extrovert in my dress to avoid that vulnerability. But it's more difficult at a mixed gig. It's got to feel safe at mixed gigs. I'm much more flamboyant dressing for a women-only gig.

Figure 3: Skirts and guitars.

Above: Teresa Hooker of Beaker, The Elm Tree, Oxford, 1995.

Right: Sharon of Pooka, The Zodiac, Oxford, 1996.

Below: Gayl Harrison and Claire Lemmon of Sidi Bou Said, The Venue, New Cross, London 1995.

Above: Valley of the Dolls,
The Punch Bowl, Woodstock 1995.

Left: Sidi Bou Said, The Venue,
New Cross 1995.

Below: Kim of Beaker, The Elm Tree,
Oxford 1995.

Dressing in a skirt and 'feminine' clothes made most interviewees feel more at risk, whereas tough and traditionally 'masculine' clothes often made women feel tough themselves, which might be particularly useful for some performing to a mixed audience. For instance, 1990s bands Twist and Atomic Candy both embraced a boyish look. Claire (Atomic Candy): 'I don't like skirts particularly. I don't feel powerful in a skirt. It's like putting on a mask or costume if you're an actor. I become something else when I'm on stage. So I put on my leather jeans and I become Claire Ross, rather than Claire Smith the double-glazing woman. It's about power.' However, most were worried about looking too masculine: 'I don't want to come across as being too butch. On the other hand I don't want to be seen as too "fem"' (Alison Rayner, of Jam Today). Indeed, this wish to avoid either end of the spectrum of gendered clothing was something of a dilemma for many feminists, who recognized that, as both poles were male-defined, their space for manœuvre was narrow:

> **SHAREEN** (Ms45): I have to think too hard. I shouldn't have to. All female dress is drag. All female dress is some kind of signifier and the thing that pisses me off is as a band if we showed up in a little gold lamé dress and false eyelashes we would be heard differently than if we show up in jeans and t-shirts. And, goddamn it, there are some days that I want to wear a gold lamé dress and false eyelashes. Then there's the ridiculous cat fight mythology. If one of them is wearing a pretty little gold lamé dress and the other one's wearing jeans, they say, 'Oh, that's the pretty one and that's the dykey one'. And it's like, 'What? No, I really want to wear comfy shoes today. Give me a fucking break. . . . Since clothing is such a signifier, I'm trying to figure out ways that I can have a better sense of humour without putting myself into the Barbie category. That's taken some manipulation.

In the 1980s, for some women the choice was either to become a sex object or 'one of the boys' so that, in a mixed band, where the only other woman had chosen the former role, 'Heather' felt in a quandary:

> The problem was she had an image as a singer which was a sort of sex kitten, which put me in a really odd position. Because—I don't know, I might have had some other bad idea, like I was one of the boys or something like that— but I turned into some really in-between, asexual sort of figure. Because there were the two boys, and me drumming, and Liz. Maybe, in a way, she didn't mean it seriously. But it still put me in a difficult position.

'Veronica' was also a feminist in a mixed band:

> I don't want to have to appear not as a woman. . . . I don't like the idea of, if you're a woman in a band you've got to be one of the lads and be completely indistinguishable from them. I think that's bad and just avoiding the issue completely. And it's good to be seen as a woman. In a normal day I wear a lot of skirts and dresses . . . but it becomes much more of a dilemma when you're going on stage.

One way of circumventing these image-traps is to 'go over the top' as a parody. 'Sylvia': 'The one time we wore skirts was the Suffragette number and that was very deliberate. It was hats and stockings and high heels—very feminine. . . . Playing bass in high heels was weird. It was really funny. And it was odd, playing drums in a short skirt.' On the other hand, whilst some feminists have worn dresses as a way of sending up femininity, other interviewees (in the 1980s) deliberately wore dresses to women-only gigs as a way of reacting against what they have perceived as the 'orthodox' feminist line of anti-feminine dressing.

BECKY : When we go and do all-women gigs I particularly put my skirt on . . . because I'm so totally against those who are so fucked up in their heads because of what I wear, or because I've got a boyfriend, that they won't accept me as a woman. . . . That really upsets me because they don't see it inside— what I'm really like. They just think, 'Ah, she's a heterosexual. She's wearing skirts. She's got a boyfriend.'

This latter position has become more predominant during the 1990s, particularly amongst younger women performers, reflecting either a backlash against perceived feminist 'political correctness' or an attempt to redefine feminism in a new way.[1] Some women wish to assert their right to wear clothes which are as feminine or sexy as they please. (After all, 'whatever I wear, wherever I go, "yes" means "yes" and "no" means "no" '.) Young women in the 1990s are more sexually confident on and off stage. Cerys Matthews (Catatonia): 'What I don't like is people reckon that if you want to be like a "strong girl" you almost become like— like Justine, she looks like a bloke. But I like jewellery and I've always got make-up on and I love it . . . I may look like a tart or something but . . .'

The risk, however, is verbal abuse or worse. Courtney Love has been called a 'slag', 'dirtbag', and 'whore' and when stage-diving she has been sexually assaulted. Others keep their body covered, either through caution or because they simply have no desire to display it. Chrissie Hynde, Joan Armatrading, and Elastica have all become highly successful despite staying relatively covered up. So, just as some women defy prescriptions of 'politically correct' clothes, others reject the more traditional and long-standing pressures on women performers to capitalize on their physical attractiveness by exposing their arms, legs, and breasts.

The 1980s parodic approach has developed into a 1990s fully postmodern ironic playfulness. Women have employed a number of strategies to produce exactly the sort of 'gender trouble' which Judith Butler (1990) suggests, upsetting the notion of a fixed, true, or real gender and revealing it to be, in itself, a fabricated performance. As the rock stage provides an ideal public space for innovative gender performance a number of subversive strategies are utilized.

[1] American Riot Grrrls seem to have refused to worry about these problems. Amelia: 'Kathleen Hanna is a striptease artist and I think two out of three of Bikini Kill work at the striptease club and one of the girls in Bratmobile, which is a really peculiar thing for me, that the main feminist inspirations in America strip at this strip club.' Courtney Love has also made money from stripping with which to finance her musical career. After such experience, expressing your sexuality on stage does not seem such an issue.

Some women performers (like Annie Lennox, Madonna, and P. J. Harvey) continually reinvent themselves, producing a variety of stylized gender performances. Others have deliberately tried to devise and work with contradictory (and often humorous) images: the ballgowns plus Doc Martens approach. (The six women in my last band, Oxford's fleeting Mothers With Attitude, employed this approach of 'dissonant juxtaposition', whilst the two men were in drag.) Yet others have created an ironic pastiche of traditional symbols of femininity such as handbags and high heels. Punky 1990s pop band Mambo Taxi employed tarty yet theatrical images: 1940s hairdos, mermaid costumes, green false eyelashes, lurex, glitter, ultra-glam. However, such irony is not always recognized, for some men simply do not understand the context and just 'read' the miniskirts as sexual availability. Amelia of Heavenly told me that the meaning of her band's use of children's clothes had been lost on 'the vast majority of people'. Clare Howard, the drummer in Beaker, who enjoys combining girly dresses and petticoats with big boots and a 'psychotic glare', has great fun deliberately conveying a scary image. Clare and many other women have enjoyed the power that comes from being anybody you want to be on stage, quite different from everyday life. Charlotte of Tampasm expressed similar sentiments. However, as Manda Rin has been criticized for being fat and ugly, the basic issues remain: 'If I wanted to be a model, I might be upset, but I don't, I want to be in a band, so why does it matter? People say, "You're too overweight to be in a band," which I don't understand. I mean, I've not broken through a stage yet. I can still get through doorways and stuff' (*Melody Maker*, 29 June 1996).

Treacle, from Sheffield, were faced with male musicians saying that they only got gigs because of the way they dressed and, as they were not taken seriously, they felt obliged to wear jeans. They, like some other bands, bemoaned the long-standing sexual double standard whereby a man can strip down to his underpants, whilst a woman wearing a miniskirt is called a 'slag':

SARA WATTS : It seems so sad that we have to dress down just to prove a point. . . . I want to dress how I feel comfortable. . . . I just think the whole thing of 'You're blonde, you're bimbos' needs to be broken down and if you have to go to the extremes of dressing down and not making yourself look as nice— which is a sad thing to have to do—but if it gets the point across that you're there to play the music and you're not there to be gawped at, it's gotta be done. When you get on stage, if you're wearing a skirt then you're playing on being a girl and so then you have to revert back into wearing jeans. It's mad to me but you do get more respect wearing jeans. When you put ripped jeans on, para boots and a T-shirt you get more respect than if you're wearing a little skirt and a little top.

Sidi Bou Said also 'dress down' in order to be taken seriously. Every Woman said they had to tone down their clothes in an attempt to minimize verbal abuse and Skin made a big effort to look as ugly as possible when she first started singing in Skunk Anansie, so that the band would be taken seriously: 'Because people remember you as how you first came out for a very long time . . . so I knew that once we'd gotten over that phase, then I could be anything I wanted to be, because we were already seen as a heavy band with a strong lead singer. So now I can be as sexual as I want to be because people don't expect it.'

There is resentment that male bands, like Oasis, can go on stage in very casual clothes and a pair of trainers, whilst women are expected to dress up. Caroline Appleyard (of Treacle) was once asked to wear a leather miniskirt and leather basque in a male blues band: 'I says, "Yes, of course I will. But you can buy 'em and you can wear 'em as well!" And he didn't know what to say. . . . Sometimes you feel like packing it in, you know, with things like that . . . you seem to be just banging your head against a wall.' These quotations serve to illustrate a general rule. The woman musician, especially a singer, is expected to be attractive; however, the catch is the more attractive she is judged to be the less respect she is given as a musician and the lower her music is rated in terms of any intrinsic worth.[2]

The question of whether to wear make-up or not also presents itself to every woman who starts gigging. Again, in the 1980s views were polarized. Generally speaking, the positions were identical to the ones discussed regarding clothes. One view amongst feminists was that the wearing of make-up of any kind, either on or off stage, was 'ideologically unsound'. It was making yourself over in the ('unnatural') male-created image of what a woman should look like to please men.

> **TERRY HUNT** : I am totally and utterly opposed to make-up of any kind. . . .
> It's not a thing of being boring and we should all look the same and nobody
> should have fun, but I don't think the whole point of make-up is for fun,
> [but] to make women look a particular way and have a look which actually
> has very little to do with women. . . . It's a caricature of a woman.

At the opposite end of the continuum, one non-feminist and commercially successful band had a policy that everyone should wear make-up:

> **'SUKE'** : When it comes to photos—when you've got the whole band and some
> are wearing make-up and some aren't . . . it makes people that haven't got it
> covering up their spots look awful. Bags under their eyes. And if it's just a
> black and white photograph you should just have make-up on that smooths
> out the lines. Because you're trying hard to publicize the band and trying
> to make it look to the best advantage. . . . It is awful if people don't like
> wearing make-up. But, then, if you're in a band and you're in a unit, and
> you're all trying to reach the same goal, you've got to compromise. I suppose
> make-up attracts men and that's why feminists don't like it . . . but then
> that's only natural, as far as I'm concerned.

---

[2] Lucy Green also makes this point 'What often happens in the sort of situation where display is forefronted is that the mere fact of the delineated attractiveness of the female singer causes listeners to downplay her ability and commitment with respect to the execution of inherent meaning. The more she goes in for displaying her body, the less likely it is that she is a "good" musician. Likewise, the overt forefronting of display leads listeners to assume that the inherent meanings of the music are of relatively little importance or value. Listeners then hear the inherent meanings in a way which is influenced by their understanding of the delineated display' (1997: 39).

However, some feminists defended wearing make-up too, arguing that it all hinged on why, and to what effect, it is used:

VI SUBVERSA : Well, I think there are ways of presenting yourself on stage that are unsound. But I don't think that the way I use make-up or clothes is unsound. I'm not trying to make myself anxious to please. That's where it's ideologically unsound; if I was just doing it so I would please the men. But I do it in a completely different way. I usually put a lot of make-up on and it's all run by the end of the set. And I work with that. I use make-up that runs easily, 'cause I sweat. I start off with a mask, a beautiful face, and the make-up gets ravaged.

This contrasts starkly with the conventional reasons for wearing make-up. And here is another interesting solution:

JUDY PARSONS : I didn't [wear make-up] for a long time and from the band it was hassle, hassle, 'why don't you wear some make-up?' And they think that I'm completely mad. But my idea is they're completely mad—about make-up and image. . . . Anyway, now I've discovered mirrored sunglasses, which means I don't have to put any make-up on.

The situation is different in the 1990s. The question, 'do you wear make-up on stage?', when I asked it, felt strange and redundant. Nearly everyone said 'yes' and it simply was not a significant issue any more, even amongst feminists.

This whole issue of clothes and make-up, as is shown in the quote from 'Suke' above, involves the question of the band's corporate image, which, in turn, raises the question of commitment, so that compromise is inevitable. Amongst the amateur and semi-professional bands I studied, a common compromise was having a theme, such as a colour. Bands further along the career ladder usually imposed stronger rules upon their members regarding appearance. Feminists in the 1970s and 1980s often believed that it was important not to submerge members' individual physical differences since clothes and make-up can make women look identical. Moreover, as this is an image which fans copy, it becomes normative for both the band and other women.

As discussed earlier, women typically come together to play in a different way from their male counterparts. There are few women musicians about, and so they get together to play with others who are available, rather than clustering into stylistic tendencies as boys do. Thus a women's band is likely to reflect a variety of diverse backgrounds and aesthetic tastes, which, together with the strong theme within feminism of expressing your own personality, lends weight to the anti-corporate-image position.

Apart from clothes, other more subtle issues emerge: how shall I stand/hold my instrument/move my body. Typically, until women musicians commence gigging they have never contemplated these questions and are surprised at just how many points there are to consider. Most of my interviewees were keen to discuss these matters, which were often experienced as unresolved dilemmas. Feminists were very concerned to avoid presenting themselves as sex objects for men, but they also rejected stereotyped 'male' poses on stage. Many drew a distinction between 'sexy' and 'sensual':

DEIRDRE CARTWRIGHT (Jam Today): I like to feel that our performance is sexual in the sense that we're projecting ourselves, but it's not sexy or sexist. It's not deliberately trying to be titillating to the audience. I think that everybody has their own sexuality, and sometimes you define it as personality or charisma, and I think it's nice. . . . We're just trying to be ourselves. And I think, in that way, we're being sexual. But that's such a big part of everybody, I think.

SHAREEN (Ms45): I have never been a frontperson before in my life, so I'm trying to figure this out as I go along. I have such ambivalence. Of course, I'm a functioning human being; I am sexual. But as soon as you *use* sexuality you're treading on thin ice. You have to be careful and people don't seem to have a sense of humour about female sexuality. You can easily be put in the 'Barbie' category.

A woman faced with all these ideological and practical dilemmas can become so self-conscious that she just does not move at all:

'VERONICA' : I don't want to convey anything . . . so I've just tended to stand still—which I don't really enjoy doing. I would like to move about but I am worried that I'd feel embarrassed about my body shape and size, and things like that, and that people would pass comment on it. I think it's a problem being a woman on stage. I think it's made very much easier if you've got a very boyish figure. You can stand on stage and you can move about quite freely and no one notices the way you're moving. Whereas, if you look more shapely, it's much more difficult because your body movements can suggest much more to the audience, especially to the men.

And these issues have not disappeared in the UK in the 1990s. Amelia Fletcher (of Heavenly) has been sometimes accused of flirting with the audience, when she was merely trying to be entertaining:

It's very tricky because, obviously, if you just stand there and not do anything it's not very entertaining to watch! I wouldn't use my body to be sexy because it seems like cheating in some way. . . . I couldn't act sexy for a long time because people would say, 'You're just trying to get boys the easy way. You're exploiting your femaleness in a sexist society.'

Playing an instrument means that your body is less on show. Not much can be seen behind a drumkit (although drummers do sometimes worry about their breasts moving, which is why Clare of Beaker sometimes wears three bras). Whilst a guitar is ostensibly a thin piece of wood, covering only a narrow band of one's body, it can feel like a shield: you are less physically exposed and you are hidden behind a weight of symbolic signification. Furthermore, the audience have a variety of expectations. A woman playing a rock instrument is breaking the gender code. She is deviant to the male-as-norm and is not seen simply as a

Figure 4: Low-slung guitars.

Above: Twist, The Point, Oxford, 1995.

Right: The Gymslips, London, 1983.

Below: Jennifer Bishop of Tampasm,
do tongues Club, The Lift, Brighton, 1995.

Above: The Androids of Mu, London, 1982.

Below: Belladonna, Halifax, 1982.

guitarist but as a *female* guitarist. She faces a set of low expectations concerning her competence (woman with guitar = fish with bicycle) and yet she is somewhat liberated from the *different* set of expectations associated with women who 'just' sing. A different code is operating, according to which she is not expected to move about and display her body to the same extent as a singer. The skills and concentration required in order to play the instrument are expected to take precedence over bodily display. Indeed, in the case of keyboards or drums, it physically limits the range of her spatial movements. In contrast, women singers are supposed to be heterosexually 'sexual', sexually pleasing and available. They are usually frontpersons and therefore expected to dance and move their bodies to provide a visual focus for the audience and the camera.

Instrumentalists face other dilemmas. Since the electric guitar, in the masculinist discourse of rock, is seen virtually as an extension of the male body, feminist guitarists have, perhaps, the biggest problem—avoiding the male guitar-hero stance which features the guitar-as-phallus.[3]

ALISON RAYNER : For guys, the lower you play it the more it is a phallus. It can never be a phallus if you play it high. It's the rock thing, when you have it slung right down there, where it becomes a phallus. Women don't often seem to play guitars and basses so low down. . . . I don't think it's true that women can't do it. I think there are very few women who would choose to do it, feminist or not. . . . I think a lot of women find using your guitar like that very obnoxious or objectionable, and if you're a feminist it's that much worse, because you can see that much more in it.

This is always implicit and sometimes explicit, as when men mime masturbating their 'axes'. Heavy metal guitarists unashamedly hold their guitars like a penis. (Prince even has a substance being 'ejaculated' from his guitar.)

The problem is partly one of a lack of female role models. Although a female musician might not be consciously copying anyone, there is no doubt that she is unconsciously influenced by other (male) guitarists. The middle-aged punk performer Vi Subversa developed an ironic solution to this problem, subverting the meaning of stereotypical macho guitar hero movements: 'I know when I go in for some big chords that this is what men do. And my feeling when I do it is irony, because I know that you don't have to strut around to make a good sound. I know that you can do it anyway. For boys to see a woman doing it is feeding them an image they haven't had before.' And in Vi Subversa's case not only are the boys seeing a woman playing 'power-chords' but an older woman at that.

It is interesting that most players find the guitar easier to play when held at chest or waist level. The main reason given for playing it at pelvic level or lower is that it 'just looks right', holding it higher up is seen as less 'masculine'. I would argue that the only reason for this is the silent encoded phallocentric message that a woman with an electric guitar looks 'wrong' anyway and, if she then plays

---

[3] Within other musical discourses, the guitar does not necessary have these connotations. In classical music, jazz, and African music, for instance, the guitar (although overwhelmingly played by men and thus perceived as masculine) does not typically suggest the penis because it is not typically played at pelvic level.

it at chest height, looks even more so. Thus, to look 'good' she has to play in a 'masculine' way. Sara Watts: 'When I record I have it really short, up here. Because it's easier to play. But when I'm on stage, obviously, I have it—not really low down like a big heavy rocker—but in the middle, so it doesn't look stupid up round my boobs.' As Heavenly is a band unconcerned about being 'girly', it is ironic that Amelia told me the following: 'I would say that if I had been a better feminist I would have been more determined to hold it correctly. I don't hold it well. . . . I used to play quite high and it was considered very sissy. So I now wear it probably lower than I should do. It *is* an issue, definitely. Pete's always trying to get me to wear it higher, because he says I play it better when it's higher. But I refuse to do it 'cause I look too silly.' Most female guitarists I spoke to (whether in the 1980 or the 1990s) had considered these problems.

CLAIRE LEMMON (Sidi Bou Said): **If you wear your guitar too low you are incapable of moving anywhere and because I play lots of bar chords and stuff up the neck it's easier to have the guitar higher. But I feel a bit 'poncey' with the guitar too high. . . . I do like the idea of women playing guitars slung like men. . . . I've always thought guitars are really sexy and really strong things and I like the fact they're slung where they are. I couldn't play it up here; it wouldn't feel right. It's all about sex, really.**

Debbie Smith (of Echobelly) even risked her health by playing her guitar very low: 'I started getting RSI [repetitive strain injury]. It's really bad. So my guitar started getting higher and higher. But it's really bad. I get a huge swelling up here from fretting.' Breasts are also a physical issue here. If you hold your guitar at chest level you risk crushing them, which is particularly painful if you are premenstrual. Both Juliet and Kate from Twist, for instance, mentioned this problem.

ANNA POWER (Sub Rosa): **They've got that kind of slot at the top which you hook your tit over the top of. You can either squash it against your stomach, which is going to hurt, or you can hook it over the appropriate bit. . . . I'm going to work on a funk rhythm guitar with a concave back that you fit your tits into!**

How you stand when you play guitar is also an issue since, although with your legs apart you are in a more stable position, it is a so-called 'masculine' one, and some women felt straightforward antipathy towards the strutting and posturing of the traditional male guitar poses.

Lastly, after the gig women musicians coming down off the stage carry with them some of the sexual connotations of the performance, so that, as with male musicians, they are more fanciable, chatted up by strangers and, sadly, their musicianship often passed over. Sara Watts: 'After the gig, people come up to you and, instead of saying, "I really liked what you did", they'll say, "I like your hair". Like, when has a male musician ever got, "You've got nice eyes" instead of . . . They'd never say that to a male person.' Furthermore, even when the comments seem to be about a woman's musicianship they may mean something different:

ANNA POWER : The times I've gone on stage and been wearing miniskirts or looking fairly girly, I've got more compliments on my playing than if I had been wearing jeans and a T-shirt. I've got a friend who says, 'Them right dead-legs who come up to you after gigs and go, "I thought your playing was really good", what they actually mean is, 'I fancy you in that skirt'.

Sexism and Sexual Harassment

Whatever their musical style, all-women bands face an extra dimension—the sexism in which the rock world is steeped. It is patently clear from my interviews that men have different expectations of women musicians, whom they define primarily in terms of their gender, the sign 'woman' obscuring 'musician'. What exactly are these different expectations?

1. Women are expected to be less good at playing than men.
2. Women are supposed to be sexy and attractive, to wear revealing clothes and display their bodies. They are pictured doing just that in the multitude of advertising images which surround us and subtly categorize women as 'bodies'.

In sum, a women's band is expected to be sexy and incompetent, expectations which form a de facto hurdle facing women musicians and, especially, all-women bands. They represent a set of assumptions which must be coped with or combated in some way. The audience must be won over from these sexist preconceptions, which may be difficult as, if they expect an all-women band to be 'bad', that may be what they hear. On the other hand, they might be impressed by the fact that women can play at all. Either way, women's music and playing abilities are viewed through a lens of patriarchal assumptions. However, probably the most rampant sexism is encountered in interaction with technicians.

JUDY PARSONS : PA crews are sort of macho . . . and I'm sure they all have a good titter about us. We're a particularly stroppy band from the point of view of PA and lights. I know they think, 'Oh, this'll be a piece of cake. These girls won't know a monitor from a mike-stand. We can have a bit of a kip at the side of the stage'. . . . [But] we're quite a bunch of hasslers and we show them that they can't get away with rubbish with us. And the band take great pride in upsetting these people who think, 'Oh, we're onto an easy thing here'.

Sexist attitudes of the sound crew lead to women's bands being undersold on time and attention. They may get their soundcheck very late, when the audience is already present, posing problems of negotiation of the two realities of practice and performance, which can be daunting, especially for novice bands. Sexist prejudice acts as a handicap. Male bands do not face the same kind of hostility, sneering, or jokes, but even women in mixed bands are singled out for differential treatment.

'VERONICA' : People tend to take you less seriously. It's all very well for boys to be in bands; that's what they've always done. But if you're a girl—oh, you're doing it because your friends are doing it, or because the person you are going out with is doing it. Therefore you are not taken seriously. Like, if you're talking to the PA they ask the men what sound they want. They don't ask you what sound you want. There have been many times when I've said, 'We want a sharper sound on the bass' or 'Take more off the bass drum', and the PA men turn round and look at you and think, 'How can she know about this? What does she know?'

The problems are most marked when playing support when the crew, perhaps hired by the main band or by the venue, often behave as if their job is only to mix the main band. To save work, they set the controls as the main band likes them, and leave them like that for the whole of the early part of the evening. What they should do is set the controls for each band and then write down all the settings so that they can reset the mixing board for each band's performance. 'Support-banditis', of course, affects male bands too, but as Vi Subversa points out,

If you're a woman, you are a support, anyway! They are interconnected. In the beginning they treated us shabbily and patronizingly, and we were always the support. It's difficult to work out whether it's to do with being a woman, whether it's to do with being older, or whether it's to do with being a support. As far as I am concerned, they're all the same: they're all part of a hierarchy and a system of privilege.

My recent research suggests that the increased visibility of women musicians in the 1990s has not changed attitudes. Interviewees told me of being deliberately blinded by techno-talk, constantly patronized, and ignored, while some had even experienced sabotage. Most women musicians had encountered some kind of problem, even commercially successful ones. Manda Rin (Bis): 'A lot of sound engineers think you don't have a clue what you're doing with equipment and stuff. It's like, "I'll do that. I'll do that." I think, "God! Do I have a brain?" And that gets to me quite a lot sometimes.' Women musicians have, of course, retaliated. In particular, the strong female performers in the 1990s have used their power to tackle this problem unreservedly: Katherine Garrett (the Mystics): 'There was one particular roadie who definitely was having a problem with the fact that I was female. . . . He came up and he pinched my arse. And a few days later, he was fiddling around with a case and there were quite few blokes looking around, I just went up to him and I squeezed his bum really hard. And he jumped out of his skin and walked out and he didn't touch me again. That's the way I deal with the thing if I do get it.' When a sound engineer patronized Debbie Smith and then messed up her equipment during the course of a gig she simply hit him with her guitar. And it would be a very foolish technician who dared to mess with Skin from Skunk Anansie: 'I just give off "Yes, I am definitely a woman, but if you fuck with me, I will fuck with you!" And so they have instant respect. They don't treat me in that typical, "Ooh, there's a woman!" and then wolf-whistle, which I've seen them do to other women.' Some bands were fortunate enough to have a 'tame' male sound engineer regularly doing their mixing. In the case of a few bands this was the husband or boyfriend of a band member (and more than one of these was a full-time sound engineer running his own business).

JUDY PARSONS : So Jim does it quite cheap. . . . He'll charge us less than he'd charge another band. . . . He cares about us a lot . . . He's always rearranging gigs—ringing up other bands. He does too much, and he gets let down when the band says, 'Oh, those Fridays are off, Jim' and he's told lots of other people.

The advantages of this situation were multiple. They would get a big PA at a cheap rate. Sometimes they would borrow bits of equipment for practices—like a small PA system for an immediate pre-gig rehearsal—and they did not suffer from sexist jibes and patronizing attitudes. Most important of all, they had a guide into that mysterious and mystifying world of sound technology, and someone who was 'on their side' at the mixing desk. Such a man was of great benefit to the bands concerned enabling the women themselves to become more confident and capable of dealing with PA systems on their own, and of dealing with other sound crews, if they had to:

JUDY PARSONS : Jim started up doing PA as a hobby. I used to go out with him; we did it together. And he explained to me how PAs worked. So he told me all the stuff that I then passed on to the band. . . . I was going back to him every night, saying, 'Help, Jim, there's this funny noise. What does it mean?'

Having the same person mixing at all or most gigs, is an enviable resource as they are familiar with the band's particular 'sound', the temperament of the various instruments (and players), the length and composition of the set. They know the songs backwards. Band members can relax and trust them to get on with it, and, because women can ask questions without fear of a put-down, a band can learn to 'talk shop'.

Feminist bands playing women-only gigs have had the particular problem of finding a female sound engineer, especially in the 1970s and 1980s. My band knew of only one female sound crew in the country—Jam Today—and, being a gigging band themselves and based in London, they were loathe to travel far afield so that one band told me they had waited thirteen months to get the crew up to their northern city in order to do a big women-only gig. Thus, large all-women gigs could only be held in London. The only alternative has been for bands to hire a PA and do it themselves, increasing the workload considerably, an option available only, in any case, for small gigs, since anything larger than a small room would require a full rig and a proper sound crew. Other compromises were tried out by some bands, like getting a male engineer to set up the mix and soundcheck, and then leave, before the audience arrived. This was unsatisfactory because they could not alter the 'mix' during the performance. Occasionally a male engineer has been allowed to stay, discreetly out of sight, at an all-women event, but this 'solution' is rare.

Thus the chronic shortage of female technicians has posed a critical limitation on all-women gigs, and thereby limited the operations of all-women bands. However, even when a band has their own woman sound engineer the problems persist since, if they are at a big gig, where a male PA firm has been hired to deal with all the bands, they will have to deal with a male crew who may resent another person using their mixing desk. This resentment is even greater if the interloper is a woman whose skills the technicians are likely to doubt so that they may be reluctant to let her near their equipment.

FRAN RAYNER (Jam Today): I've worked on a lot of PAs, but convincing blokes . . . it's very difficult. You have to really get into this frame of mind and go up to them. And sometimes I don't feel like that. . . . If you eventually convince them you can do the mixing . . . you're sitting there and he's right behind you, waiting for you to make a mistake and go, 'Oh, no, you can't do that!' So it's really nerve-wracking.

Another reason for this reluctance is simply a sexist possessiveness which is actually more disturbed by female competence than ineptitude:

JACKIE CREW (Jam Today): He was freaked out that there were all these women running around, looking as if they knew what they were doing. And he couldn't cope with it. I think a lot of men feel freaked out.

Understanding the complex, technical world of PA can give a feeling of power to those with this 'superior' knowledge. Sound technicians stand, at big gigs, in their own little enclosures into which few people are allowed. I have often watched 'outsiders' attempt to enter this territory, inching their way over and being edged back again by the crew who patrol its boundaries. It is a male space in which a woman mixer is often simply denied any form of access to the desk:

'GINA' : They were making this awful balls-up of the sound. It was terrible. But they wouldn't let me be on the mixing-desk. They didn't actually give a verbal reason. Just two men. Just consolidated themselves at the desk. They basically ignored me and I gave up in the end, totally frustrated.

At other times, the sexism is less blatant:

FRAN RAYNER : On one occasion recently . . . we hired the PA on the understanding that I was doing the mixing. And he set it up on the balcony of this hall and it was very dark up there. . . . I was going to sit down and do the mixing and . . . he said, 'Oh, you'd better just tell me what you want, then.' I said, 'Hang on, I'm supposed to be doing the mixing.' And his excuse was that 'it's very dark up here'. We've got a light, so immediately someone went and got the light. So he couldn't say anything, and eventually he moved over.

Female musicians also often face sexism from male musicians who may resent the popularity of a women's band.

JUDY PARSONS : When I started off drumming I felt that there was an awful
lot of hostility from local male musicians . . . and I think there's a lot of
snideness and you have to close your sensitivity off. . . . You just become
thick-skinned. You think, 'Well, look we've done a gig and the audience really
loved it. And what are you doing?' I think those particular men don't like the
idea of women being musicians. And it is about being a woman; it's not about
you as a person. They do think women can't play. And there must be a lot of
other men like that.

Musicians in the audience can sometimes attempt to put a women's band down
by standing at the front of the stage and staring in an intimidating way. On a few
occasions men came up whilst the Mistakes were playing and drunkenly tried
to take over the drumkit. Guitarists told me about men who, after admiring their
instruments, played very fast up and down the neck to show how good they
thought they were. Because local bands are in a state of competition with each
other—for gigs, reviews, 'headlining', and so on, sexism gives male bands a built-
in advantage in this musical market-place. On the other hand, male bands are
quick to exploit the advantages of having an attractive young female in their band
as a crowd-puller. These issues were still there in the 1990s. Beaker were supported by male musicians until they began to look like serious competition,
when there was some resentment. Likewise, Frances Belle told me that local
musicians, despite initially helping them, were relieved when their band split
up, while some of the 'help' was patronizing, taking the form of boys storming
on stage during a gig and, unasked, altering their amp and microphone levels.
Atomic Candy entered a rock open competition and their success elicited violence from male bands competing against them:

FRAN (Sub Rosa): We won the first heat, knocking out Scunthorpe's main
contingent. The next heat came along and we knew they were going to be
trouble. We had various phone calls telling us not to turn up, that we were
going to get into trouble when we got there. And we thought, 'Fuck that, we
are going to go and hopefully we are going to win it!' We got in there, started
playing and some of our equipment got nicked off the stage even though
there was security round the stage. We were halfway through one of the
numbers and beer glasses started getting thrown at us. And we didn't win—
surprise, surprise. . . . These lads had just got it into their heads that no
woman was going to win the competition over them and it got really out of
hand.

Male musicians like to have female bands as support acts in the expectation that
they will be useless and thus make the male (main) band look better. Tampasm
told me this, as did Ms45. Mandy: 'You get other bands going, "Hah! Girls!" and
then they watch you play and you can see them going . . . pulling faces, a smirky
look when they think, "Oh, great! We're gonna blow this lot off the stage." '
On the other hand, some male bands resent supporting a female band. Every
Woman, a vocals and dance group working the northern club circuit, found some

male musicians jealous of their success and refusing to 'play second fiddle to four tarts'. Jealousy increases if the female band gains commercial success.

> **DELIA** (Mambo Taxi): We'd had some male bands that'd go, 'How come *you* got in the *Chart Show*? How come you got a record deal?' 'Cause there were times when we didn't play that well and they'd be really resentful that we'd got somewhere, when they had possibly thousand quid drumkits and massive Marshall stacks and widdly guitar solos and they didn't. And they didn't understand why we got a record deal or had people coming to see us, or got paid £200 and they only got fifty quid. . . . We had quite a few blokes saying to us, 'We're gonna dress up as girls next time we play and maybe we'll get some press' and things like that. And I'd say, 'Well, I'll dress up as a boy next time and maybe someone will take me seriously.'

Treacle were constantly criticized by male musicians in Sheffield and when they were filmed for Channel Four they were accused of only getting on television because they were, basically, 'ten tits and five cunts'.

Musician boyfriends were sometimes jealous of their girlfriends' success. Mary Genis's past boyfriend had accused her of being 'just a decorative guitar stand' and told her, 'I'm a better musician than you are, but you get more gigs because you're a woman and the guys wanna fuck you'.

Promoters are a further source of problems. Alison Rayner recollects the pre-punk mid-1970s: 'Promoters . . . didn't use to believe that a women's band could play. So they wouldn't want to take a women's band. Unless the women's group at the college would book you, it was difficult to get a gig.' Every Woman, who had trouble with promoters advertising them as 'raunchy' and 'sexational', were also told to improve their act by removing their clothes. Promoters showed little respect, wandering into their dressing room, so that the band had to paste up a notice at all their gigs: 'Every Woman. Please knock and wait'. Other bands told me that they had sometimes obtained gigs simply because the promoter was under the delusion that he would be able to have sex with one of them.

Some of my interviewees mentioned the sexism of male DJs. I remember playing at a well-known London club where the resident DJ deliberately provoked the feminist audience by playing records with the most sexist lyrics he could find. Sometimes retaliation is possible:

> **CAROLINE APPLEYARD** : 'He was a sexist old fart and kept bugging me when we were packing. [So] I kept unplugging his DJ desk and all his lights and music went off about three times. That's partly why there was a riot. I felt great, 'Oh, I didn't know. I'm sorry, I'm a dumb blonde. I didn't know you weren't supposed to take that lead out'.

Lastly, women's bands have to contend with sexism from audiences, which comes in a variety of forms, one manifestation being the way that audiences typically expect women to be incompetent or less good at playing than men. Many interviewees had been patronized. 'Sylvia': 'When I first started playing the bass you'd get men come up after the gig and comment on your bass playing, saying how good it was. They were really just saying, "You're a woman playing bass! This is amazing!" This was in 1976/77.' This type of comment was less common but still around in the 1990s. Men in the audience are much more likely to comment on a woman performer than a man:

'HILDA' (Noisy Neighbours): I've heard lots of remarks about, 'Oh, she can't play her instrument, she can't do this, she can't do that . . . she's a hopeless singer', from people who wouldn't normally pass any comment on men. And, in fact, specifically when there's a mixed band, they don't say anything about the men, positive or negative, but they make a point of saying, 'She can't do this, she can't do that'.

This also affects women doing the mixing, women who are often gradually learning to get confidence in the equipment, and constitutes another obstacle men do not have to face:

FRAN RAYNER : There used to be a stage when a lot of blokes used to come up at mixed gigs and give their advice. They might know nothing about it at all, but they always thought they'd give their advice anyway. . . . You can get a really hostile atmosphere from them, just because you're carrying out the gear and you don't need them to help you.

Women also get more comments made on their personal appearance than men do. (Feminist bands who do not conform to the normal trappings of femininity come in for a lot of criticism on that score.) The most common form of harassment is verbal abuse of the 'show us yer tits' variety, evaluation being based as much on the size of the musician's breasts as on her guitar playing, and such comments are meant to be heard by the performers. It can be startling and offputting for the novice band to be told to strip. Sometimes the promoters of gigs have been partly to blame, by laying the emphasis so heavily on gender. 'Becky': 'On the first tour the angle was, "An all-girl band. Wow!" And we got to the place . . . and there was all the young punks and they said, "Take it off! Take it off!" And Karen was saying, "You go and take it off!" So they just backed off. There was so much anger.' In the 1990s this kind of abuse is still common. Singers and front-women are apt to receive it more than instrumentalists.[4] Marcella Detroit told me that she had had men miming oral sex at her when she was singing in a solo spot, but had experienced no hassle when she was playing in Shakespeare's Sister.

FRAN (Sub Rosa): I used to get a lot more hassle when I was singing. Blokes trying to pull me off the stage, fucking trying to snog me and that kind of stuff, trying to get the mike out of my hands. 'Can I touch you?' Which is one of the reasons I stopped being lead singer. Usually men respect me more because I'm a bass player, because bass is seen as a male instrument for some reason. . . . You get the odd one who's a bit narky, but I ignore it.

---

[4] Lucy Green points out that 'the image of the paid female singer who puts body and voice on public display has inevitably been associated in practically all known societies with that of sexual temptress or prostitute. Although not engaged in a fully intentional act of display, the singing woman in a public arena is dangerously, and tantalisingly, close to doing so. For this reason she is a threat and, as such, is open to abuse' (1997: 29).

Younger women are liable to to get more abuse than older women:

YOLANDE CHARLES : **When I first started playing I think I wore a short skirt and a pair of high heeled shoes—I was 16 or something—and you feel awful because somebody gives a wolf whistle and shouts 'lovely legs' and you just played your arse off and they didn't take a blind bit of notice. . . . It did make me think twice about wearing a short skirt again. But that was then, and I was 16. Now I wouldn't give a shit.**

My youngest interviewees, the 16-year-olds in Tampasm and the 18-year-olds in Kid Candy regularly get 'show us yer tits'. The experiences of the two women in Echobelly make an interesting contrast: Debbie (guitar-player and lesbian, with a tough image) has never had any abuse, whilst Sonya (vocalist and frontwoman, with a softer image) faces it regularly:

DEBBIE SMITH : **That happens at every single gig. Every single gig. They don't direct it at me. They direct it at Sonya because she's the frontperson. That happens all the time. It's one of the hazards of being a woman in a band. As long as women have tits they will be shouting 'Show us your tits!' All you have to do is either have a good putdown ready, or ignore it, or jump in and fight them; three options. I just look menacingly in the direction from which it came, but Sonya has a couple of good putdowns which she uses.**

Older women, women who play instruments and those with a 'hard' or less feminine image tend not to get abuse. Skin, who is a strong female with a tough uncompromising image fronting a 'heavy' band, could not remember a single occasion where she received sexist abuse. Gail Greenwood from Belly, who is 'totally flat chested', 36 years of age, a bass player, and (she says) not considered pretty or cute, never has any hassle, but frontwoman Tanya Donelly apparently has had a lot. Fluffy, with their 'girly' image, get regular mammary requests (despite playing instruments), whilst the cerebral Stereolab instrumentalists, Laetitia and Mary, have never once experienced it. It seems that image and stage presentation can be a factor affecting the degree of abuse received:

LAETITIA : **If you position yourself a bit vulnerably, then people feel it and it opens up this situation where they're gonna attack you. Whereas, if you come in as a wall or something that is unattackable, then they won't even think about it. The same in the streets. If you walk and you look like you're the aggressor, people aren't gonna give you shit. But if you walk and you're scared then of course they're gonna . . .**

The problem with this argument, however, as with the allied argument about rape and 'asking for it', is that non-sexy clothes and a hard image, although offering some degree of protection, are no guarantee. Whilst it is true that some women regularly receive more abuse than others, *all* are ultimately vulnerable to it, simply by virtue of their sex.

Younger women in the 1990s have been strongly retaliating. Actively drawing the audience's attention to the perpetrator and confronting him usually works.

L7 apparently like to suggest that the man save his breath for blowing up his inflatable sheep when he gets home. My interviewees supplied me with a number of effective one-line retorts which they had used: for instance, 'You come up here and get your trousers off and we'll get our tits out' (Jill Myhill of Valley of the Dolls); 'It's alright. I remember what it was like when I had my first drink' (Caroline Scallon of Soul Devotion). 'Loads of people would say, "Sit on me face" and I'd say, "Why? Is your nose bigger than your dick?"' (Mandy of Ms45). Although older women performers are less likely to be asked to expose their breasts, they do have to confront sexism combined with ageism:

VI SUBVERSA : I can't separate being female from being an old female. As you're about to go on stage—you know how you feel—some bloody little bugger at the side of the stage is saying, 'Here come the old age pensioners' or 'Who's that old bag? . . . Cor, she must be 90 years old!' Now, it just feeds my strength, but in the early days it put me off my stroke for the first few songs.

Pregnancy seems to be an even greater source for mockery:

ALISON RAYNER : We did a gig a few months ago at Bart's medical school. When we started, there was a row of medical students standing straight along the front . . . with their arms folded and a kind of sneer on their faces. . . . Julia was extremely pregnant at the time and a couple of them, particularly in front of her, were making laughs and jokes. You know, what a laugh—a very large pregnant woman playing saxophone.

Direct racist abuse did not surface as a significant issue, but then I only interviewed seven non-white musicians as (despite white music's extensive 'borrowing' from black music) there are very few black and Asian women musicians in the indie/rock/pop worlds.

Male hostility often makes women musicians determined to show how good they are, although there is usually an accompanying resentment.

JUDY PARSONS : 'Get 'em down!' You don't get that at a male band's gigs . . . and they've only come along because 'Cor, it's an all-girl band!' We probably all feel a huge amount of depression and a lot of aggression. We think, 'You bloody stupid idiots, we'll show you!' And we plod on throughout the set. Every now and then you feel your confidence wavering and you wonder whether you can do it. And then it comes back, you know, 'We're gonna play our songs' and 'We're a good band and you can like us or not!'

Sometimes harassment goes further than verbal insults. If it is true that aggression stems from a dislike of women's independence, then it is not surprising that the feminist and lesbian bands have a lot of such stories to recount.

TERRY HUNT : We were playing on a lorry and this male photographer was trying to get on the lorry with us. We were in the middle of a song and he wanted us to move something so he could get on the lorry. We said, 'Piss off!' And he was really put out. He couldn't believe that we wouldn't want him to take our photos. He made a swipe at somebody.

Some men are enraged by being excluded from women-only gigs. When I was playing in a the Mistakes we did some gigs which men tried to invade. When, on the worst occasion, a crowd of drunks did manage to gain access, the women resisted and there was a serious fight, during which our bass player was punched in the face, and our drummer was so beaten up she had to go to hospital. We were forced to cancel a number of gigs. Other feminist bands have had similar experiences, for example, 'A bunch of cricket club boys tried to gatecrash when we were doing a gig in an education college. They broke windows. It was really heavy' (Ros Davis, of Rash and Contraband). Because men are not used to women being encouraged to come down to the front of the audience and take over some space, they sometimes react aggressively.

TERRY HUNT : A lot of students from the Poly came down—male students. And the women had done what they quite often used to do in those days. They'd formed a semicircle in the front and were dancing with linked arms. And the blokes linked arms behind them and were dancing, kicking their legs up and were actually kicking the women and children. They were just being hateful. They were making fun of them. They just couldn't understand what was going on.

Often the women in the audience become the victims of this sexual violence, rather than the band. However, bands do retaliate:

'SUKE' : There was one wally at Bristol that came up with a camera and said, 'Let me take a photo of between your legs' to one of us at the front. And we threw a bucket of water over him. And some girls that were fans of ours got hold of him and tried to smash his camera up.

Interviewees recounted particularly scary stories of gigs abroad.

SHAREEN (Ms45): I remember once when I was 18. I was doing a gig in Colorado. Some guy actually came up to the stage and picked me up and started to carry me off. . . . It was scary! I hit him on the head with my guitar and a big fight started.

EMMA ANDERSON (Lush): We just did a tour in America and we walked off the stage at one gig. Because there are these weird radio festivals and people are just moshing and punching each other senseless. And people were just throwing things at us. Not like 'Get off the stage'; it was just a sport for them at these festivals. . . . It was a really violent atmosphere. . . . I was afraid when this massive shoe came hurtling towards my head. That's when I walked off.

There is one band which stands out in my sample for having received the worst abuse and that is Every Woman, who were young, singers, and played no instruments. They also danced, which further emphasized their bodies as being on display and undermined their status as musicians. The northern working men's club circuit, in which they worked, has traditional chauvinist expectations of women 'entertainers'. However, in line with the experiences of other women musicians, their worst gigs have been at armed services clubs. Dee: 'Oh, God, if we play squaddies do's, that's it straight away: "Get your tits out for the lads!" They all just sing that. "Get your liver out" "Show us yer monkey head". Oh, it's terrible. All the time.' One can imagine the kind of racist abuse that would have been added to this had any of the band members been black or Asian. Every Woman (who, unlike most of my 1990s interviewees, unreservedly define themselves as feminists) take care not to go on stage scantily clad or wearing revealing clothes. Dee: 'But there again, there are places where we do go and it doesn't matter what you've got on. Just because you're a woman, you get abuse. You could be there in a rainmac and a pair of galoshes. You're female, so you're a sex object. Especially on the RAF, navy, that kind of circuit.' They accept these gigs simply because they are very well paid, but they have to take the precaution of staying in the dressing room all the time they are not on stage. They do the show, smile, and pay no attention to their abusers, some of whom openly masturbate in the front rows of the audience. Marie told me that she had had two rape attempts at gigs and a man masturbating in her dressing room: 'Basically, you become musical prostitutes. You just take the money and run.'

Because of the widespread sexist abuse and potential dangers at gigs, women musicians typically look out for and protect each other, which increases the members' commitment to each other: 'We take care of each other, stick up for each other at rehearsals and look out for each other at pub gigs. I feel safe' (Caroline Scallon). Dramatic incidents are rare, but all kinds of non-overt violence and general harassment were commonplace and taken for granted in the 1980s:

TERRY HUNT (Jam Today): There's always either a comment or some uneasy atmosphere or something. Every gig there'll be some little something that has to be dealt with. [But] a lot of women just have that experience happen to them so much of the time that they block it out. And it's the victim syndrome. It's like almost that you draw that kind of attention to yourself, that somehow women are responsible for those things. Or, 'Oh, it's not serious, dear. It doesn't matter.' We're so used to being harassed.

And, similarly, in the 1990s, such incidents were still so routine that they barely required a comment. Practically every woman musician that I interviewed had experienced them. For instance, Clare Howard from Death By Crimpers referred in passing to the 'inevitably silly remarks' and Charlotte Clark from Tampasm told me, 'We've had the usual "You're girls, you're shit" kind of thing.' However, despite the sexism that women musicians encounter, some laid stress on the advantages of being a female in the rock world. They stood more of a chance of getting gigs because of their 'novelty value' and their looks, and their bands are seen as 'more commercial' by promoters. Treacle, whose publicity photos show them to be five attractive blonde young women, face the problem of ingrained assumptions that they will be musically incompetent, and yet sexism offers them advantages, as well: 'If you're a male band you're ten a penny, but if you're a female band, as soon as somebody who books gigs hears that you are a female band, without even listening to the tape, 90 per cent of the time they'll offer you a gig' (Sara Watts). Some bands debated whether to exploit the fact that they were female, some arguing that, as there were so many disadvantages stacked against them, they might as well utilize their advantages.

Working Conditions and Masculinity

Gigging in the early 1980s:

VI SUBVERSA : There isn't a changing room. There's beer spilt all over the place. You're gonna get gobbed on. Maybe, climbing into a van, without being able to change, and driving to somewhere where you're gonna sleep on someone's floor. Bad conditions. The lack of care. The lack of tenderness, warmth . . . the whole kind of macho thing of having to survive on a shoestring and heroic treks through the bloody snow to get to a gig on time, or whatever it is. I think it's really awful.

And a rehearsal room in the 1990s:

'VANESSA' : The floor's an ashtray and there are beer cans everywhere and it stinks and it is cold and the guys don't clean up after them. So on two or three occasions I've gone down to the desk and said, 'would somebody come and clean it up before we work in here?'

The important factor, here, is not so much the physical conditions per se as the value-system which romanticizes and sustains them. As rock venues are organized entirely around the notion that rock bands are male, inadequate dressing rooms are a particular bugbear for women. Well-known and prestigious venues often lack even minimal facilities. When the Mistakes played at the Rock Garden in London the only place to change was a tiny toilet which smelt of Jeyes fluid since the official 'changing room' was dirty, and contained dozens of beer kegs and a thirteen-piece male band. As 'Suke' (of a prominent 1980s all-female pop band) told me, 'Dressing rooms have never catered for women, because they've always catered for men. So they've never thought of a mirror, or a nice toilet. It's awful. I hate them.' It is not simply a question of clubs failing to provide reasonable facilities for performers: by smashing up the facilities male bands create a 'masculine' environment which works to exclude women:

ALISON RAYNER (Jam Today): At the Greyhound one time they did up the dressing room and it was quite nice. It had a basin and sink and a few chairs and it was quite reasonably decorated. And there was a toilet next door. Gradually over the months it deteriorated and deteriorated. They didn't bother to clean it up properly. And the bands who used it must have been really shitty, because there was graffiti all over the walls and the sink was permanently blocked. They never bothered to put soap or towels out anymore. And it was just awful in the end: the chairs were broken, the toilet smashed up. I hate that kind of thing. Men seem to be much more like that than women.

The world of rock does not have to be like this; many women musicians try to change it. Every Woman *insist* on the following in their contract 'rider': 'two dressing rooms with lockable doors, wash basin, hot and cold water, table and chairs, adequate heating and lighting, toilets, full length mirrors'. On the other hand, a band would find it hard to obtain these conditions on the indie and rock circuits until they were successful enough to play really big venues. Moreover, other bands criticized Every Woman: 'Who do you think you are expecting such conditions? Superstars?'

NATASHA ATLAS (Transglobal Underground): At the level we've been touring at the moment—like, no dressing room facilities, that kind of shit really gets on your nerves. . . . Like, I won't be able to do very much dancing tonight because there's a great big hole in the stage and unless they fix it first I can't deliver my best. If we were selling a lot more records and doing really big gigs then I don't think I would find it a problem at all. It's the level. . . . [The crew] take the piss out of me sometimes because, you know, we'll walk into a venue and it's dark, dingy and black and smelly and horrible and there's me, Arabic singer, and they call me the Queen of Egypt—which is fine by me. They say, 'Oh, HRH Egypt is here. Oh God, she's not gonna like this place is she?' No. I'm carrying my little handbag and my nose is turned up.

The Musicians' Union is committed to equal opportunities and has fought hard to try to improve pay and working conditions but proportionally low membership amongst rock and pop musicians and the effect of the large number of amateur and semi-professional bands undermines collective action. Moreover, I believe that male musicians accept bad conditions because they endow masculinity, making the life of a rock musician one which most women would not choose. It is, then, another way of excluding women, as is language which a single woman in a male band may find herself under pressure to use in order to become 'one of the lads'. Both members of Ms45 had done this.

SHAREEN : One of the earliest camouflage devices that I learned being a girl in a band with guys is to become a foul-mouthed crass bastard, simply so that I wouldn't have a separate language for the 'treehouse' and then when the girl came in. On the other hand, it's sad that I had to change myself that way. But, on the other hand, I didn't want to feel that marginalized because everyone was being polite around me.

Other women have made attempts to deliberately 'feminize' gigs: at one stage with the Mistakes, two of us were knitting before going on stage. Sue had her period come on unexpectedly and asked from the stage, 'Has anyone got a sanitary towel?' However, the most significant clash between women's needs and the masculine code of rock gigs revolves around children.

Gigging Mothers

I have already discussed how the role responsibilities of being a mother tend to interfere with band involvement. At the gigging stage these problems ramify.

> **'JANICE'** (1980s Yorkshire pop band): It makes life difficult with family. Because there were occasions when we had a couple of gigs a week and we had to have a practice. And then we'd be loading up the day before and it seemed to be taking the week over, and our life over. . . . You get keyed up before a gig. You tend to throw everything else to the wind and concentrate on that . . . I do find it difficult when I'm full-time at college, having to fit family things in and kids.

As this example illustrates, being a mother and either doing paid work or being a student as well poses the most acute problems of all. Many women need their jobs for the money (which gigging does not supply) but are restricted in the number of gigs they can do because of work and childcare commitments. Given these competing commitments, it is amazing they were playing gigs at all.

Rock venues do not usually accommodate children. Many gigs take place in pubs, from which environment children are legally barred. Gigs are typically unsuitable for children from the point of view of health and safety, being dirty, cramped, and full of potential dangers such as electrical cables and leads. Electric shocks are not unheard of, people tripping up is commonplace. Aside from these physical dangers, the audience poses a possible threat. Thefts and fighting may occur. A baby could not be safely left in a changing room. Indeed, there is usually no safe place for a baby or young child. Some venues, even reputable ones, lack dressing rooms; they certainly do not cater for children. Furthermore, babies, nappies, and breastfeeding are anathema to the protagonists of the 'heroic' vision of rock'n'roll life. On the other hand, some women did take their children to gigs and on tour and thus showed that these hurdles could be overcome.

> **VI SUBVERSA** : It hasn't limited my involvement with music because I haven't let it. I demanded that other people shared responsibility for my children . . . and, because of my commitment to the band, I demanded of my children that they respected my needs. Actually, it was a wonderful experience for them. Some of those gigs were frightening—where there was violence—and a lot of the time I was telling them to keep out of the way of the bogs and where there was likely to be scuffles . . . What gave me courage was the feeling that I was allowing my children to have some awareness of danger—that people were not always to be trusted, that fights did happen . . . and, looking at my children now, I feel good about what I did . . . They are really strong individuals.

Women like Vi were fully aware of the role they were playing for other women— as was Terry of Jam Today, who felt it was important to 'be gigging live and showing other women that it's possible to be a musician and a woman, including having babies'. Co-band member, Alison Rayner detailed the problems her band faced and how they organized to overcome them:

> **Gigs vary. Some gigs are fine and some are extremely difficult. If there's a dressing room—at the moment he's very young, he's only a few months old— if he's not asleep, then we have to have somebody come and sit with him while we're playing . . . or if the dressing room's near enough to the stage, and he's asleep, then he can be left for half an hour or three-quarters of an hour when we're playing. But sometimes it's difficult. There's been once or twice we've come to gigs and it was entirely unsuitable. . . . When I book gigs now I have to remember, that's another thing to mention, after you've discussed the money, the PA, the dressing room, the lights, the stage, the times, etc., then I have to say, 'Right, the other thing is that we have a baby. And is there a suitable room? And if the baby's asleep will there be somebody who can sit with the baby?' Sometimes, like a pub, you just get a kind of blank look and they say, 'Oh, it's nothing to do with us'. So that's when you have to make alternative arrangements.**

Some women managed to incorporate their children into their performances. I have seen both Sue and Ali Smith's children (of varying ages) on stage. Sue's partner is also a musician and is very supportive of her involvement, sharing responsibility for the children. Once Ali had three little children, she knew she just had to go on playing in order to 'stay alive', so she always takes her young children to gigs where kids are allowed. She played one on the day her daughter was due, advertising the gig as probably including a birth, and three weeks after that she was playing again, with her baby in her sister's arms in the audience. I have even witnessed her playing the sax with her baby on her hip at the same time. On the other hand, Ali stresses how difficult this juggling act is: 'You're a mother first and a musician second, always'. This makes it extremely difficult for such women to turn their hobby into a career and become professional.

Band Meetings

In the beginning, bands are often split about what is a 'good' or 'bad' gig. Arguments can erupt over these evaluations. But with experience values, attitudes, perception, expectations, and aspirations become transformed. A joint understanding is reached about what is a 'good' or a 'bad' gig, and other group definitions of this sort develop. Band members learn from their experiences at gigs and the development of a shared view is accelerated by the post-mortems which inevitably follow. Analysis of gigs takes place spontaneously afterwards and is an important group learning experience during which members pass comments on each other's performances. The playing is a subject for minute dissection, as is the total behaviour of all band members, so that even bodily movements and off-stage behaviour are scrutinized. Arguments often occur, and, as one area of common contention is, simply, what actually did and did not happen during the performance, gigs are taped, since, despite the practical problems in trying to get a reasonable reproduction of a performance, a more objective rendering is possible via this practice. (Some bands might also video their performances, although expense usually rules this out.)

Bands feel the need to set up meetings, to analyse the band's past and present, to air grievances, and to plan for the future. As a band progresses, administrative tasks increase and, if a democratic way of working is adopted, group decisions are necessary. Many women's bands take pains to introduce some home comforts into meetings.

FRAN (of Sub Rosa): In this band we meet, have a cup of coffee—real coffee— and talk about any administration that needs doing: who's heard of any gigs to do, any PA that needs sorting out, photo session, radio programmes, that sort of thing. We discuss that. We discuss the structure of the songs, if they need changing, what can be improved. . . . Band meetings with men used to be a big piss-up session, sitting around talking about who they wanted to screw next, basically; anything apart from the music.

In this way 'band meetings' become institutionalized as a normal part of band life. However, they may begin to take up an increasing amount of time which can cause problems and even precipitate a crisis. I have already explained how time becomes increasingly taken up by rehearsing and gigging. When meetings are added onto this, individuals have to reorder their lives and think seriously about their desires and commitments. There may well be objections from some members who would rather be rehearsing or who cannot see the need for meetings while others simply feel they do not have any more time to give the band. For most interviewees (whether in the 1980s or in the 1990s) the band simply always came first in their lives: before other leisure activities, before social life, before relationships. One which does not plan and evaluate will be disadvantaged in career terms and, predictably, it was the band composed entirely of mothers who fell into this category as they simply did not have the time so that problems never got resolved. 'Sandra' (1980s Yorkshire pop band): 'We start talking about washing or nappies or something when it gets bad. We just fume quietly, I think, all of us. We just sit there and stew over things. It's terrible.'

Remuneration

Bands just starting to gig tend to get little or nothing in the way of financial rewards, a factor which band members have to learn to come to terms with. Some women are surprised by the paucity of payment, given the popular myth that rock bands are rolling in loot. There are also hidden costs:

ALISON RAYNER : By the time you've rattled around a bit doing rehearsals, buying strings or sticks or whatever you need, getting to the gig, probably having something to eat, buying a couple of drinks—you've probably spent more than £10 [each].

ALI WEST (the Mistakes): You spend an hour playing the gig and then you spend anything from 12 to 15—getting ready for it, or driving down, or humping gear, driving back . . . or whatever. And so the amount of work that goes into any one gig is phenomenal, really. And I don't think most people realize that. And the hourly rate that you get is probably, practically nil. . . . I didn't do it for the money because there wasn't any money!

However, most bands starting out are so happy just to be playing that they are willing to do some gigs for no money at all. Rewards are intrinsic: 'You put a lot in and you don't get anything out. But you come to accept that quite early on —that you're playing for fun' ('Janice'). Yet a lot of women did voice dissatisfaction at the lack of remuneration, particularly as money was seen as a necessary resource in order for bands to progress:

'KASSANDRA' : If we did have a little bit more money we could make our gigs a hell of a lot better . . . We want to use slides and we want to have a few extra things—certain pedals . . . just expand a bit on our sound. . . . I think, if we had some money, the first thing we would get would be a van, 'cause every time we do a gig we have to hire one and it's really expensive. . . . There's one or two PAs we've come across we really like, but we can't always afford them . . . and we want to go in a good studio, and work under circumstances where it's not the middle of the night, so we can do our best.

Lack of money was one of the reasons which led Sandra to leave her band:

'SANDRA' : Most of the time we've not got any money at all. Sometimes it's been so much of a hassle you just think, 'That's it. We're not doing it again.' If you can't even get your petrol money when you're as poor as we all are to start with. . . . We've ended up paying out of our pockets and got minus a fiver each! . . . If you've got to pay for your petrol and your beer and you don't get anything back you wonder whether it's worth it. . . . The most we've ever got was £8.50 each, and we thought that was wonderful. So we all went and got a bag of chips!

Even at some well-known venues bands get so little money that they cannot cover costs. Sometimes they even pay to play. This, again, reflects the low level of unionization amongst popular musicians with competition and price under-cutting militating against collective action.

Benefit Gigs

These financial problems face all bands, regardless of sex, but one aspect which is more gender-specific is that, during the 1970s and 1980s, all-women bands seemed to have been pushed towards doing benefit gigs, unlike male bands (apart from specifically political ones and, interestingly, reggae bands). Women and black musicians (both disadvantaged groups themselves) often felt morally obliged to do benefits. Most of the women I interviewed during the 1980s had done benefit gigs, some a large number. 'Sarah' (of 1980s Brighton pop band): 'We've done lots of Rock Against Sexism and Rock Against Thatcher, Rock Against Racism. . . . We've done rock against everything you can rock against!' Benefits throw up particular sets of problems as bands are expected to play just for 'expenses', although some found they were not even getting this. Terry Hunt (Jam Today): 'Women musicians are always being asked to sponsor everything—from one extreme to the other. You get terribly ripped off. What they expect you to give up, of what is equivalently your wages, they would never dream of asking the people on the door to give up at all.' Some women felt particularly indignant that they were sometimes taken for granted by other *women*:

> **'HILARY'** (of 1980s Yorkshire rock band): I got fed up with not getting any money. Like, people kept asking you to go places and saying that they'll pay you and it's, 'Oh, well, we didn't get enough people to this conference. We can't pay you'. . . . It really gets up my nose. It's not as if you want to earn thousands from it. You just want a fair deal. [So, nowadays] we'll only play, not just for expenses, but for money as well, even if it's just a fiver each. We need to get paid. It's also just something about getting paid—I like the feeling of it.

Often the organizers of benefits are inexperienced and underestimate the problems such ventures involve. Gigs may be disorganized—with inadequate PA and lighting, poor advertising and a low audience turnout which may mean they fail to make enough money to pay the band's expenses. Benefits sometimes lose money and benefit no one. 'Sylvia': 'The people that you're dealing with are even less experienced than you are, so you end up ringing up and saying, "Have you done the publicity yet". . . . It happens all the time—it's a shambles. You turn up and—God, it's the same story.' Nevertheless, a benefit gig is still a gig, which, for an unknown or new band, competing in a limited local market, is often difficult to get. Also, many band members believed fervently in the causes they were supporting and saw gigging as a way of giving those organizations large amounts of money—which would otherwise be impossible for them to donate. For some bands, a very large proportion of their gigs were benefits.

> **'KASSANDRA'** : You usually get really good audiences . . . you've already got a point of contact with them. If it's Rock Against Racism, then you're not going to get a bunch of racist pigs. And it's a very nice feeling to know that the money's going to something good. Because, otherwise, the money's just going into someone's pocket, anyway. And finance-wise they usually make sure your expenses are covered. With commercial gigs it's a totally different scene. You make a bit of money but, on the other hand, they don't give a damn whether you cover your expenses or not. The whole transaction becomes a big sort of 'I'll sell you this and you sell me that'. I'm not a great one for going on demonstrations . . . so it really makes me feel good that I can do a gig for a cause . . . and it's a much nicer way for me to contribute to it.

In the apolitical 1990s, some bands did benefits (for environmental groups, women's organizations, and against the Poll Tax) but the 'benefit syndrome' of the 1970s–1980s no longer existed.

Band Fund

In order to accumulate enough funds, bands often develop a joint fund/bank account. This pooling of resources marks a very important step: the band has a financial embodiment as well as a social one, which adds to the band's stability and represents a considerable financial investment on the part of each member. The possibility of collecting such sums from individuals as a donation would be most unlikely, but a regular sum taken out of band fees is usually quite painless:

'BECKY' : We put [the money] into a fund. . . . We get two quid every gig to give everybody pocket money. . . . If we didn't have this hundred quid I wouldn't be able to buy video cassettes or buy make-up stuff [for the band as a whole]. I'd have to go round and collect the money and it would be a big hassle: 'Oh, I've only got fifty pence this week.'

In one city during the 1980s the women's big band put all their fees into a fund which was also used by two other women's bands in the area. Splitting the big band's fee between twenty-odd people would have meant each member receiving only a tiny sum, whereas pooling it meant that a sizeable amount could be accumulated, which could then be used to purchase equipment which would be of use to a lot of women.

The moment at which a band fund emerges is an important point of transition since it ceases to play just for the fun of it and considers long-term goals, so that it is precisely at this point that the question of financial management is considered. If it isn't someone will have to take on the task of administering the fund, and perhaps other related tasks.

Rationalizations

Band members who generally hope to cover their costs and make some money on top also expect an audience, preferably a large one, and to be received favourably. When, as often happens, these expectations are not met, a crisis is precipitated, the perception of failure leading people to make decisions which determine whether the band will continue or not. Some bands decide that the returns (in all senses) simply do not justify the investment and they break up. Others decide to make a determined attempt to break out of existing limitations (local gigs and inadequate PA) by stepping up the scale of the operation and investing considerably more time, energy, and money. The ones which take this path are making a commitment to some sort of professionalism. However, there is a third option. Some bands scale down their aspirations, relinquishing all vague notions of 'making it' and settle for playing 'just for fun'. Music-making is conceptualized as a 'hobby' rather than a possible career and a 'musician' identity does not emerge. Such an adaptation involves bands subscribing to a set of beliefs and values which, in a sense, rationalize their experience of failure. Disappointment at being badly paid may be offset by having a good time, as in this case: 'We've done a festival in Cornwall which was only expenses. But we had such a nice time on the beach. It was a nice experience' ('Kassandra'). A typical rationalization is to view the gig as a 'practice'. This enables a band to carry on gigging in an otherwise unrewarding situation, but lack of money *or* fun erodes motivation, while the lack of an audience is even more threatening to a band's continuance. In such a situation satisfaction can only come from aspects extrinsic to the actual playing and the gig itself.

> **'JANICE'** : It was well publicized but no one turned up. [We got] no money in the end but only five pounds expenses shared out between the band. [We] wouldn't have minded not being paid, but we didn't enjoy it either—which is most important. . . . I wasn't disappointed because I always think the worst, after so many gigs where you turn up and there's nobody there. I always think it's going to be hopeless, anyway. So if there's half a dozen people there it's quite nice. . . . Usually, however bad they are, you think, 'Oh, well, I had a good chat with so-and-so'. . . . Last night was a flop. But the curry was good— so it was worth it!

This same band had, previously, undergone the humiliation of having to tout for business:

> **'SANDRA'** : We did a pub in Manchester and there wasn't anybody. . . . We'd got the PA and it was going to be really good. And there wasn't a soul. And we literally went into the pubs and clubs and [said], 'Do you fancy coming to see a band? It's a women's band' to try and get them there. We ended up with an audience and it was a right bunch—never seen such a mixture. But we had a good time in the end.

Continuance of this situation for any length of time will lead to one or more members leaving:

> **'SANDRA'** : I'm leaving this band. I do like playing and if I felt that it was worthwhile. . . . But we've had so many gigs like last night. They've nearly all been bad gigs. Nobody seems to be bothered. It's just pathetic. You put up all these posters; you make an effort and you want to do gigs so that people can have a good time, and nobody ever turns up.

But, for most bands, gigs were usually fun and that was the major reward: 'It's a great feeling being on stage because we have a really good laugh and we have a really good time' ('Julia'). For some, playing music together as women is a different kind of experience from their usual music-making context (in mixed bands). 'Beth': 'This is our relaxation! I think that is why it's working. We always thoroughly enjoy the gigs—even bad gigs, I've enjoyed—because on stage you get a good feeling going together. We know what's happening and we're all laughing at each other and it's great. It's good fun.' Some bands are conceptualized simply as hobbies from the start. For the members of Kid Candy, the band had only a temporary existence as they were going on to university at the end of their A levels course.

MIRIAM COHEN : The reason I'm still in a band is that it's a hobby that's really productive . . . something you get a really good sense of achievement from . . . . It's just everything you could get from a hobby: you can do it with people; you can do it without people; you can do it in front of people; you can learn from it; you can do it for people.

Conflicts and Contradictions

Problems arise once the gigging stage is reached, some revolving around the issue of power. Many male bands set out from the start with an established 'leader' whose band, in a sense, it is. Some mixed bands start on this footing too (and may have a woman as the leader), but women's bands (both in the 1980s and 1990s) have tended to be more democratic, possibly due in part to the sheer lack of female musicians: a band may be composed of novices all learning together. However, whatever the reasons, the absence of clearly defined leaders in all-women bands has a number of implications.

In a typical male band the existence of one or two highly committed people, who more or less 'run' the band, means that it can survive a high rate of turnover in membership, the leaders 'carrying' the rest. Thus, in a male band where personnel change is frequent it is rarely composed of the same members at the moment of signing a record deal as it was when it started, whereas women's bands find it more difficult to survive the crisis of a member leaving since they rarely have clearly defined leaders and the shortage of female musicians means that members take longer to replace. (It can take so long that the band dissolves in the meantime.) For this reason the Valley of the Dolls made a pact that if one member left they would split up: 'You go through ups and downs and if you're going through a down, you think twice about leaving the band because you'll mess it up for everybody else as well. We described ourselves as four legs on a table' (Jill Myhill).

Despite their democratic origins, however, over time bands tend to develop power imbalances, which may be based upon a number of factors, for example the ownership of equipment or songwriting. Once a woman becomes established as the main, or sole, writer, then power tends to accrue to her. (In male bands the 'leader' who sets up the band is probably the songwriter from the start, anyway.)

Over time, as it becomes apparent that not everyone is going to write, one or two individuals are inclined to predominate as, in arranging a song, the writer usually has more influence than other band members, particularly if there is a lack of songs and a fear of the only source drying up: 'I think the person who's written the song tends to have last say. Like it's their baby and if they really don't like it you won't do it' ('Sylvia'). Power may also descend upon those who work hardest, either in terms of administration or in terms of physical labour, although this is often connected to the amount of time members have available.

> **'VERONICA'** : The two of us who have the most power work [only] part-time. Therefore I think we expect the others to think about it as much as we do, to put more effort into it and be prepared to give up more time for it. Commitment's the main thing we argue about . . . I think everyone in the band wants to go in the same direction, but we push it along, just saying, 'Now, we do need another practice next week'. When people might be saying, 'Oh, I don't think we really need it', we say, 'Yes we do need it, otherwise I'm not playing the gig.'

Thus, over time, as the number of gigs increases, there may develop a split between those who wish to spend more time on the band and those who do not (or cannot), and, if this widens, the band will break up. A further set of problems revolves around the issue of time because once a band starts gigging there are (usually) more practices and meetings as well as gigs. The increase in time a woman must commit to her band is considerable and it is often on weekends. I heard many tales of broken relationships, lesbian and heterosexual.

> **FRAN** (Atomic Candy): It has split up one relationship that I had, because they can't be doing with it. It was 'either me or the band'. So I am afraid it was the band. . . . I limit my relationships. Music comes first.

> **ALISON RAYNER** (Jam Today): It was something so separate from the woman I was involved with, there was nothing she could relate to, or be involved in. And it took up a lot of time and I was terribly excited by it, and it wasn't anything to do with her. People I know who are musicians who have relationships with people who aren't musicians find it very difficult.

Perhaps this is why most of the women I interviewed had relationships with other musicians, who would be more likely to empathize with the problems involved. Some musician husbands took on a greater share of domestic labour once their wives started performing:

> **'SANDRA'** : I'm very lucky, because he's played in bands and he's had so much time, anyway, he can't really say anything! If he's working, I do everything, and vice versa. He does a lot of the housework if I'm busy. When he and I were both in bands together it was a real hassle getting babysitters and that was very difficult. But [now] if he's not playing he's quite happy to babysit. So most of the time it's been quite easy. And because he's self-employed he can always be home in time for me to go.

But others were less fortunate.

'JANICE' : He resents me practising on my own. Because when he's here and I'm here he expects me to spend the time with him. I mean, he doesn't think anything of going in there and getting his guitar out. But if I was to go in there and start playing he'd be really pissed off: 'Not much of a life we lead!' He'd start moaning about me not spending time with him.

'KASSANDRA' : There's this big battle of whose trip is more important. So I think my next boyfriend is not going to be a musician. Musicians are so selfish. To be a musician you've got to be really selfish. You've got to ignore everything.

Having a sexual relationship *within* the band can be a solution for some, although when such a relationship ends the band is liable to break up and, anyway, the relationship may impose a strain on the other musicians. When Caroline (from Treacle) was in a mixed band and she and her boyfriend split up she had to leave. Some women I interviewed said that they felt they could not afford to have any kind of sexual relationship whilst in a band. For instance, Ali West: 'I think it was quite a factor in ruining our relationship and I haven't had any serious ones since. Because I did make a decision, after that, that I just couldn't cope with both. The band is like a relationship in a lot of ways.' Whilst others discovered for the first time, through band membership, a new and rewarding emotional independence:

'KASSANDRA' : I think, what would have happened if I wasn't getting into any of these things. I'd probably get a boyfriend and I'd worry about 'what is he doing now? Where has he gone?' But now, because I've got something in my life, he doesn't come first. It changed my life. He can go off and not see me for a week. It doesn't bother me. I think it happens in a lot of women's bands. It's something fulfilled in your life. You have got something going for you. If you haven't got anything else, all you rely on is your love.

A more specific problem develops in bands over how to allocate the (limited) amount of time that individuals have jointly available: for instance, a conflict typically develops between gigging and practising. Before the first gig much time is spent practising and working on the full 'set'. However, once gigging becomes regular the need for new material soon develops which creates a problem in finding the time to write, arrange, and rehearse a new set. There is thus an ongoing tension between doing gigs and having practices, so that sometimes a band may decide to refuse gigs for a period of weeks (or even months) in order to write more material. One particular aspect of this conflict is the need to write and arrange 'new' material versus the desire to go over, and rearrange, existing material. Clashes can also develop, because people become attached to particular numbers and are loath to see them dropped in order to make way for new ones. Another tension often develops between gigging/practising and day jobs as there is a limit to the number of gigs a woman can do if she is working in a full-time job.

'HILARY' : I work shifts. I work till 9 o'clock some nights. . . . That is one of the really hard things, trying to get everybody free at the same time. Also, if we've got a gig coming up we'll play twice a week and it's really difficult to get it all in. Sometimes I can't do them because I'm working and I can't always get somebody to swap with me.

This issue of time, raises (again) the question of commitment and future aspirations. If the band decides to go professional, then members in day jobs will have to either relinquish those jobs or leave. The time issue is linked to money since when a band is starting off members cannot afford to give up their day jobs as their wages are needed to finance the escalating outlay. However the band will only improve if it practises more, which people find is eating up their spare time and money and, if the problem becomes too acute, they may leave. Some of my interviewees deliberately did casual work, such as waitressing, whilst others felt forced onto the dole in order to progress musically:

CANDIDA DOYLE (Pulp): We weren't successful for ages. And yet, we couldn't have a job, because you'd lose your job because you were having to pack it in to go and do a date. Then you wouldn't do nothing for months, but you wouldn't have a job. . . . I lived in Manchester at one point, working in a shop, and I had to pack it in and go and live in Sheffield for a year on the dole. It was horrible. That was really hard, because I never wanted to sign on again. I signed on for about seven years of my life. I hope I don't have to sign on again ever.

Meanwhile, school student bands have particularly acute problems of time and money, plus parental restrictions. Tampasm found themselves getting back from a London gig at five o'clock in the morning and then having to get up for school at seven. Some of my interviewees were playing in bands, going to classes and doing paid work before and after school.

As band members develop increasing aspirations, 'better' gigs are sought, which, for non-London bands typically means out-of-town gigs. For London bands it means more prestigious venues. The snag is that, for such gigs, the band find they need to spend more money on a more expensive rehearsal facility, a high-quality demo tape or CD, or a bigger or better PA. Thus, although they may be getting more money for these gigs, most of it will probably be going on the increased expenditure which such gigs necessitate. For instance,

'SOPHIE' : Our rehearsals cost us twenty pound every time. So we lose that money; that comes out of out our own money. [Consequently, practices are rare.] Generally, about once every three weeks, 'cause it costs so much: four hours for twenty quid. We used to go to a place down Leyton . . . but we never used to get a good rehearsal. The place we go to now is [more expensive] and you've got to take all your own equipment. But it's such a good place.

This, then, is the central contradiction at the gigging stage: rewards are outweighed by costs. Band members quickly find that gigging is expensive and actually lose money on it. Being in a band eats into all spare time and completely disrupts social life, many activities and even relationships being sacrificed for the sake of the band. If you are in a job you do not have enough time; if you are on the dole you do not have enough money. Band members start to ask themselves 'is it all worth it?', despondency which may be reinforced by parents, friends, and partners who cannot understand all the hard work for no pay. There is a log-jam of bands all spending more and more money on better and better equipment in the fierce competition for gigs and record deals, Valley of the Dolls being a typical case. In 1995 they were gigging a lot and reinvesting all of their money into the band fund but, with no record deal, they could not afford a soundman, roadies, guitar technicians, slides, lights, and were not able to practise more than once a week. Their day jobs, for all of them, came firmly second to the band and were ones chosen because they could be dropped easily. The band had been waiting to be 'signed' for five years. Only a few are able to break through this situation to the richer pastures where expenditure on the band is justified by the rewards, and the very first step on this path must be to go professional. For the only way to make a living out of music-making is to make it your sole career.

7 Going Professional

'Going professional' is commonly held to mean making a living from music, giving up other, non-musical, careers or jobs in order to devote oneself solely to performing. Becoming a professional involves making a substantial commitment to music and it typically necessitates making considerable sacrifices in other areas of life. The most immediate one is often financial. For Shareen (of Ms45), it was law school. A woman may leave a secure non-musical career in the certain knowledge that it would be difficult, or impossible, to return should her musical venture fail. Judy Parsons (of the Belle Stars) relinquished a 'marvellous career' in civil engineering. 'I decided that that's what I wanted to do with my life . . . So I've lost lots of money by being in a band . . . I think it's wrong if you think, "I want to be a millionaire. I'll play in a rock band". It's not the same. You think, "I don't care if I'm starving. I'm gonna play in a rock and roll band".' Making a living from music is quite an achievement, for it is the unrealized goal of innumerable local bands. Judy was lucky in that her job had given her the means to purchase high-quality musical equipment. The irony here is that it is often only by having a well-paid non-musical career that a woman can get the necessary equipment in order to launch herself.

The 'moment' of going professional is both a moment of choice and crisis. Immediate financial rewards are likely to be limited. So why do women do it? The decision comes with the dawning realization that to 'succeed' one must move forward. The semi-professional band will be faced with the escalating costs of 'better' gigs and the perceived need for more expensive equipment. The band is taking up an increasing amount of time, often eating into band members' non-musical careers as making music and a living begin to clash. Thus, paradoxically, it is the inability to earn a living wage at the semi-pro stage which makes band members give up all other forms of money-making activity and commit themselves to making the band a financial success.

Implicit in most notions of the career trajectory is that bands follow the time-honoured route to rock success: 'paying your dues' by gigging for a number of years, gradually building a fan base and doing better paid gigs, until a major record contract is achieved. On the other hand, some bands are set up as professional from the start, usually composed of musicians who have already been in professional bands and define themselves as such. This situation is rarely applicable to women's bands, as professional women musicians are so rare. However, 'cultural capital' in the form of knowledge and connections from playing in a previous high-profile band has helped some female performers. Belly had a good start because Tanya Donnelly had just left Throwing Muses. Likewise, Elastica was helped by Justine Frischmann's past membership of Suede and her relationship with Damon of Blur. Elastica's career (along with Fluffy's, Pulp's, and Suede's) has been carefully planned and synchronized by Savage and Best, a leading management team and skilled ex-press officers.

However, partly owing to the rise of global pop and the record industry's response to international market demand (Frith 1993) the tradition of 'paying your dues' has been changing, so that, increasingly, bands are signed before they have ever walked onto a stage. *Who* you know is crucial. Garbage (put together by Nirvana's producer) had completed their album before their first gig. Skin had a clear agenda from the start, and Skunk Anansie did only two gigs before being signed. This fast track has also been taken by some female bands. The Spice Girls' first single raced up the charts before they had gigged. Kenickie were not yet musicians when Lauren Laverne met people from Slampt Records at a party and lied that she was in a band. Within weeks fiction became reality: there was a band, a demo, a contract. Fluffy started by acquiring a publishing deal and did their first gig, not at their local pub, but in CGBG's in America. In contrast, L7 had neither a manager nor major record deal for seven years. The vast majority of female bands plough away at local gigs for years with neither indie nor major record deals and absolutely no significant connections.

Although much that can be said about being in a professional band applies equally to male and female musicians, there are some significant differences. Men are more likely to start out thinking, 'I am going to be a rock musician and make hit records and become a star by the time I am 21'. If their band is not moving fast enough along the career ladder, then they will simply find another. Male musicians tend to have more of a sense of themselves as 'musicians', developing their individual professional careers. Most of the women in my research joined bands first, and only then began to see themselves as musicians and think in terms of developing a musical career. Thus their band is not a mere staging post, but bound up with their very identity as a musician in the first place. Kim McAuliffe (Girlschool): 'We didn't think, at the beginning, "We're gonna make an album and go to number one" . . . We took one step at a time . . . When we realized it was happening, we just thought, "Great!" ' Indeed (and surprising), some female professional women, who had toured and had record contracts, did not actually regard themselves as musicians, let alone professional. In the 1980s, the Mission Belles had been living from gigging continuously since 1962 and yet were loathe to call themselves musicians. A decade later, some of my interviewees felt the same. Anna (of Sub Rosa), who plays guitar, bass, and keyboards and who has been in at least half a dozen bands, had inhibitions about using the term: 'It's odd, isn't it? Before I came in here I was saying, "I don't know why she wants to interview me, I'm not a musician". . . . I think it's because I can't read music. It's because I can't compose on paper. . . . It's to do with confidence.' As most women drift into playing in 'local' bands without giving much thought to the long term, or having any kind of strategy, aspirations are learned via the process of band involvement, through informal socialization. At first, band members are simply glad of the opportunity to play, but, after a long succession of low-paid gigs, the musicians come increasingly to resent the fact that their playing and rewards are restricted and that they need day jobs in order to support themselves.

The desire for success in the long term enables a band to survive short-term financial deterioration, although musicians will only go professional if they believe in their music and the potential of the band, regardless of the reactions of others. This critical moment is the same for both male and female musicians, but women are less likely to take the plunge and give music their total commitment. They are held back by a range of factors, some external and others subjective, ones which have operated at earlier stages in the career process but which, at this point, become particularly crucial: lack of self-confidence, lack of role models, domestic and personal responsibilities, and so on.

One problem for bands is that the critical moment may evoke different responses from their various members. Some hate their jobs, and so going professional is an easy decision, while for others, already committed to their non-musical careers, the decision may prove impossible. When in the 1980s a 'major' offered her band a contract, Amelia Fletcher (of Heavenly) was not prepared to give up her place at Oxford University. Women musicians may have a mortgage and family obligations which limit their mobility. Many male musicians, especially in the world of jazz and improvisation, are financially dependent upon their wives, an arrangement which is seen as perfectly acceptable, probably because it is hidden. In sharp contrast, although women may be supported in order to raise children, this is rarely extended to the development of their musical talents. Thus, bands often become deeply divided on the issue of going professional and the ensuing arguments can tear them apart, with some women dropping out of playing music altogether.

If a band chooses not to go all out for a record contract and commercial success, it may scale down its aspirations and settle for just being a 'local band'. The notion of becoming professional is raised and rejected, but the band continues to play, far more aware of the value of the hobby it is engaged in. Teresa Hooker and Clare Howard, having experienced the pressures of being a recording band 'getting somewhere' in Death By Crimpers, were wary that their next band, Beaker, would become 'more serious' than a local fun band.

Going professional involves increasing expenditure on equipment, studio time, rehearsal space, and probably an agent and a manager. It will certainly mean entering fully into the world of the professional musician, which means, consequently, being cut off from others.

JUDY PARSONS (Belle Stars): If you decide that it's your life and your career you haven't got time to do anything else: you're on call. If someone rings up now and says, 'You've got to do an interview in two hours time', I'd have to be there. It's my job. I'm available all day and every day.

Becoming a professional musician involves subjective changes: radical shifts in self-conception and ways of seeing the world. A set of professional attitudes will be internalized, such as punctuality; deferred gratification; being 'serious' about music-making; single-mindedness in the pursuit of success; hard work to improve one's musical skills. Only by giving up everything else can one hope to succeed in the competitive world of rock music, and this sacrifice and dedication is at the centre of the professional world-view. Because becoming a professional musician involves thinking about one's playing in the long term, strategies emerge which inhibit the spontaneity of playing music as a day-to-day affair and make a band's orientation more businesslike.

Age becomes an important constraining factor at the point of going professional. The older a woman is the less likely she is to go professional, partly because age tends to bring responsibilities and obligations, both financial and social, and also affects self-conception. The music business is youth-orientated and ageism is pervasive, making older women feel pressurized into hiding their age or being vague about it in interviews.

JUDY PARSONS : It was just a hobby. I thought, when I started, I'm learning far too late—I haven't got a hope. . . . Ever since I started I thought 'I'm too old'. And I get depressed 'cause I think, 'what's the point of me working really hard? 'Cause my drumming career will end next year.' I have that dilemma and I really can't see how long I'll go on playing. I'd have never thought that I'd be playing drums in a rock band at 31. You wouldn't have thought it was possible, really. And I think, 'I will carry on, bugger it! I've got so far and in a year's time I'm going to be really proud of myself for doing something that I feel is worthwhile.'

However, if you are not bothered about commercial success age ceases to be such a problem. Jam Today had no intention of signing up with a record company and so experienced none of these commercial pressures: 'We're all around 30 and there's no precedent, really, for women musicians who aren't wearing dresses and doing harmonies. I don't know if we will, but I really hope we'll be going in ten years' time, 'cause I think that's really nice—a band full of women who are 40' (Alison Rayner). One woman in a punk band has turned her age into a positive force. Although playing and selling records to a very young audience, she did not attempt to look younger than her 47 years. It is a political gesture:

VI SUBVERSA (Poison Girls): I'm looking forward to being really old and doing it. There is a kind of power that will come because you're older. At the beginning I thought people would resent me for being older and say, 'Get off!

**This is a young person's music . . . It's like your bloody auntie turning up!'
. . . But a lot of young people say they really like it. I think, that what ageism
is about is the same as what sexism is about: the sheer waste. Half the human
race being written off. . . . It's the way that we're all divided against one
another, compartmentalized into marketable, manageable, manipulable
groups. So, now, I feel the older I am the more power I'll have to put in—You
know, 60-year-old woman guitarist!**

Ethnicity is also a factor, given that the world of guitar bands, rock, and indie
music is overwhelmingly white. If there is a lack of female rock role models, then
there is an even greater lack of black female role models, so I made a point of
interviewing four black female professional musicians, in order to get their perspective: Mary Genis (bassist in Dread Warlock), Skin (lead vocalist in Skunk
Anansie), Debbie Smith (guitarist in Echobelly), and Yolande Charles (who has
played bass with Paul Weller and with Marcella Detroit). Tellingly, the only contemporary black British female guitarist either Skin or Yolande could think of
was Debbie and the only contemporary black British female performer Debbie
could think of was Skin.

Black women tend to be socialized into 'black music' (soul, reggae, R'n'B, hip
hop, etc.) rather than rock or indie. They are also encouraged to be singers, rather
than instrumentalists. Men dominate the black music-making scene, just as they
dominate white music. Mary Genis: 'I think it's to do with black men's delusions
of sexual grandeur. Women aren't encouraged to get involved unless there's
an ulterior motive. That does sound off the wall but, unfortunately, that is the
case. . . . I think music is a man's world, black or white and if they can keep it
that way they will.' The obvious role for a black female is backing vocalist for
session work:

**SKIN : That was what I was pushed into, very gently and slowly, and what I was
offered when I first starting singing. It's to do with being a black female. It's
'Oh, alright, this is what you do, you sing soul music, you sing dance music,
you do back-up and look pretty behind other people.' And if you actually
want to do something a bit different you have to fight quite hard and break
out of a lot of pigeonholes that people think you should be in.**

Skin was convinced that being black was a handicap in her professional career as
a rock performer: 'It made things a lot harder. It took us twice as long to get on *Top
of the Pops* and it took twice as long to get radio play and all those things. Because
it's just not a typical established thing. There was a lot of ground to break before
we were taken seriously.' Natasha Atlas (Arabic singer), too, feels that she has
suffered from an underlying musical racial prejudice from the music press. She
also said that it was difficult to separate the racism from the sexism and has sometimes 'felt like the exotic bird in the corner', rather than being taken seriously as
a musician.

Definitional Complexity

So far, I have simply defined professional as making one's living solely from music. In practice, however, the distinction between 'amateur' and 'professional' is not all that straightforward and the transition from one state to the next is by no means an easy one to make. Between playing in a band as a 'hobby' whilst supporting oneself from a non-musical job/career, and being a successful professional, there are a variety of states of existence. Some women who do not earn all of their money from music nevertheless adamantly insist on being defined as 'professional'. This is possible for, as I have shown, being a professional seems to be not merely an objective state of existence, but also a state of mind, the latter being sometimes more important. Ofen these are women who have given up something to play music—a career or well-paid job—knowing full well that they would be very lucky to earn a living wage from playing. They are prepared to go on the 'dole' or do a variety of jobs in order to support themselves. What distinguishes this group as professionals is their commitment to the musical path. For these women, non-musical work, which is seen as a form of 'moonlighting' from their musical career, is fitted around their music and, even if full-time, viewed as insignificant. As music is the central preoccupation and focus of their lives, this is what marks them off from the category of women who play as a hobby, the fact that they do not live entirely from the proceeds of music-making is considered irrelevant: 'It's my life. . . . If you spend all your time doing it, then you're professional, as far as I'm concerned' (Terry Hunt of Jam Today). Often the financial pattern of such women's lives is a patchwork of gig money, part-time temporary jobs, and signing on and off the dole. One might get a run of good gigs and be able to 'sign off' for a while, or give up one's temporary job; but one never knows how long this period will last. Although going on the dole makes sense, for it allows women time to devote to music, it can give rise to problems. Gig money may only be covering one's expenses and, as the DSS is likely to dispute this, many do not declare their gig earnings. Asking for cash payments can pose problems with, for example, student unions, who will often only pay via cheques. Eventually, a point is reached where such bands must 'sign off', despite the fact that they may still be only just covering their expenses. If you are featured in the media everyone, from the taxman to the social security office, will think you are rolling in money, whereas you are probably only just surviving below the poverty line. The dole office tends not to take the occupation 'musician' seriously and just see it as an excuse for someone dossing around and, to women taking their musical careers seriously, this is depressing. However, many women would rather stay poor and carry on being a musician than do any other job. Thus, some have remained unemployed for years. This, however, is no longer a realistic option with the introduction of the Job Seekers' Allowance, which will increasingly force people off benefit into jobs.

Different Ways of Being a Professional

In the world of pop, making money involves selling a musical service which means coming into contact, either directly or indirectly, with the consumer. There are a number of services which can be sold, and so there is more than one way of being a professional musician.

ENTERTAINMENT

Many bands perform this function, which has been a tradition in rock from its earliest years. The problem for women's bands operating in this context is that, because of their rarity, they are typically seen as a novelty act and are less likely to define themselves as 'serious' or 'proper' musicians. One clear example of this from my research was the Mission Belles.

CRAFT

Another group of women sell their skills as studio 'session' players, and are recruited to play on tour with various bands. These women (mainly vocalists) do define themselves as musicians and have a very high level of musical skills. Mary Genis, for instance, is a session musician, doing vocals and playing steel pans and bass. She also does reggae, MIDI (computers and synthesizers), and percussion workshops.

RECORDING/SONGWRITING

This is the way of being a professional musician to which most budding musicians aspire. It is extremely competitive, yet offers great financial success, the goal being to win a contract with a record company and publishing company and live off the initial 'advance' and eventual royalties from hit records. These bands tour in order to promote their records, rather than touring for its own sake, the money being made on record sales, publishing royalties, and merchandising, rather than from gigs. Bands also make additional sums from TV, radio appearances, and promotional advertising.

   Analytically, these three categories can be seen as distinct ways of being professional. However, as, in practice, the categories overlap, a band may disagree about its function and goals. Musicians may operate on more than one level since some band members may, for instance, also be session players, which, if the band has a recording contract, can pose problems. Musicians may have to use a pseudonym in order to engage in session work or to perform with another band. There may also be a clash of commitments. Furthermore, bands do not necessarily start off from a clear-cut premiss about what kind they wish to be. They may have a period of brief success recording and then change to entertainment.

Similarly, women may combine one or more of these options with part-time music-related jobs. A sessionist may also teach, as happens frequently with women who are classically trained, while others manage to squeeze a living out of music by combining gigs, recording, and doing technical work for other bands.

Division of Labour

At the professional stage of the musician's career, she finds herself entering a whole new institutional world: the recording studio, the record company, the television studio. Important new roles are encountered, such as the producer, the studio engineer, and the press officer, people who act as intermediaries between the band and its audience, and the band and its record company. However, they also impose constraints.

When bands start out, they do everything themselves. At the opposite end of the career ladder, the successful 'name' band only plays. It has a manager, an agent, and a road manager. Artwork is contracted out or done by the record company's publicity department. Thus, success involves an increasing division of labour, a multitude of tasks which could be called 'bandwork' being passed on to specialists. Decisions are made in the light of some long-term strategy based upon intensive discussion between band members, the decision to go professional leading to much of this farming out of tasks.

'SYLVIA' (of 1980s Yorkshire pop band): I think, when you go professional and you're working full-time at it, that's when you don't want to be bothered with [the practical] side of it, or you haven't got the time. That's what happened with my first band. I think that's the difference—doing it full-time.

However, there is a dilemma here. The conscious aim of musicians is to employ a manager, an agent, and so on, and yet retain control over their sound, their publicity, their finances, and their general direction; but the more intermediaries are employed, the harder this becomes and so power tends to leak away.

Getting a Manager

The actual order in which a band gets a record deal, manager, and agent varies. Often, the manager is the first acquisition and then she or he tries to secure good deals in records, agency, and publishing. Indeed, often a band decides to get a manager because she or he is someone with the right contacts, since who you know is crucial. Having a manager when 'signing' is a distinct advantage, particularly for a new band, whose members may not know their legal rights. (Alternatively, you need a good solicitor.)

When a band begins to realize that they are being exploited by promoters they often decide to employ a manager, a decision which indicates a businesslike frame of mind, a determination to make a reasonable living from music, and a refusal to be 'messed around'. It is a key moment in a band's career, and this step is only taken if its members have faith in their joint ability to progress. Sometimes, it is the record company who suggest using a manager. Record companies, and also booking agencies, expect bands to have managers since they prefer to deal with just one person:

KIM McAULIFFE **(Girlschool): We were doing it by ourselves and it was getting too much. We found we couldn't talk to people—record companies—'cause they just don't deal with bands directly. Well, they didn't then, definitely not then. We needed somebody to look after our affairs, basically, and help us along.**

A manager can give a sense of direction to a band and formulate a long-term plan of action, which can make the band much more efficient. On the other hand, some told tales of incompetent or even corrupt management.

'SUKE' **(of 1980s all-female commercially successful pop band): We had a manager once who was incompetent. He'd say, 'Well, girls, all I want you to concern yourselves with is the music, and let me concern myself with everything else.' And he didn't! Things never got done. We found out later that we'd got offers and they'd never passed through, and all sorts of people had been phoning up, trying to get hold of us . . . money had been paid to us but it hadn't gone through the books.**

Thus, many women are wary of managers and emphasize the importance of finding someone trustworthy. Some bands have simply not been able to find the right person.

VI SUBVERSA **: Nobody's bloody turned up who's willing to do it. Some people say that we are unmanageable, because we're not young and naive. But I'd love to have somebody who looked out for that side of things, and who worked with us. And I think that's essential, in a way. What I think we need to do is get a proper marketing policy and we are totally unprepared to deal with that side of it . . . It feels to me that we're not engaged properly; we are not in gear for a lot of the stuff we are doing, and so we are being ripped off and we are wasting energy.**

Others had been offered management deals with unwelcome strings attached:

FRAN **(Sub Rosa): The only thing with managers and agents is hopefully they are promoting you for the right reasons, not just trying to get in your knickers. I've been offered endless tours, really good money and stuff, but basically the bottom line is you sleep with the manager, and I'm not doing that. That is crap. Even though it's going to be harder, and I might never get there, I'd rather do it on my own ability and my personality.**

On the other hand, some choose not to have a manager. Many feminist bands in the 1980s, aspiring to internal democracy, were against having a manager for political reasons. Others have simply felt that they do not need one. 'Suke''s band, who were able to deal with most of the administration by themselves, viewed management as an unnecessary expense. They did their own accounts, sleeve and poster design, and generally kept a watchful eye over everything. Meanwhile, their tour manager had an expanded role:

'SUKE' : I felt there were enough people in the band that had their heads screwed on the right way. And we'd also got both our publishing and record deal by ourselves—which is another reason for having a manager—and didn't see any point in paying someone 25 per cent for something we'd already done. We just needed this magical coordinator that could help keep us all together, do diaries with us, and just keep the whole band as one. [So] we don't have a manager as most people know it, who takes 25 per cent of your earnings and ploughs money into you, and says, 'You will dress like this, girls' and 'You will do this!' What we do have, though, is an excellent tour manager . . . who manages us only after instruction by us. And we have the final say on everything.

However, even with an administrator, some members of the Belle Stars found themselves very busy: 'Doing accounts last time took about ten hours solid. The time before it took about twenty hours. We worked until five o'clock one morning and we got up at ten and we started again. That's just the monthly thing. It's just hours and hours of really hard work, and your head is swimming' (Judy Parsons). Like record companies, managers can have an influence on the band's image. Emma Anderson told me that Lush had once had a manager who tried to make them look too glamorous and slick on their video, while Pooka, after some initial resistance, were persuaded to change their image by the logic of market:

NATASHA (Pooka): You get a lot of people and they say, 'You should have an image like this'. Or you feel pressurized to dress up in a certain way and you go along with it. But then, at the end of the day, you just think, 'Well, fuck it! What's it all mean, anyway? It's just clothes.' It comes from management, really. It's a thing to do with selling yourself. Because pop is all about selling yourself—to look good. . . . I did use to have a lot of arguments with people about it. But I think if you're gonna survive in the pop business then you've either got to rebel against it so much that people notice you for it, or you just give in and you wear nice things just to sell yourself in a different way. But both of them are towards the same aim, really, to sell yourself, because that's what the job is, I suppose.

The women in Ms45 had resisted more strongly. Mandy recalled her experience in an all-girl band in the 1980s, but Shareen was talking about the 1990s:

MANDY : A manager wanted us to look all pretty and 'if you don't do this I won't take you on', and 'I'm not going to pay for this'. And we went, 'Oh, fuck you then! You wear the dress!' . . . They wanted us to be like Vixen. They wanted us all tarted up.

SHAREEN : Actually, the label we're on now started to approach the issue and I shut it down really fast. It's like, 'So, what are you saying then? Do you want a band of Barbies? You hired the wrong band!' Yeah, it's dangerous . . . I smelled a rat.

Male management can also have a potentially disruptive effect on female friendships in mixed bands, according to Gail Greenwood (of Belly):

I may be paranoid, but I always felt that there was the need for the men in the organization . . . management, to sort of feel like they needed to create competition between the two women in the band. And that became a really big issue. Like, how could two women in a band be friends? Why shouldn't it be more competitive? And it felt like there was unnecessary shit, starting to create some tension between the women. And luckily it didn't happen and Tanya and I are still very good friends. I've talked about this to so many other women players now, that I know . . . other men or their management is somehow trying to demean one or the other women. Like, there can't be more than one leader or one strong women in a band.

It was maybe for these sorts of reasons that a handful of my 1990s interviewees welcomed a female manager: Natasha Atlas, Sidi Bou Said, and Skin.

NATASHA ATLAS : My manager is a woman and she's black as well. She's the head of Nation Records. She's my manager as well as my record company boss. Generally, I've never had a problem and it's nice having a female manager because I can talk to her about female problems and she understands.

Getting an Agent

As I have shown, a manager facilitates getting an agent. So does a recording contract: 'Until our first record deal nobody would take us on. . . . The first agency we had were really good, but when we got thrown off the record deal they didn't want anything to do with us' ('Brenda'). Bands want an agent for two main reasons. First, it relieves them of the time and strain of trying to get gigs. Secondly, individual clubs and circuits often work only through agents. 'Suke': 'It's like a catch-22, you can't get in on those good gigs unless you are with an agency. We wanted to go into it far more professionally . . . that's why we decided to go for an agent, especially as we didn't have a manager.' It is another hallmark of professionalism and helps the band get respect within the industry. Furthermore, if a band does not have a manager in the conventional sense, then an agent is clearly vital. Also agents can get bands better fees. Suke's band got some good 'support' gigs from being with this agency, which, in turn, helped them to establish themselves and get a big 'following'. 'They hardly ever put completely incongruous bands together just for the money's sake. They actually do try and provide a package deal or put us in a situation where we're gonna reap the benefits. There's been so much advantage just from being with that particular agency, because the bands that we've supported are huge.' However, some bands are as opposed to having an agent as to a manager or major record deal.

ALISON RAYNER (Jam Today): **Politically, we'd have problems, because we're not an 'all-girl group' and we're not interested in being 'sold' in any kind of way like that. There are groups of women who are definitely used to promote an image of women which isn't threatening to men, very girly—a very sexist image—to make money. Record companies do it a lot, and agencies do it. We can't be associated with anything like that. We wouldn't have anything to do with it.**

Apart from 'sexploitation', many bands fear being used and not getting anything out of it.

VI SUBVERSA : The trouble with an agency is that you become one of a bunch of bands and you've still got to work for yourself. I don't actually think that anybody will do anything for you. That's what's held us back from getting involved with any major deal with an agency or [record company]. . . . Because they've got a stable of bands. Why should they look after you more than anybody else?

Record Companies and Recording

Bands want record contracts for a number of reasons: to widen their audience, for the 'advance' money (in order to buy new equipment), for effective promotion (via the links record companies have with DJs). Most of all, record contracts are perceived as the route to financial stability.

VI SUBVERSA : I think recording is essential and important. A lot of people who I want to address will not go to our gigs. A lot of women don't want to go to mixed gigs. A lot of people are too old to feel comfortable at our gigs. More than that, selling records, is the only way a band can hope to get some money together. And I know it's a chancy thing, but it's the only way that a band can make money. And I don't know any bands, apart from the very, very rare few, who can demand fees of any significance for performing.

To a new band, signing to a record company implies financial solvency: you receive a big 'advance' and your troubles are over. In most cases, however, this is a delusion since costs escalate. Some spend the advance on equipment. (It is ironic that only the megastars get free or cheap equipment from the manufacturers, in promotional ventures.) Bands also need to hire better PA and rehearsal studios: 'Now we pay £30 a day to rehearse [and yet] most of the band haven't got anywhere to live! They haven't got any money to pay for a proper place' (Judy Parsons). Those on a smaller advance may receive only slightly more than 'the dole', some telling me that they were living on 'a pittance' or 'just keeping their heads above water'. Katherine Garrett of the Mystics told me that it was 'difficult to survive', eking out their advance for a year. Besides which, as Shareen (of Ms45) put it, 'an "advance" is just a sexy word for debt'. There is an argument against the very idea of advances because they inspire immediate gratification and an unrealistic feeling of wealth, creating the pressure to live up to the 'now we've made it, we're rock stars' expectations of the press and public: 'Everyone says, "You're rich now"'. And we're not. We're miles off it. It's gonna be two years before we pay the record company back their money and start getting royalties through' (Judy Parsons). Even after a band has had a hit they can still be hard up since a whole string of hits is necessary before all the recording costs are paid. On the other hand, as Cerys Matthews (of Catatonia) pointed out, if you have been used to living on £45 a week from the dole for four years, then £150 a week is excellent. It is also a relief, for many, not to have to have to 'sign on' or do boring 'day jobs' anymore: 'I was getting a wage and it was coming from the record company—an advance. . . . It was like, Wow! I don't have to belly dance in restaurants anymore. All the income comes from this' (Natasha Atlas).

A record contract is a benchmark of progress in a band's career, taking it out of the league of 'local bands', and, even if the aim was not originally to go full-time, that desire may now be seen for the first time as an option. Indeed, the record company may suggest it. Thus, signing a record contract is a crucial moment in the career of a band, crucial for its objective effects and for its subjective meanings and consequent implications for identity. However, some of my interviewees had reservations about 'signing', fearing loss of artistic freedom: 'Hilary': 'I can't imagine me wanting to get involved with people in the music business. . . . I suppose I have a purist idea. I'd rather do it like I'm doing it now, with all its frustrations, and keep some sense of . . . sincerity . . . I just imagine they would want total control and tell us what kind of music to make and how to be.' Bands feared record company interference in areas well beyond the music per se:

EMMA ANDERSON (Lush): **I think right at the beginning when we signed we didn't want to sign to a major label because we didn't want to be turned into Tracey and the Primitives or the Darling Buds. . . . Tracy from the Primitives, her manager told her exactly what to wear, exactly how to do her hair, and sent her to acting school and completely changed her.**

From some women there was much cynicism about the benefits which supposedly accrued from a record contract:

'BECKY' : **They've got a hold on you, but they don't actually think of doing anything. That's my experience. I've seen a lot of bands get mistreated . . . say they've got a big main band—they put all their energy into that big band, and you're pushed about, supporting this and that. If there's a record company who's gonna spend a lot of time on us and do good publicity we will do it. But you can never guarantee that, unless we get a good advance. . . . In**

the beginning we didn't jump. We could have signed up, because all-girl
bands were terribly rare at that time.

For many women in bands, especially in the 1980s, signing to a major label
has implied a series of compromises leading to loss of integrity and alienation.
Many, whilst rejecting major record companies, were prepared to sign with an
'independent' company. Indeed, many were keen to get a deal with an 'indie',
believing that fewer compromises (whether aesthetic or political) would be
involved, and that they would have more control over both the product and the
production process. To sign with a 'major' was to sell out, whilst to sign with an
'indie' was not: 'Our view is that big record companies put you into packages and
just get the most out of you they can. Whereas a small label are more interested
in you as a group and what you wanna do, rather than making money out of you'
('Kath').

I found this view to be prevalent among women's bands who had not yet
reached the recording stage or had only done one or two demos. Women higher
up the career ladder felt differently:

'BRENDA' : You have to make more compromises with small labels . . . because
people who run small labels actually get more close to the bands. They feel
that it reflects on them personally, what the band does. So, if the band is
singing about things that they, personally, don't like, then they don't want it
and they'll try and stop that. Whereas, on a major label it doesn't reflect back
on anybody personally at all . . . they'll give you the money, they'll tell you to
go away and they'll leave you alone.

Amelia Fletcher (of Heavenly) believed that many 'indies' were honest and in the
business for the music, whilst others were as exploitative as the 'majors' can be.
Mambo Taxi initially thought that by signing with an indie they would have
little money but ample control, whereas in reality they were messed around by
the indie just as much as any major and at least a major would have given them
plenty of money. Indeed, a particular drawback of signing with an independent company is that they tend to give bands smaller advances (or none at all),
making it harder for bands to pay themselves a living wage until they become
commercially successful.

In order to get a record contract, a band makes a 'demo' tape or CD which also
demonstrates what they play like to promoters, agents, radio stations, and music
journalists, and as a succession are often made it can be exensive. The cheapest
method is DIY, although this can be fraught with problems, especially if the
musicians are mothers:

'JANICE' : We'd play in the living room and we'd have the mixer out here [in
the kitchen]. And it took ages to set up. . . . We'd start off at nine o'clock in
the morning, as soon as we'd got the kids to school. We'd all turn up, set the
equipment up, get it all set out. And we'd just be playing the first number
when it was time to get the kids back from school at 3 o'clock. It was totally
frustrating. We had all the multi-core out the windows and coming through

here! This table would be full of equipment. And the kids would come in and I'd try and get them some tea and get them to go out of the way somewhere. And we'd come back and carry on into the night.

Bands typically start with a home-produced demo before hiring studio time. If they have no luck with their tapes then they move to an even better studio and do another, and so the process spirals, the only limit being lack of funds.

The usual way of winning a contract is to hawk demos around record companies. If an established company does not respond, a small entrepreneur may act as intermediary with a 'major', but sometimes, a band is simply fortunate enough to be in the right place at the right time: 'Total and utter luck! We used to play the Moonlight every three or four weeks and A&R men used to get in contact with them, 'cause they always had new bands that weren't really on the circuit' ('Brenda'). If a band receives no favourable response from record companies, they may consider setting up their own label as a stepping stone to making a record deal. Vi Subversa: 'We took a demo tape around to the local label and they weren't interested. So we formed our own company and recorded the first record ourselves. . . . When the company heard it again, through the grapevine, they said they'd like to join in with us.' A band's first recording experience marks its entry into a new technological and a social world, which is, initially, both stimulating and intimidating. This is exacerbated by the way the recording process is typically divided up: each part is recorded separately, with only a backing track to guide the individual musician, which means that she is physically isolated in the studio, able to communicate with the producer/engineer/rest of the band only through a microphone. Alone in the soundproofed room, she has time to worry and become self-conscious and, after two or three 'takes', may begin to lose confidence:

JUDY PARSONS : As soon as it says, 'tape rolling' and the red light goes on I just get so tense. And you think, afterwards, 'I could have done so much better'. And I find that a terrible pressure. . . . When the red light's on and the tape's rolling I feel a bit inferior.

This insecurity is often increased by lack of time:

ROS DAVIS (Rash and Contraband): It was really terrible, a pretty bad experience, just 'cause there was such a lot of pressure. We'd learnt it and played it within two weeks. . . . The numbers weren't bedded in at all. They were really still new. It was terrifying.

Time pressure is often due to lack of money. At the beginning of a session things might be relaxed, but towards the end short cuts are taken.

JUDY PARSONS : You go into the studio and you play your particular part fairly badly and the time runs out: 'I'm afraid your time's run out for your guitar bit. We've been doing you for an hour. We've got to get the saxophones in now.' So the guitarist is left feeling, 'I haven't done my best'. Things that shouldn't be left on the record are left on because of time and money.

The studio brings out perfectionism in musicians, because they are aware that almost anything can be done with the sound: mistakes can be altered and the 'good bits' from a number of takes can be simply welded together to make one version. The possibility for improvement seems infinite until the money runs out, which means the atmosphere in the studio becomes increasingly tense towards the end.

Many recording studios are permeated by sexism and a masculinist culture. Engineers and even tape-ops may make disparaging remarks about women's playing, upsetting the women concerned, or looking down on their playing style and boasting about their own ability to play 'really heavy'. On the other hand, I did detect more confidence and assertiveness amongst my 1990s interviewees and there were less tales of obvious studio sexism. As many also had more technical knowledge they could demand exactly the sound they wanted. Andrea of Mambo Taxi, for instance, went on a short sound engineering course in order to understand the recording process better, although the band had one particularly bad experience when their record label boss unexpectedly took over the final mix and wouldn't let them near the desk: 'They just sat there as two blokes over the desk, cracking rude jokes at us and fiddling around. We couldn't believe it was happening. You'd go out of the room and come back and they'd done something that we'd asked them not to. They'd think we wouldn't notice.' Skin had learnt sound engineering and production by building her own sixteen-track studio (whilst she was still on the dole): 'When I walk into a studio people take me seriously, because I know exactly how a studio works and runs. And I'm not sitting there going, "What does that button mean?"' Mandy (of Ms45) had worked in studios doing sound: 'I always get taken seriously. 'Cause you go in and you know your shit. I've taken the time to learn something about it and to know exactly what I want to hear. I know how to ask for it.' Bands who were not clear on the sound they were trying to achieve, and who knew little of what a studio can do, were much more likely to have their sound moulded into an unforeseen and undesirable shape.

Production and Promotion

Conflict often occurs between bands and record companies over who should produce the record. The producer can be the fulcrum of record company pressure and influence over artistic output because she or he has more power than any band member, able to help achieve commercial success, or, alternatively, wreck the sound. However, there are a number of different production options available to a band which first embarks upon recording, depending on whether or not a record contract has been signed and the wording of that contract. At one end of the continuum, a band might choose to produce itself and those who are not signed but wish to make records often do this. Usually ones with a contract may self-produce if they can convince the record company of their capabilities since, although it increases pressure, it gives more control over achieving exactly the sort of sound desired. From the company's point of view, this saves on costs, although they are usually unwilling to allow an unproven band to do its own production. Nevertheless, self-production can be problematic as individual members may disagree, and often bands find it easier when an outsider produces them, especially as, the more democratic the atmosphere, the more disagreements there are likely to be. In the end, pressure of time may cut out debate, which creates resentment, widening latent splits within the band and even bringing about its demise:

ALI WEST (the Mistakes): We foolishly, naively, thought that we should produce our own records. So the agreement was that [our manager] and us would produce. But that just led to such rows as you could never have imagined, because people had different ideas about what they should have sounded like. Different people wanted to do different numbers. Invariably, not everyone would like the mix, and you ended up mixing some numbers three or four times and still not being satisfied. And I now think that we should have just got a producer that we were vaguely happy with and left them to it. There was far too much [of] everybody wanting to sound perfect and you can't expect that.

Agreement has to be reached on who is to produce, which can sometimes hold up the recording process for months, depending on how democratic a band is and how many musicians there are to consult:

ALI WEST : I think [our record company] found us quite difficult to deal with because of the fact that we were so collective. . . . [Our manager] had to go back to us all the time and say, 'This is what they think. What do you think?' And I think they got quite annoyed with that in the end. Probably, as a women's band, we were more collective than a lot of mixed or male bands.

This tendency for women's bands to be highly democratic has certain disadvantageous effects since, the more disunity there is, the more power they inadvertently hand over to the record company. Divisions within the Belle Stars prevented them from acting in a concerted way and developing a long-term strategy, for both their future as a band, and for dealing with the record industry.

JUDY PARSON (Belle Stars): In our record contract it says that we have 'mutual agreement' on a producer, which studio, what songs. . . . The record company kept putting forward people and the band kept turning them down. Yet the band could not come to an agreement amongst themselves. We've got a democracy, but in fact it's a veto system as well, which it's not meant to be. Like one person in the band throws a complete wobbly. . . . So, eventually, we came up with this completely unrealistic list. We went along to the record company and they said 'no' to the three people that we'd actually agreed on. And we'd been going around for three months rejecting the record company's people. Later on we were in the same dilemma of what producer we were going to use for our next record. The record company mentioned someone that we hate. So we said 'no' and they were furious. And that was two months suspended in the band's career, where nothing happened. So in the end, everybody said yes [to the company's choice]. . . . So basically we start off saying no and, in every case, [eventually say yes].

Furthermore, as in many other women's bands, the members of the Belle Stars all liked different kinds of music and they were only together because their individual musical careers depended upon the band's success. The lack of women's bands and the sexism of the rock world meant that there were few other musical options available to them. The fragility of the band also led to the avoidance of change:

JUDY PARSONS : The band is horribly weak. If it was a strong band we would say, 'No, we will not do another cover'. We could be sufficiently bolshie that they'd say, 'Well, get off our label then!', and we'd go to another record label. But the band would split up. The band is very fragilely held together. So, because we have to stay, we have to have money to survive, and so we're doing more or less what they want us to.

Some interviewees felt that they had considerable power and freedom in their relationship with their record companies, a number saying they had 'total' or 'complete' artistic control: over what songs were released, over posters, T-shirts, record sleeves, and photographs. But is this just rhetoric? The potential for real everyday control by the record company seems to be built into the system:

'SUKE' (of 1980s professional all-female pop band): In our contract we have agreements which are mutually agreed, but you know darn well that the record company has the last say. . . . I've been very disillusioned. You run with the tide in the end. [It's] just the way record deals are done. . . . You hear that they're poised to rip you off, and it's true. But when it's actually happening, it's done with such . . . you don't actually realize that it's happening. And, in a way, the other party aren't doing it deliberately. It's just part and parcel of the whole thing that's happened before. It's just an existing thing, and you try and get as many points as possible.

The very speed at which things happen in the rock industry means there is simply not time to check everything:

EMMA ANDERSON (Lush): I think anyone in a band, unless they were putting out their own record in a plastic bag, would be lying if they said they had 100 per cent control over everything. I know they're lying because you can't. To be honest, there's not enough time to have control over every single thing. . . . You approve things. Like the record sleeves. We don't do them ourselves, but we say 'Yes. We like that' or 'No. We don't like that.' More often than not, they just get done anyway. . . . When it comes to promotion, promotion people set things up for you and you do them.

Bands are often faced with a fait accompli. Here are two instances from my interviews:

JUDY PARSONS : We're meant to be at the 'cut', when they cut the final master. [But] he's always told us that it's happening in half an hour's time, when we're doing a soundcheck. You know, we can't do it. We can't get there.

ENID WILLIAMS (Girlschool): I think most of the album covers were vile. They were always being done at the last minute, and generally disorganized. It's quite possible that it was done earlier and they didn't tell us till the last moment so that it was too late for us to stop anything. I mean, that's quite conceivable. We did complain a few times. There's one single that had a cover of a woman with stilettos on her feet, tied together. We didn't like that at all and we made a bit of a fuss about that. But it was a bit too late at that point. If you're on tour for six months—like you've sorted your album cover out and you sort the single cover out and then you go off for a few months and then they want a follow up single. They release something and there isn't really time for you to get back and they've got to send a picture out . . .

Moreover, record companies often persuade bands to comply with a whole lot of features they do not like by claiming that otherwise they will not sell records and, anyway, it's just 'the standard thing'.

Gender and Record Companies

To what extent does gender have any bearing on the relationship between bands and record companies? Some of my interviewees did feel that they were treated differently from male bands, while a few thought that being female was an advantage. For instance: 'Because you're women, you can get away with certain things. I don't mean playing badly. I mean, we can get our way round him' ('Sophie'). Most women musicians had experienced some sexism, however.

MARCELLA DETROIT : I've worked with people who've been in the business who've said very chauvinistic things. . . . I was out to dinner with a really big executive from the company I was with . . . and he said, 'Ooh, did you see the tits on that one?' Just all these really horrible, disgusting comments about women. I just found it absolutely disgusting and I'm sure that it goes on all the time. . . . I've had people I worked with make comments about my tits or this and that, when it's really none of their business what my body is like. I'm there to sing; it's nothing to do with what my body is.

In the early 1990s, the 'majors' were interested in getting at least a token 'girl band' on their books, but in the 1980s it was a different story:

JUDY PARSONS : He was a bit dubious about signing us because . . . he'd never signed another all-girl band before. Then he decided that we were going to make a lot of money and he'd better sign us, anyway, and we might be tricky to work with but that was too bad. [He was worried] and still is, that we're a load of irrational women and that we're not controllable. . . . I know he still thinks that we're a different cup of tea to a male band and it's because we're female.

Female musicians argue that it is important to challenge this sexist stereotyping:

'SUKE' : I think we've proved our worth, both as musicians and on the business angle as well—the fact that we did our own record deal and publishing deals. I think we have respect in that way. Rather than being the sort of little-girls-lost-in-the-studio, or have somebody do it for us—You know, flutter-the-eyelids and trying to do it like that.

Others tell of how they have challenged gender stereotyping by behaving in as aggressive a manner as male bands, when occasion demanded.

'BRENDA' (of 1980s professional new wave band): I have got a reputation. There's no doubt about it. It surprises me. I always hear it back—how 'heavy' I am—'what an unpleasant person she is, this man-hating feminist'. But I'm not a man-hater at all. I just don't like what they do to women.

I think it is true to say that women have to fight harder than men to avoid being controlled by their record companies. Skin told me that she thought people tried (unsuccessfully) to manipulate her 'every second of the day' and that all women in bands experience this. There are so few women musicians and the industry has only come up with a few stereotyped marketing strategies for them. Judy recounted the way in which the Belle Stars had been subjected to such a moulding exercise, the record company selecting the songs, and these were not their own numbers but 1960s covers. They were told what to play on their instruments and, indeed, sometimes not allowed to do so on the record at all. Judy viewed their records as 'synthetic, commercial music', the final product of an alienated production process in which the artists had very little control:

JUDY PARSONS (Belle Stars): We hate [our producer] because he makes you feel really low and inferior. And it might just be to do with being female, that he can't handle women. But I'll never know. He just makes you feel that you are a shitty musician and if only he could replace the whole band with session players and computers it would be much better. . . . It's not the whole band playing together; it's a cold, calculated, commercial type of approach. . . . The records that have had success haven't had much of the band playing on them. They haven't been a band sound. They've been a recording studio concoction job. . . . I've programmed the computer and I've gone off, 'cause I couldn't stand listening to those awful songs. I can't take them seriously. I think what the band is doing at the moment is rubbish.

Yet Judy was trapped in this situation because the records were, in fact, successful:

> **The whole experience is just miserable and you feel like committing suicide
> at the end. And then you see your record in the American charts and you get
> your royalty cheque and you say, 'Oh, let's use him again'. And halfway
> through you think, 'Oh, Christ, I think I've got to kill myself. I can't carry on.'
> Then you go back.**

Judy felt that, because their record company had a very strong image of what the
band should sound and look like, they were allowing themselves to be packaged
and thus stunting their own creativity. If they could bring their own songs out on
record they would, she believed, be able to resist this moulding process and, at
the same time, to express themselves artistically:

> **You very easily get out of the area where you're a musician and get into, what
> you could call the Bananarama-area, where you are merely a commercial
> entity . . . you don't write your own songs and you don't establish your own
> thing. . . . Normally, [people] think if you don't write your own songs, you
> haven't got your own identity, your own style. And then, if you're a woman,
> you quickly get branded as being some sort of quick ruse to make money.**

Alienated from the music itself, Judy substituted financial rewards for personal
fulfilment—'my musical principles have gone by the board'—and eventually,
the stress of living this contradiction led to her leave the band.

Record companies, do, of course, package male bands too, but the range of
images and options is much wider. It also seems that women's bands may be
easier to manipulate. The Belle Stars went along with what was happening partly
because they lacked confidence in their own songs, ideas, and musical skills and
because they were, as explained, disunited, and failed to present the company
with any cohesive alternative strategy which they all believed in. Furthermore,
with mounting debts, they needed commercial success, which made the tempta-
tion to go along with the 'master plan' too great: 'We've been desperately short of
money and it's such that we've had to try and have a record that sells. We could
have said, "No, we will not do one of your shitty, horrible covers". . . . [But] the
band do what we're told by the record company. The record company books all
our radio, press, TV type things and we do whatever they say' (Judy Parsons).
Mambo Taxi had quite a good relationship with their record company, but they
were not happy with an early press release which referred to them as 'wild
handbag-waving females'.

At the professional stage, the pressure to conform to a band image increases.
There are more photo sessions and promotional videos, in which appearance has
to be considered and choices made, and during which women musicians may
find themselves edged closer and closer towards a more 'sexy' or glamorous presentation of themselves. At photo sessions they might be expected to wear make-
up and perhaps 'show a bit of leg' or other parts of their anatomy. The extent to
which a band willingly collaborates with this or, alternatively, resists it, depends
partly on how far members have a feminist political outlook. It is also affected by

how desperate they are to make money or get out of debt. Ms45 were prepared to make some financial sacrifice in order to have 'final say' over choice of songs, final covers, etc. written into their contract: 'It's worth it for your dignity. . . . That was something really important to me. That was the main stipulation and I'm incredibly sensitive to it because of the things that can be done with female images can be so insidious that we have final veto power over everything' (Shareen). Record companies often emphasize the importance of sexually attractive photos on album sleeves and how these tend to boost sales. For example,

JUDY PARSONS : We had a photo session and the record company said, 'Let's use live snakes'. And I said, 'I'm going to leave the band if you have snakes in this photo session'. . . . Because it just seemed to me that we were getting so blatant-commercial-sex type thing that it was the end!

Other women told me similar stories. For example,

KIM MCAULIFFE (Girlschool): We did have a bit of a problem when we signed to this American record company. They wanted us to change our image and be more glamorous and all that sort of thing. And we actually got a 'front' singer in then—a blonde front singer! . . . It was a total disaster. We weren't happy with it and we ended up parting with her. And now we're back to being how we were originally and we're getting a lot more success than we have had for ages, because we're back to being ourselves. . . . They wanted us to glamorize ourselves. But it just didn't work. We're not into all that.

A previous record company had told Marcella Detroit not to wear her glasses on a TV programme because it was de-glamorizing, but, as Marcella was allergic to her contact lenses and simply could not see without her glasses, she felt that wearing them was quite human, a fact of life, so she overrode the instruction. Emma had make-up artists trying to get her to wear false eyelashes and there was pressure on Miki to shave her armpits.

EMMA ANDERSON (Lush): We actually recently had a terrible time at a photo session in America, where they got all these clothes in which we were terribly wrong. . . . Miki was nearly in tears, because they were all so sort of coming down on her hard saying, 'you should wear this'. And the make-up was terrible. The other three members of the band were just sitting there saying, 'Miki, just don't wear it. Take the make-up off. Do what you want.' And she was practically in tears. It was awful, a really bad day . . . because you think, 'Well, they've spent all this money on these people'.

Many women, in fact, told me of the pressures and problems of photo shoots. In this case, for instance, a band member was left out of the photos altogether because she was deemed to be overweight.

ANDREA (Mambo Taxi): When the photographs came back there were several of them that Delia wasn't in. He'd got her to stand behind one of the tallest members of the band and you couldn't see her at all. And he didn't even notice she wasn't in them. And it was just horrific.

For some interviewees, it has been important that there were women in key record company posts. Shareen told me that one of the deciding factors in Ms45's decision to sign with Virgin Records was their having a female A&R: 'because we had a feeling we were gonna be handed a case of push-up bras the moment we signed'. Emma Anderson praised the ethics and integrity of indie record company 4AD, which has a lot of women in its employ and many female-led acts on its roster: 'I mean, they wouldn't say "we think you should wear a short skirt in this video" and they're not the sort of label who would think, "right, we're going to have a hit with this band, so we'll put them in with a producer who will completely revamp their sound". They're not like that.' Some of my 1990s interviewees had a 'hard' image which helped them resist manipulation. Debbie Smith (of Echobelly) told me that no one has ever tried to force her to grow her hair, or wear a dress or shut up about being a lesbian, while Skin makes her resistance to any 'girly, flirty, sexy' image abundantly clear. It was to this end that she deliberately made herself as ugly as possible from the start of her career:

SKIN : I think the record company would *like* to, but they wouldn't dare ask. In a much more girly, sexy way. They'd be happier. They had the idea, at one time, of having a big poster campaign with just me, with my arms folded and no clothes on from the waist up. And they thought that would be a really good idea. They'd like me to be a lot more sexual and appeal to more men in that way. And, you know, I see myself as *very* sexual. I don't run from my sexuality at all, but *I'm* in control of my sexuality. I'm not gonna let someone else take my image and turn it into the phantom perfection thing.

The Media

Professional bands find themselves inextricably involved with journalists, TV producers, and disc-jockeys who mediate between the music and its consumers. A band puts out a record, but without media attention people do not know of its existence, and to sell, it must have publicity. As I have already discussed, there is a tendency for women's bands and female performers to be trivialized in the media, being presented as sex objects in glamour shots, and as scatty girls in interviews. In fact, both male and female artists at the pop end of the spectrum are treated as lightweight. However, as I have shown, women are more heavily concentrated in pop and consequently there is a far higher proportion of female (than of male) performers who get the 'mindless pop' treatment. Furthermore, videos of women have been made specifically for the 'male gaze', with a fetishistic focus on the female body which has been used in the videos of all-male bands along 'woman as ornament' lines.

Because pop stars are simply not taken seriously they are discussed in terms of their personalities, lifestyle, and fashion, and asked superficial questions about their taste in everything from clothes to food, whereas their music and skills do not receive serious treatment. Judy Parsons found that her technical comments in interviews were completely ignored: 'I was telling him stuff about the PA—information and plain, straight stuff, which they don't like. . . . The general thing that comes over in all the interviews is, "Here's a bunch of silly girls". . . . You can't do anything about it. . . . They're gonna write, "The sizzling sextrovert bunch of women . . ."' Judy preferred not to do interviews with sexist papers, but the rest of the band did not mind: 'They'd do it whatever it was. Even if they said, "They're awful and they can't play for toffee". We say, "Any press is good press" and we go for it.' This was also the attitude of Cerys Matthews of Catatonia (usually portrayed as an excessively hard drinker) in the mid-1990s: 'As long as they keep writing about us they can say what they want. As long as they write about us and we get our records in the shop—that's my business.'

However, even those women not at the 'pop' end of the spectrum complain about being trivialized. Natasha Atlas takes her Arabic performance very seriously and when she appeared on *The Girly Show* it was insisted that she wear her belly dancing costume yet none of her dancing was shown, so she felt a bit 'objectified'. Heavy rock is taken seriously by music journalists, although those very few women's bands who have ventured into this 'male' enclave have been treated as a novelty act, their gender appearing to be more important than their music:

ENID WILLIAMS (Girlschool): In the beginning we got a lot of press because of being female. We had lots and lots of music press and we wouldn't have got anything like that much if we hadn't have been women. But, at the same time. . . . I don't think we were ever taken very seriously. It's much harder for people to take women seriously. So it's easier to get through the door, but then to prove that you're doing something worthwhile is a lot more difficult. And there's always this image pressure, of looking glamorous and beautiful. And I think that that's, perhaps, getting worse.

DJs behave in the same way. When faced with women musicians they typically slip into talking about their bodies and 'looks', rather than their music. Whereas, male performers seem more able to avoid being discussed in these terms. It is only when a female performer becomes really successful that the image question ceases to matter so much. Lower down the career ladder a woman tends to be judged first and foremost in terms of her sexual attractiveness.

Because there are so few female reference points, journalists are inclined to pigeonhole women and their bands into a narrow range of stereotyped categories. Women performers are always being compared to other women performers. Many of my interviewees spoke of 'lazy journalists':

MANDA RIN (Bis): When people try to compare our music to something, the first thing they think about is either Bikini Kill, Huggy Bear or Shampoo . . . this is totally lazy. They're not looking into the music at all. They just think, 'Oh, here's a female. Let's compare it to Shampoo.' It's not fair.

SHAREEN (Ms45): The 'B' bands: Belly, the Bangles, Blondie, and the Breeders, we're constantly getting compared to. We don't really have that much in common. I get sick of being stuck in the girl band ghetto. I want to be taken in the context of the history of rock and roll, god damn it. There's a lack of vision. How many times has Deborah Harry been referred to on the vocals? Deborah Harry is a wonderful woman, I'm sure, but we don't sound anything like Blondie. Nothing. We both have the same reproductive organs, that's about where the similarities end.

Shareen also told me that she is consistently referred to as singer and not as a guitar player, despite being both. The focus, from the predominantly male journalists, is on the woman-as-body (including voice).

EMMA ANDERSON (Lush): Some are worse than others. You do sometimes read these things where people are going on about 'her sparkling blue eyes looked at me over the table' blah, blah, blah. And they do write about your looks probably a lot more than if you were a man, you know . . . and some of them apply these sort of things in their writing: 'Afterwards we went out and she hung out with me'. Like, 'she fancied me a bit' or something.

The emphasis in photos of women musicians is on their bodies. I asked for a photo of Candida Doyle (of Pulp) actually playing her instrument (the keyboard) but her record company could not locate one. Women are often photographed from below, with the camera looking up their skirts. Even Skin was featured thus, on the *Melody Maker* front cover (9 November 1996), with heavy innuendo in the accompanying headline: 'Going down under Skunk Anansie in Australia'. However, there is resistance to this sexual objectification. Sometimes, photographers, caught in the act of taking offensive shots, have had their cameras confiscated. When Oxford's Beaker were asked to supply a photograph to a local newspaper they sent a picture of four beakers (i.e. drinking mugs). Some bands, like Huggy Bear, have refused to give press interviews, whilst others have only granted them to selected journalists. After an offensive caption in the local paper, the Mistakes insisted on (and succeeded in) writing their own copy.

Publishing

The common pattern amongst male musicians is to try to get a publishing deal before a record contract. Selling your publishing rights is a way of solving immediate financial problems, the money being used to cover living expenses whilst gigging and doing demos. However, only a minority of the women I interviewed took this path, which may be partly due to ignorance of the financial importance of publishing deals amongst some of the inexperienced musicians I interviewed. (A woman who had done it all before would be far more likely to go for a publishing contract at the outset.) In particular, things just seemed to have 'happened' to many of the 1980s bands, rather than their developing any clear-cut long-term career strategy.

As many male musicians see themselves primarily as songwriters, they arrange their own publishing contract and then set about forming a group to record their songs, the band becoming the vehicle for the songwriter, the showcase for his material. In the 1990s, some of my interviewees were in this sort of position. Emma told me that Lush were living on their (large) publishing advance rather than the record company advance (which was only small). However in the 1980s, there was not a single instance of this amongst my interviewees: women saw themselves as band members, first and foremost.

KIM MCAULIFFE (Girlschool): It's basically me and the main guitarist who does most of the writing . . . but we've always credited the other members on at least half the album. . . . I always think it's astounding that a lot of these bands who are successful just have one songwriter who gets all the money, and yet if there hadn't been [that] band, then who's to say that they would be that successful? I think that's very unfair. So we've always credited.

Lastly, like other intermediaries, a publisher might not actually accomplish much for a band. For instance, Mambo Taxi ended up doing the work themselves. Some 1990s bands (like Sidi Bou Said) held back from signing a publishing deal, thereby creating a 'bidding competition' as a mechanism for achieving a large advance.

Touring

For the recording band, touring is a necessity: tours promote record sales. Touring conditions vary widely, depending on the finances of the band. For the commercially successful, tours can be very comfortable, with specially equipped tour buses (with stereos and videos) and good hotels. It is like a holiday, there being no responsibilities except to play. Gail Greenwood: 'With Belly touring, for me, it was wonderful! It was tour buses and hotels and being taken care of really well. I'm not saying lavishly, but I was used to touring in a van and sleeping on floors. So to me it was a great escape from reality. . . . It was really fun touring that way.' However, for the not-yet-successful band, it is often a gruelling experience. For instance,

KIM MCAULIFFE (Girlschool): We'd go for two days without anything to eat at all. We used to break down constantly in the middle of nowhere with no money. Sometimes we'd have enough money for a bed and breakfast. But quite a lot [of times] we didn't and we used to sleep on top of the gear in the van—all of us, with these two guys we had with us, too, our roadies. We had this great idea that we'd go away and do gigs and make some money. But things always turned out very wrong and we lost [money].

Bands which have signed to a record company may find themselves touring with others on that label, a women's band being used sometimes as a gimmick to pull in the crowds for a male one. Certainly, being female can help a band get support tours, although such novelty-value tends to be short-lived and may harm a long-term career since one packaged in this way may not be taken seriously.

Another particular problem which women's bands can face is that of staying in the 'support' spot for ever:

ENID WILLIAMS (Girlschool): People usually do one support tour and then start headlining. We did a lot of support tours. . . . We went through quite a long period where we were supporting major bands before we started headlining the major circuit. Maybe at one point it was concerning—whether we'd be able to make that transition, really. We were very much the ideal support band. . . . We weren't good enough, or professional enough, to blast the main band off, but we were good enough to bring people in.

The rock tour (like a ship at sea) is a kind of moving 'total institution'. Band members are working, eating, sleeping, and engaging in leisure pursuits within the same confined space with minimal privacy. When working they are behind a barricade of security systems; when not working, they're stuck on the bus. It is very different from normal life, all decisions and tasks being taken by others. Candida Doyle (of Pulp) describes the mental discipline required in order to maintain a sense of self under these circumstances: 'You don't have to use your brain. You have to get into a routine of washing your underwear and cleaning your teeth and keeping your things neat in your bag, otherwise you'd crack up. It's like you have to get some kind of army discipline.' In a normal job, if you are sick you can stay at home and recover. On tour, you are rarely allowed time off work, the livelihood of the whole touring entourage depending on your labour. Whether with period pains or flu, musicians are dosed up with drugs and have to continue to perform.

EMMA ANDERSON (Lush): You can't plan your life as an individual, as in, 'I'd like to take a holiday in July'. Every single thing is linked to the band. Your whole life is linked to the schedule and campaign of your band or record. And that can be a bit—especially as you get older and you've been doing it for a long time. When you're young and you first start doing it it doesn't matter because you're so excited about it. But it can get a bit of a drag.

It is easy to find yourself in a situation where all of your friends are in the music business. Some interviewees told me that they tried to keep their friendships going with non-musicians in order to have a more balanced life or, as one or two put it, 'to keep sane'. They needed other conversations than just ones about music. Kathryn Garrett (of the Mystics), for instance, enjoys 'the party side of it', but she sometimes wants to 'be with women and kids' just to have a different perspective. However, keeping non-music scene friendships can be a struggle as there simply isn't enough time. When asked about their 'social life', some women (like Debbie Smith and Natasha Atlas) said that they simply did not have one outside the band. Professional musicians are typically almost constantly on tour as one merges into another, with only a few days in between. With perhaps only three weeks off a year, 'home' is somewhere you rarely are and, not surprisingly, the transition to a 'normal' life provokes disorientation, taking days to acclimatize to.

> **STEPH HILLIER** (London sound engineer): I come back completely knackered. I get bad 'touritis'. Every night you've been gigging and you're really hyper and then you come back and it's like—straight down, like, really bad depression. And it can last for days or weeks. You really feel that you must do a gig!

Candida Doyle said that she thought musicians should have a psychiatrist waiting for them at home when they came off tour. Stadium bands, like Pulp, are insulated (and isolated) more fully than bands that are less successful as the 'front-stage'/'backstage' line is tightly policed by bodyguards and security.

> **CANDIDA** : Basically, it's so big now. I had hell when I played at Manchester recently. I couldn't get my friends to where I was and I couldn't get them in free. It's not just that I can't see my friends when I'm on tour, because you're not your normal self; you can't relax. It's better seeing people away from the tour.

If physical escape is impossible in the temporary total institution of the tour, so is escape from the pervading rock value system. The masculinist lifestyle of rock becomes even more apparent on tours which, according to the archetype, involve partying and high levels of indulgence in alcohol, sex, and drugs. Undoubtedly, some women musicians throw themselves into this lifestyle as much as any man and it is easy to become a victim of the whole mythology, for trying to live up to the expected lifestyle can be fatal. Yet, interestingly, many I interviewed told me they had chosen to limit their involvement and that, amongst the sea of drink and drugs, the one thing you really needed and could never get on a tour was a simple cup of tea. For instance, Natasha reflected on Pooka's European tour with the Levellers: 'I remember the Levellers were really party-type people and we were—at the time—we wanted to get to bed early . . . Whereas they liked their drugs and their jokes and their friends around them. So, in that respect, we were really quiet . . . We were into drinking tea and coffee and sitting having a little chat around the coffee table.'

Sidi Bou Said have consciously tried to challenge and subvert the normative structures:

> **CLAIRE LEMMON** : We actually try very hard. They had a microwave on the bus on the last tour and we were the laughing stock of the Cardiacs. Because they got up at eleven, had a beer, and that was that for the day. Me and Mel get up and organize a salad and get the microwave going. And it is important to do that. And also with the singing you have to, with your smoking and drinking and stuff. With this rock and roll lifestyle thing, I go for two days and I'm completely dead. . . . Performance does come first to me. . . . It is very male

that rock and roll thing. But we like to challenge that. . . . I don't need to
have fifteen beers before lunch. I don't feel that people might think you're
a weed or whatever.

Women's bands can try to insulate themselves from the general atmosphere, but
when there is only one or two women in an all-male entourage life on the road
can be lonely and alienating. Candida Doyle, usually the only woman on the bus
when Pulp go on tour, told me she hates touring and only does it because she is
'forced to'. She misses female company: 'You just can't talk to boys like you can
to girls. . . . Just chatting about how you're feeling or how your life is. It's really
hard to get boys to do that.' Skin also missed her women friends and female company, while Manda Rin (of Bis) found it weird not having her mother or female
friends to talk to when she had female problems. Gail Greenwood (of Belly) gets
homesick and misses her dog, whilst Candida explained how she misses the
small daily comforts of life:

It's nice to have normal things. Small things can really make me happy. On
tour everything is so big and it's the really big things that get you excited. It's
like you can play this massive date, you can stay in this wonderful hotel, you
can get taken out for a free meal, you can have loads of champagne. Or you're
going to make loads of money from this concert. Or you're going to meet
someone really famous. . . . But it's usually pretty simple things that make
me happy, and that's what you miss on tour . . . like owning a nice bubble
bath or a really nice cup of tea after a good meal.

The following two quotes get closest to conveying the all-pervasive 'maleness' of
the typical tour.

DEBBIE SMITH (Echobelly): From a woman's point of view it's hell, isn't it? . . .
It's such a male atmosphere on tour because all the crew, all the band and all
that, after the show you just sit back and you drink beer or you take drugs or
whatever . . . it's just the testosterone pervades the air, basically, and you
can't escape it. And either you go with it or you go to bed early, really. Toilets
are the worst thing because the bus is always moving and men spray and they
don't put the seat back down. The lights hardly work. It always stinks.

Natasha Atlas (of Transglobal Underground) finds the men forget that she's a
woman and expect her to be 'one of the guys':

Once a tour I just freak. Like, on a tour bus, we're all in bunks and I'm the
only female and just hearing them in the morning. They're coughing—men
sort of thing, 'cause they smoke too many fags and because they drink too
much. . . . Every night they've got to smoke loads of spliff and drink loads of
beers and the bus just gets filled with this drinking-beer smell and loads of
cans of beer. And it's such a male sort of rock thing. And I hate it. And
sometimes I think, 'this is a really shit way to live'.

Skin (of Skunk Anansie), on the other hand, has insisted that the men on tour remember that she is a woman and treat her with respect:

> The band are very female-centred, so they're very aware of my privacy and
> things like that. And they're very aware that I'm a girl. I *am* one of the lads
> but they remember that I'm a woman. If you're around lots of men sometimes
> a certain kind of man can be quite disrespectful and . . . talk about women in
> quite negative ways. And *you're* there and they forget that you're there. . . .
> I'm not gonna ignore the little sexist things that go on.

With more women the masculine atmosphere diminishes. Even the presence of
two or three extra women can make a crucial difference, as when Sidi Bou Said
did their first tour with a male band: 'On the first tour I had to stay up with the
tour when the rest of the girls went down home for a little break for a couple of
days. And the atmosphere changed quite dramatically on that tour. Everyone
started yelling out of the windows at women all of a sudden and it got a bit
laddish, which it hadn't while we were there' (Claire Lemmon).

One hidden aspect of touring is sex on the road. Clearly many male musicians
do have casual sex and female 'groupies' exist to supply it, but, although female
musicians engage in sex with strangers on tour, none of my interviewees admitted
to this. Mandy (of Ms45): 'I think women don't really sleep around as much on
tour as men. Men, definitely, are just out there looking for that on tour, a lot of
the time', which is hardly surprising in a patriarchal society with a continuing
sexual double standard. Moreover, the age and power dynamic helps to ensure
this. Most fans are young. Male rock stars (older and powerful) sleep with female
fans (younger and powerless). Most women in their twenties are not attracted
to 14- or 16-year-old boys, yet this is the age of the fans who write to 33-year-
old Candida Doyle, for instance. In Liverpool, Shareen (of Ms45) got offers of
marriage from 12-year-olds when she told the audience about her work permit
situation.

> **ANDREA** (Mambo Taxi): One of the things I found weirdest was touring,
> because most of the 17-year-old boys who liked indie music—they'd come up
> to you and go, 'You're lovely' and you're thinking, 'You're a 17-year-old boy! . . .
> All the blokes I know are always getting laid on tour, but it's like, 'Er, it's a
> little boy. Go away!' And you go, 'Do you know how old I am?' and they say,
> '18 or 19?' And you say, '28' and they say, 'that's really old!' . . . A lot of men
> would find this wildly exciting. I wasn't attracted to 17-year-old boys. If a
> man marries a young girl it's 'well done'.

Lastly, there is the danger. As Shareen (of Ms45) said, 'there are some sincere
psychopaths out there'.

Yet despite the problems which women face on the road, some loved touring
and mentioned the comradeship and unusual closeness which develops: 'It was
brilliant fun and we got on really well with the two bands we were playing with
. . . like a huge family. It was really sad to say goodbye' (Katherine Garrett of the
Mystics). Women (like Mary Genis of Dread Warlock) who tour with their sexual
partners and/or their family find it easier. Whilst all-women bands touring by
themselves do not have to subscribe to masculinist values at all.

Professionals' Problems

The new way of organizing time can cause unforeseen problems for band members since there is less chance for spontaneity, for 'play', and while the band is touring, it can't be recording or writing. For a newly released record, touring is imperative. There are also videos, artwork, and press interviews. If one of the reasons for being in a band is to express your creativity, then long periods where you do not have the time to either practise or write can be very frustrating and a source of alienation.

> **'SUKE'** : We did about three or four tours. So that was a gig every night over periods of four to six weeks. Too many gigs and not enough working in a studio or working together as a band. Not enough jams. Too much getting out there and just playing. . . . I would have liked to have done a lot more experimental stuff, just jamming around with people, instead of just having to come up with finished products and out you go.

As a band moves along the career route, time and other pressures increase. What begins, commonly, as a bit of fun turns into a very serious business indeed with which some women feel they just cannot cope. It's easy to get burnt out.

> **ALI WEST** (the Mistakes): We started off just being amazed that we could actually play gigs at all. . . . There was very little pressure at the beginning and it was a lot more fun before we started getting involved in all this record business and everything. On one level, I'm pissed off that we didn't get further, because I think our music was good enough. On another level, I'm quite glad we didn't, because I don't know if I could have coped with that, personally. The pressures were bad enough as it was.

However, the contradictions and pressures are different for bands depending on the level of 'professionalism'. There is, in fact, far less pressure on the superstars for, as Frith (1983) points out, 'the biggest acts have contracts that let them do much as they musically like'. Bands lower down the ladder are the most constrained by pressure from the record company and are unlikely to have control over their 'product'. This is the level at which most bands (male and female) get stuck, but there are very few female bands who make it through to the next stage.

The role conflicts so far discussed in previous chapters—musician vs. mother, gigging vs. boyfriends—were between various roles, and these are obviously exacerbated by going professional. Another sort of conflict emerges when gigging becomes subsidiary to recording, which can present problems for those members who get their 'fix' from live performance and do not much enjoy the sterile conditions of the modern studio. Forced to spend increasing time in the studio, they may miss the live performance that drew them into the occupation in the first place. On the other hand, the really successful band may prefer to make records rather than endure the stress and disorientation of touring.

Another, quite subtle conflict is between the public's expectations of the rock performer and the studio's and record company's expectations: the romantic bohemian ideal versus the everyday realities of bandwork. I think there is an interesting contradiction here. The public values of rock and roll are all about youth rebellion against the adult structures of school and work, the manifest values being spontaneity, hedonism, and a devil-may-care attitude. But the 'backstage' reality of rock as work is antithetical to those values since success in the highly competitive world of rock music requires discipline, organization, punctuality, persistence, and deferred gratification. Now, it is true that bands' behaviour in studios can be notoriously riotous. However, each minute costs the record company (and, ultimately, the band) money, so there is also a pressure to be disciplined and work conscientiously, especially so today, for record production costs have escalated and companies have had to exert pressure on their bands. The crucial point here is that people may get drawn into playing rock by a set of motives which are lost as they progress along the career path, as comes out in musicians' definitions of what makes a 'good gig'. For the novice in a local band a 'good gig' may be one where she got drunk and had an enjoyable time, playing, dancing, and socializing. But a professional attitude to gigs means, among other things, not allowing one's personal enjoyment to affect the quality of music being delivered to the audience. It might mean not drinking at all.

At the professional stage, all of a musician's life revolves around music. The distinction between 'work' and 'leisure' becomes blurred:

'SUKE' : It's a social life that's part of my career. It's not a social life [where] you leave work and then you go out and have this other type of life. It's all part and parcel of the same thing. You mix with the same people. You go to gigs because it's part of what you should be doing; listening out for new bands and listening out for new sounds. And meeting people, and making sure your face is shown and you're seen to be out and about. Guys there with cameras; get your photo taken. It's proof that you were there. Because it's good press. It's great. It's a total thing.

On the other hand, some women found the endless work-socializing, the 'meet-and-greets', and the parties claustrophobic, while the sheer numbers of people you meet on tour can be overwhelming: 'It can drive me a little barmy knowing too many people. Because you meet so many people and you have an overload' (Mary of Stereolab). Stardom brings its own set of pressures: endlessly being in the public eye and your private life held up to scrutiny, and being mobbed by fans. I did not interview any established rock stars, but I did capture the feelings of some women who were in the process of becoming stars. For instance, Skin told me that success ruined her relationship and turned her world upside down:

The way that people look at you. They look at you and think you're a rock star. They assume you have lots of money and they assume that you're used to a certain lifestyle. . . . I really try not to surround myself with those kind of people who look at you in that kind of rock star thing. . . . I feel that people are looking at me from one perspective but I'm being very real about what I am and not letting people's perception of me—you know, that thing that people turn into. I don't want to do that, turn into what people think I am.

Relationships

One problem which has a gender specific slant is balancing playing in a touring band and maintaining personal relationships: sexual and familial. The Cocteau Twins take their baby and nanny on tour and, unusually, Throwing Muses take their children on the tour bus. Normally, male musicians leave their offspring at home with their wives or girlfriends, whilst female musicians cut back on their careers or drop out completely. It is well known that Chrissie Hynde has taken her children on tour, although she has had to curtail the amount of time she spends on the road: 'Because I have children, I can't go out on the year-long tours I would like to do. So I thought one way we could stay in London and keep things ticking over was to do this acoustic album' (*Making Music*, November 1995). Shakespeare's Sister had to curtail their tour in 1992 because one of Marcella's children had an accident.

CLARE KENNY : Siobhan and Marcy both have very young children, and over a year's worth of promotion for an album represents a substantial part of a child's life at eighteen months old . . . and it gradually got more and more difficult for them to balance their family needs with touring. Then, towards the end of the tour, one of Marcy's kids had an accident in LA and that stopped the tour in its tracks. (*Guitarist*, April 1993)

Katherine Garrett (of the Mystics) told me that, worried about having babies, she could not envisage having one unless her partner did at least half of the childcare work. Otherwise, she would not be prepared to compromise her time. Andrea (from Mambo Taxi) said that she had no time or space to fit children in. Whilst Emma Anderson (of Lush) said that if she had a baby she would not want to be in a band that was touring. Moreover, the general masculinist atmosphere of the professional rock world makes the idea of taking babies on tour seem impossibly unhealthy to many women.

YOLANDE CHARLES : I've just had a baby. He's four and a half months old, so I won't be touring unless I can take him with me. There's certain gigs that I've been offered that I wouldn't take him to because I think it's too rock and roll. . . . Some gigs I just wouldn't feel comfortable. I guess although people say they don't mind, they're probably secretly rolling their eye up to the ceiling going, 'Oh, she's going off again; the baby's demanding her time'. And I think women are less likely to do that because they've either been through it

themselves so they are sympathetic, or they imagine themselves going through it, or are just more sensitive to that in some ways. . . . I just wouldn't want my baby to be travelling on a coach that's full of drugs and smoke, because it's not really fair on him.

Some women were lucky enough to have a relationship with another member of the band (for example, Laetitia from Stereolab and Mary Genis) or someone else in their entourage. Sharon's boyfriend is her band's sound engineer. Marcella Detroit is married to her manager and her previous boyfriend was in the crew: 'Before I was married I always used to have a boyfriend on the road, you know, someone that was with the band, because it made it a lot easier to do, you know. You get lonely.' For the other women, however, sexual relationships were problematic, principally because touring splits the couple for most of the year. It is only at the superstar level that you can afford to take three-month breaks or take your partner with you on tour, and my subjects were too busy 'trying to get somewhere'. Any boyfriends touring with the bands I interviewed were either paying their own way or temporarily working for the crew for low pay. A secondary reason is the inability of the partner to cope with feelings of insecurity and fear brought about by the knowledge of 'what goes on on tour'. Indeed, it is difficult to stay faithful on tour and one of the 'perks' is, of course, 'celebrity sex'. Furthermore, a woman musician in a relationship with a less successful male musician typically has to cope with jealousy, envy, and competitiveness. On the other hand, non-musicians do not understand the lifestyle and find it difficult to cope with the woman's drive and focus on music all the time. Some women told me that there was no point in being in a relationship with a non-musician and that they would not even contemplate it. Often there is no choice: once on the road, the only people you meet are musicians or in the music world. It even becomes difficult to relate to and to get to know non-musicians while, although musicians understand the lifestyle, they still think that the relationship should come first. If both partners are gigging then the likelihood of being free at the same time may be limited. Well-known pop couple Damon (of Blur) and Justine (of Elastica) spent only three weeks of 1995 together: 'It's a relationship of absenteeism' (*Big Issue*, 28 November–4 December 1995).

ANDREA (Mambo Taxi): **You spend your whole life checking diaries to see when you've got a free night to get together. I find that quite stressful.**

MANDY (Ms45): **In a way, you don't really have a relationship. It's like being single until you're together.**

In a society where men are still supposed to be the main breadwinner, a further problem arises when a successful female musician is in a relationship with a man who earns significantly less: 'My boyfriend who I go out with doesn't work. He's not working and I've got loads of money, which doesn't make it easy' (Candida Doyle of Pulp). Anyone would find it difficult being left behind whilst their partner goes off on world tours for most of the year, but again men seem to find it harder than a woman being the one who is left behind. Yet, although it is easier to be the one who is living the exciting, glamorous life, women in love miss their partners and can find it difficult to channel themselves into the music. They also run up huge telephone bills. Consequently, many women did not have a relationship. Some (like Natasha Atlas) told me that they actively chose not to have one because they felt that a relationship would not work out under the circumstances. 'Right now I have a wonderful exuberant opportunity for big noisy fun and I don't want to lose myself in something else [fun as it may be]' (Shareen of Ms45). Many others (like the members of Sidi Bou Said) had found that a relationship was simply impossible to sustain whilst being in a professional touring band. Emma told me that, sadly, her last relationship had been fine until she went on tour, and now she is away from home so much she couldn't imagine being in a relationship. Others, heterosexual and lesbian, told me similar tales of broken relationships.

SKIN : That is what ruined my relationship. Basically, just being on tour non-stop and when I am in London, every minute being planned. The relationship just crumbled under the weight. . . . I think it's very difficult to keep the thing running unless you're going out with someone who's connected to what you're doing. I think its incredibly difficult to keep a long-term relationship going when you're never in the country. Last year I must have spent, let's say, two months in London. I tried everything to keep it going, but it's just impossible to have a relationship if you're never there. It's easier if they're in the business but then you have a whole set of other problems.

I have shown that being in a band requires sacrifices, particularly at the professional stage. For women, the biggest sacrifice is a sexual relationship.

GAYLE GREENWOOD (Belly): It's so weird. For me, a relationship and the band don't mix, because the band rules first. And if there's something that I have to do for the band, that comes first. . . . You think 'maybe I should have a relationship with somebody that would understand [i.e. a musician]', but it doesn't make any difference. They still think that your relationship with them should come first.

CLAIRE LEMMON (Sidi Bou Said): We've all had really crap love lives since we started the band.

Indeed, in a sense, for women like the members of Sidi Bou Said, the band itself takes the place of a steady relationship.

Success

First, the term 'success' needs some discussion. It means different things to different people, depending on their goals.

COMMERCIAL SUCCESS

A 'successful band' is one which has sold enough records to get into the charts, done world tours, and become rich and famous. It means building up a large following, performing in front of tens of thousands of people, becoming a 'star', and having people request your autograph. Success brings power, for it is only the commercially successful musicians who can gain 'artistic control' from their record companies. The money they earn in royalties enables them, if they so wish, to set up their own recording studios and thereby gain control of the production process. I did not interview any 'superstars', but some of my interviewees did speak of the feeling of satisfaction that came from the relative success of being able to buy their own flat or even simply pay the rent from music.

CRAFT SUCCESS

For session musicians, success could mean simply being able to get regular work in recording studios and to make a reasonable living from hiring out one's musical skills. It also means getting very good at playing and being recognized for this: 'Playing well enough to be respected by other musicians—that's my ultimate (goal) really' ('Beth').

SUCCESS AS ENTERTAINMENT

For bands who follow the path of gigging rather than recording, success is being able to get regular gigs, which pay well and enable one to make a living just by playing.

SUCCESS AS 'ART'

Success, here, is making a creative contribution to popular music which will be memorable. This, also, is linked to the desire to be appreciated by other musicians rather than by the general record purchaser.

> **JUDY PARSONS** (Belle Stars): **I would rather have made one Captain Beefheart record, personally, as my goal, something I regard as worthwhile, a valid bit of art. . . . Being on *Top of the Pops* is not one of my personal goals. . . . Even if you get to number one in the American album charts, that is something to be ashamed of—'cause they've got no taste—although you're vey rich.**

This quote illustrates the way in which band success and individual success can be quite different and even contradictory. One of the common reasons why bands break up is precisely because an individual's musical career comes into conflict with that of the band. Indeed, individuals often use bands as stepping stones in their own careers (although there is not one single instance of this amongst my interviewees).

Within the world of popular music, success is an ambiguous and contradictory concept. For a professional musician, it may mean popular commercial success via making hit records, or it may mean being able to make a steady living from playing music. For many women it means both of these things, and yet these two forms of success can be mutually exclusive; a band with hit records may be living in poverty. There are production costs to be paid back, and royalties take a long time to come in. Moreover, the chart band is only as successful as its next record. The sales of records determine the size of the next 'advance'. Thus success, in these terms, is precarious and often fleeting. Yet bands who earn a good living from entertaining in their local pub, miss out on recording success and the fame that goes with it. So bands have to make a choice; they cannot follow both paths. This leads me to other questions: does success mean something different for women than for men? Is there a feminist conception of success?

Some women regard success for female musicians as simply going out and playing, showing your presence in a 'male' world. Other bands believe that a feminist practice must be involved. Many believed that feminists would never achieve mainstream success because of the amount of compromise involved. Anna Power (Sub Rosa): 'It makes me realize I'll never be famous. I think I would be very unconformable looking sexy. . . . I think I tend to think about the message I am giving out by what I wear on stage.' Some bands feel that the very aim of commercial success is a form of political compromise which many feminist bands have rejected altogether, developing alternative strategies towards different goals. However, some feminist bands did want success in commercial terms and fell between two stools since, although they were prepared to sign a contract with a record company, they would not make many compromises with their feminist principles (on lyrics, clothes, image, and decision-making). For feminists, there is only a narrow range of options and therefore less room for manœuvre. A compromise on image is far more significant than for a non-feminist band; it could undermine their whole political stance. I think that this lack of malleability and refusal to fit into the ideological space reserved for 'all-girl band' has acted as a brake on their commercial success. But most band members have probably not thought through what kind of success they are aiming at, and so many try to be commercial, although in a half-hearted way:

JUDY PARSONS : **I think being in a local band is entirely valid, [but] there are a lot of people in local bands that are really stupid. That is really what they want to do and yet, at the same time, they're sending tapes off to record companies and failing horribly in the commercial stakes. Everyone vaguely feels that you've got to be successful, and you're a failure if you don't do this, that and the other. [But] it's two completely different things.**

Success is, of course, always relative, and a band's goals change over time. The local band may see success as getting gigs in London and a record contract. However, a band which has already been on *Top of the Pops* will see success in more ambitious terms. As a band's goals are also affected by audience response, one which starts out playing for fun may develop further goals if it finds that it is being well received. On the other hand, some bands are unable to change their initial (limited) aspirations, typically because children are involved and mothers have to think in the short term.

Breaking up

Bands stay together because they enjoy playing together, have fun, and share the same aims. The average life of a band is probably only a year or two. Those which last longer than this tend to be ones which have achieved some measure of financial success and whose continued success depends on staying together. Other factors include close bonds, especially between family members. In my research a number of women's bands included sisters. Such kinship connections weld the band together and enable it to weather the stormy patches in interpersonal relations.

Bands often break up when one or more people leave, which happens for a variety of reasons: lack of money, touring 'burnout', and so forth. Quite often a band starts off in a very unified way but camps develop over time. It is when communication breaks down between these groups and when the resentment and frustrations which build up are not expressed, that a band is in danger of having an explosive, and terminal, row. Another difference that can develop over time is in musical taste. There are a number of possible dimensions to this. It can be linked to growing musical skills. If members join as novices, as they improve their playing abilities they may wish to branch out and play an entirely different sort of music which may create conflicts. A skilled musician may feel that the band is holding her back and this frustration may eventually lead her to leave the band. Or, she may wish to move in a more commercial direction than the others.

TERRY HUNT (Jam Today): As we all got better musically, our musical tastes diverged. I felt very restricted . . . I wanted to explore other ways of playing. . . . We were playing standards and we started to write our own music, but we had to play to the limits of the weakest member. . . . We just grew apart. . . . There had been a thing that we were intrinsically feminist and that meant we were not going to be commercial [and then] Denise said she really wanted to be famous.

Relationships change within bands. Lovers may fall out and the band end because of that. The power balance also shifts as women develop their musical skills at varying speeds, musical expertise, songwriting, and administration all having the potential for conveying power. Paradoxically, some bands actually break up at the point of 'signing', or at the moment of going fully professional because members decide they are not prepared to take the risks involved, or to make the necessary sacrifices.

Some factors affect both male and female bands equally; others, such as a new sexual relationship, marriage, and parenthood, affect women far more than men, all of these events having the potential to interrupt or put a permanent end to a woman's musical career in a way that does not typically happen with men. The difficulty of finding replacements is a major problem facing a professional women's band: 'We had to get a guitarist from halfway around the world. We held auditions [but] there was only about five [worth considering]. The tapes we had sent in of girls were absolutely horrendous. They just couldn't play' (Kim McAuliffe). Usually the most difficult instrumentalist to replace (because the most rare) is the drummer. 'Becky': 'In the beginning, when Clare left us, we looked for a woman drummer for ages and ages. We spent months looking for a woman drummer. There was none.' So they recruited a man. 'Suke''s band advertised in the national press for a woman drummer and only had five replies: 'And that was over a long time: about three months. We did get people from quite a long way away answering. And guys. Regardless of the fact it said "girl". Just 'cause we were a "name" band, I suppose.' Female bands tend to be very close and so the new member must be able to fit in socially and personally:

KIM MCAULIFFE : It is quite difficult trying to find other people, especially when you've got to find somebody that you get on well with. Because we're so much involved with each other in the band. It's not like a band that comes together just to play gigs. It's our whole life. We go out for drinks together. We're always around each other's flats. It's that sort of thing.

Thus, one or two women leaving a band is far more likely to precipitate its demise than would be true of a mixed or male band. For women's bands, then, breaking up may be more traumatic than for male bands. First, women tend to be more emotionally involved with each other than male musicians typically are. Second, women have fewer chances, than men, to join other bands. For some it can mean ceasing to play music for years or for ever. Third, the very knowledge of the rarity of women's bands, and the problems of joining another one, lead to group loyalty. (Many women would not feel able to join a male or mixed band for either ideological reasons, or lack of self-confidence or experience.) The continuance of the band is perceived to depend upon everyone staying committed. Thus, when a woman leaves it may be viewed as disloyalty or emotional rejection, and it is seldom taken nonchalantly. Many of my interviewees (in both the 1980s and 1990s) commented on the way in which a women's band is like a marriage.

JUDY PARSONS : It's like being married . . . and the frustrations and the torment and the ups and downs. . . . It's an emotional involvement with other people. There's so much at stake and you get so frustrated. You get really involved in the interpersonal thing.

DELIA (Mambo Taxi): It's like being in a relationship. You have to know them that well. I guess, maybe, being in a band with them is as close to people as you can get without sex and stuff. You can get as pissed off with them as people in relationships do. I mean, an awful lot of bands that are really good musically and doing really well break up just because the people don't get on.

And when bands do split up it can resemble divorce:

JUDY PARSONS (Belle Stars): 'I hate you!' and 'Don't lay a finger on me!' . . . I
thought, 'Why can't people react in a nice, normal fashion? Never again will I
get involved with a bunch of women . . . that get so het up . . . and their
emotions in turmoil.'

Conclusion

In looking at the issues and problems which women musicians have to deal with
at the professional stage, two things strike me as important. First, there seem to
be fewer difficulties which are specifically due to gender, at this stage, than lower
down the career ladder. As a musician progresses in her career, she overcomes a
whole range of obstacles which are tied up with her being a woman. Once at the
professional stage, however, her problems become more similar to those of men.
In fact, female superstars often deny gender constraints in popular music. However, I would maintain that this is because they have either been lucky enough to
have been relatively unaffected by such difficulties, or, more likely, they were
overcome so long ago that they have simply been forgotten. P. J. Harvey says that
she has transcended gender roles; Bjork says she simply ignores them, while
Justine Frischmann, of Elastica, has stated that she has never felt that it is a disadvantage being a woman. Yet, gender does have some impact, more noticeably
at the sub-star level. My interviews have thrown light upon the routine, everyday sexism rampant throughout the male-dominated industry: in management,
agencies, record companies, recording studios, and the press. Women's bodies
are objectified and they are edged into narrow stereotyped categories. I have suggested that women have a tougher ride on the road than their male counterparts;
that they inhabit an overwhelmingly male world drenched in a masculinist culture. I have shown that women usually have to choose between continuing in a
band and having children, whilst men typically do not, and that a major sacrifice
which women, specifically, make is in their sexual relationships.

Second, common sense arguments (such as those fielded by some record companies and managers) that women cannot cope with day-to-day life in the world
of rock (because they are too weak, incapacitated by menstruation, lack stamina,
do not travel well, cannot carry heavy objects, and so on) do not hold up against
the evidence. I asked my interviewees questions about physical limitations,
but musician after musician denied having any. Many women were surprised at
my asking the question. Those few physical things which women did mention
as being problematic seem to have been very easily overcome. For example,
difficulty in carrying equipment was neutralized by learning the skills involved
in lifting heavy objects. (Moreover, for professional musicians, once you have
reached a certain level of success, working conditions improve and roadies are
hired to do all the physical work.) Regarding periods, a phenomenon which has

often been used to symbolize women's biological weakness, some mentioned PMT and/or menstrual cramps, but they have not let this deter them from playing. Indeed, women described situations where they had ploughed on through a set with, for example, flu and a raging temperature. Alison Rayner (Jam Today): 'The only time I can remember a person being ill in our band, or any physical thing, that wasn't anything to do with them being a woman. Terry once had a shocking migraine, just before we played. And Jackie (the drummer) broke her foot once. She did her gigs with a broken foot.' The gender problems my interviewees did emphasize, again and again, were the social constraints: the definitions of 'woman' imposed on them by husbands, boyfriends, and babies, on the one hand, and by the music business, men, and institutions, on the other.

Last, despite all of the constraints mentioned, most of the women playing professionally were enjoying themselves and many stressed that they felt proud and privileged to be doing music for a living. For all the pressures and discomforts of touring and so forth, at least playing in a band is not a nine-to-five job and you get to travel and see the world. In the words of Ms45:

MANDY : You can't get a better job than this! It's not even a job, is it? It's your hobby. It's what you do. It's your whole life.

SHAREEN : You do this for fun and for your own enjoyment. Beats the hell out of waiting tables! We rehearsed this morning and after the first song, I turned round and said, 'Goddamn, I love my job!'

8 Conclusion

THIS book began by examining the positioning of women within the world of popular music: consuming, decorative, and supportive roles. Whilst there is a clear role for women as vocalists in bands, there is a marked absence of women playing instruments. Although there has been an increase in the numbers of female instrumentalists since the watershed of punk, they are still hugely outnumbered by men. The first important question I addressed, then, was how can one explain the lack of female players. Biological explanations do not persuade because, as women are as capable of making music as men, all are potential musicians. This positioning of women in popular music can be explained only by social factors which I conceptualized as 'constraints' facing the potential female musician. They can be divided into 'material' and 'ideological'. However, this dichotomy is merely an analytical distinction and the dimensions are inevitably interrelated. Material constraints operating on potential female instrumentalists include: lack of money, lack of access to equipment and transport, spatial restrictions—both in terms of 'public' and 'private' space, lack of time, the 'policing' of female leisure, and regulation of female play—including restrictions imposed by parents, boyfriends, husbands, and exclusion by male musicians. The main ideological constraint is the hegemonic masculinity of rock music-making: the perceived masculinity of the musical discourse itself and that embedded within rock instruments and associated technology. Running in parallel is the ideology of hegemonic femininity, particularly in its teenage form, which encourages young women to spend a lot of time on their physical presentation of self and the pursuit of the boyfriend. For working-class girls, in particular, this ideology of femininity and romance is integrally linked to early marriage, with concomitant loss of autonomy. Both material and ideological constraints can, to varying degrees, be 'internal' in the sense of being internalized within the psyche and embodied within the individual.

Given the forces stacked against women becoming rock musicians, it is remarkable that any do, but socialization is not uniformly consistent and, anyway, it is a dialectical rather than a mechanistic process. What is interesting is the way in which women are able to overcome or evade the restraints, constraints, and exclusion. The successful struggle of some, however, does not in any way diminish the effectiveness of those social forces, although it does show that the women who do make it into rock are special and that the sexual status quo is neither inevitable nor unchangeable. This raises certain sociological questions. Under what particular social circumstances are women able to resist gender socialization and successfully break into a male enclave? How and why have they done it? What alternative strengths do they draw on to oppose gender hegemony? The answers to these questions hold out the possibility of a wider application, rather than simply to rock music. These questions are important, not least because they are rarely asked. There is a series of 'spaces' within which women are able to struggle and develop a series of strategies to overcome their socially-produced handicaps. (I have produced these in schematic form in Diagram 1 below.) Alternatively, one can conceptualize these as a series of 'escapes' or successful 'resistances': musical families, classical music training, art school, drama, gender rebellion, musician partners, higher education, accessibility of female musical role models, feminism, lesbianism, punk, and Riot Grrrl. I have not attempted to prioritize these factors, but merely to present them as indisputably operating in the lives of the women musicians that I interviewed. Clearly, more than one factor is operating in the life of any single individual and, as some are interrelated, they tend to operate in clusters. For example, early 1990s Riot Grrrl involvement would include feminism, punk, and gender rebellion. Similarly, the late 1970s punk movement made it easier for women to get into bands and on stage and simultaneously provided a marked increase in female instrumental role models. In sum, at any one point in time any one constraint or enabling factor may assume primacy over the others. They operate at different levels and at different rates in different people.

The first thing that strikes me about my 1990s sample is that many of the women had feminist mothers, while others had ones who, although not feminist, made them feel they could achieve any goal that they set themselves. An even more interesting finding is the importance of fathers, the key factor being not how they personally performed their gender, as some might assume, but the amount of leeway they allowed their daughters from the constraints of femininity. Although most of the fathers were quite traditionally 'masculine', they related to their daughters as they would to boys. In those instances where girls were taught technical skills by their fathers there was a good chance of techno-phobia being held at bay. The ramifications of this go way beyond the issue of rock music, for such young women often went on to do sciences at school and, later, traditionally masculine jobs. Thus, if girls are allowed by their parents to break gender codes from an early age, their ensuing confidence seems to be strong enough to offset the later combined onslaught of school, mass media, and peer group pressure. Many of my interviewees were rebels at school, but that rebellion seems to have been rooted in their early childhood.

Another area which has been neglected is the extent to which families today continue to pass on a specific tradition, in this case a musical one. A family

Constraints	Escapes
childhood femininity	gender rebellion
family	unusual/musical family
technophobia	unusual family/school
	women's music projects
teenage femininity	bohemian/artist
(via mass media and female peer groups)	rebel identity
material constraints:	feminist collectives
equipment space, money, time	political collectives
	women's music projects
	unusual boyfriends and husbands
ideological constraints	feminism
(dual standard of morality etc.)	lesbianism
	Riot Grrrl
	Girl Power
exclusion by male music-making peer	women's music projects
groups and by male bands	women's bands
exclusion by promoters	DIY feminist venues
male-dominated gigs	
hostile male audiences	women-only gigs
sexploitative managers	DIY administration
	supportive husbands/managers
sexist PA crew	DIY feminist PA
	feminist courses in sound engineering
female compartments	punk, Riot Grrrl, and feminist
alternatives in the record promotion	DIY record production and distribution
industry (esp. light pop/vocals)	

background in popular music was strongly associated with young women becoming rock musicians, since the normal restrictions and restraints are lifted, and girls often find strong material and emotional support in their musical careers. An unusual family background seems to be more important for working-class women, whose period of freedom from family obligations is much shorter and they are steered, by the education system and by their own peer groups, towards a particularly narrow set of options. To set out to be a rock musician means breaking out of these cultural tramlines and seeing the future as offering more than an early engagement, marriage, and motherhood. Interestingly, those working-class young women who do join bands tend to receive a lot of support from their parents, who treat rock music-making more seriously as a way of making money than middle-class parents do. It is also important to remember that female working-class culture is not monolithic, and to note the existence of alternative subcultures which afford a group context in which to engage in masculine activities such as motorbikes and rock music. This is significant as working-class girls are less likely to make significant contact with feminism, which is largely middle class.

For black women, a determined break usually has to be made from family background in order to perform in a (predominantly white) indie/rock context, since what is played in the home tends to be soul, reggae, hip-hop, gospel, and various genres of black dance music, and it is a strong expectation that musical young women will slot into the 'black backing vocalist' role. For these women, the lack of black female singers in rock is significant, let alone the complete dearth of black female instrumentalist role models. As Skin told me:

> **My whole family were horrified when they heard the music I was making. . . . It was music that was quite different from what I grew up with. . . . You know, I'd kind of hide my love of it. . . . I never had anybody that I wanted to be like, because they were so different from me that I didn't identify with them. . . . I identified with them musically, but looks-wise or anything else they were completely alien to me.**

There was a notable increase in the number of black and Asian women in rock bands during the 1980s and 1990s. Thus, women like Skin, Natasha Atlas, Yolande Charles, Mary Genis, and Debbie Smith are now acting as crucial role models for future generations of black women.

Regarding education, my research lends some support to the argument that mixed schools hold girls back in traditionally masculine subjects, so that in an all-female environment young women have more of a chance to express themselves and gain the teacher's attention, and do not fear ridicule or humiliation from boys. A women-only context in which to learn musical and technological skills has been of central importance for many, all of my evidence pointing to the importance of providing some male-free, protected spaces (in schools, community centres, youth clubs, and so forth) in which young women can be supported in learning to play.

Women's music projects are still rare. The norm tends to be a gender-blindness which serves to maintain patriarchy. For instance, Jude Sacker first set up an all-women class in Sheffield when she discovered two girls hanging around after a mixed workshop. They told her, ' "We came to play but nobody's asked us to play". They hadn't even picked up an instrument and they'd been sitting there all afternoon and these two male tutors had completely ignored them. It hadn't even occurred to them that they might want to play and a load of lads had been playing all afternoon.' Women's music projects are notoriously underfunded. They have had trouble finding buildings, and have often only kept going by the voluntarily unpaid labour of their highly committed tutors and administrators. For instance, the pioneering project Ova(tones), in London, spent two and a half years trying to find somewhere to put the equipment. In one of the two women's music projects in Sheffield in 1995 the tutor was subsidizing it by working for no pay. They used to have a saxophone but they had to sell it to raise money. Outside London, such projects also often have to face considerable local opposition. For instance, Jude Sacker, who runs the Sheffield Women's Music Project, has had to face outright hostility: 'We used to get a pile of lads staring in through the windows and trying to make fun of us. We were really up against bad attitudes.' And the opposition also came from male tutors who shared both the learning environment and the equipment: 'We had a year of battles with these two male workers who would lend us the instruments but they wouldn't be working. Or they would lend us an amp and the fuse had been taken out and they hadn't bothered to tell us. I had lot of trouble over a period of five to six years.' However, where these projects do exist, they provide a safe atmosphere in which young women can learn to play traditionally 'masculine' instruments. Such projects offset material constraints by providing (free or cheap) access to equipment, space in which to be noisy, and music tuition by women who also act as role models, showing that it is perfectly possible for them to play rock. In particular, these projects confront technophobia and give women both skills and confidence in dealing with equipment. A number of interviewees had run women-only music projects and their comments were always like this:

'LINDA' : No one here has to be embarrassed or on their guard, and there's no way you'd be able to get that if it was a mixed project. The women don't have to be concerned about making fools of themselves, like if they don't know how to use a particular piece of equipment. . . . The women don't have to battle for time. They don't have to battle for attention. They don't have to battle for space, for access to the equipment. They don't have to feel they are in competition with men.

If a women-only environment is important for learning how to play an instrument, then it is doubly important for learning sound engineering, as Rosemary Schonfeld, a founder of Ova studios, told me: 'When there are men around technology there is often an element of competitiveness and women very easily feel

Figure 5: Learning about the mixing desk. Young women's music workshop, Pegasus Theatre, Oxford 1982. Judy Parsons of the Belle Stars (extreme left) and Penny Wood of the Mistakes (extreme right).

intimidated and insecure. Women find in a women-only environment that they can generally focus on learning without those competitive things.' Consequently, my research bears witness to the strategic effectiveness of separatism as a temporary political strategy for increasing the number of young women musicians. Since the 1980s, local councils in Britain have sought to alleviate local youth employment problems in urban areas by financing music projects. Insofar as they have done this without addressing the gendered nature of rock and its institutionalized sexism, they have—in practice—been funding *men's* music-making. My research findings suggest that one important way in which the local state can challenge male hegemony in music is to substantially subsidize women-only learning environments. When gender issues are seriously addressed, the effects can be dramatic.

Feminism and lesbianism have been major routes into music-making, these subcultures providing an alternative socialization experience which enables young women to resist the culture of romance by downgrading the importance of heterosexual relationships. Because it encourages women to centre their lives on themselves, rather than depending on men, the women's movement has been a continuous wellspring for the development of musicians and, especially, women's bands over two decades. In the early 1990s, Riot Grrrl (a sort of revamped feminism for a new generation) inspired many young women to set up bands. Although press mediation stunted the movement's national spread, local pockets of musical activity remain. In the late 1990s, feminism has become part of the life-orientation of young teenage girls, with the phenomenally successful Spice Girls popularizing the slogan 'Girl Power' and making a feminist 'Attitude'

Figure 6: The Mistakes. A farewell gig (the first of many), The Caribbean Club, Oxford, 1981. Left to right: Ali West, Penny Wood, the author, Georgina Clarke.

trendy. In a sense, the Spice Girls have picked up on the Riot Grrrl theme, whilst diluting and commercializing it. Young girls have been encouraged to see themselves as potential performers, although as singers and dancers rather than instrumentalists. (Kenickie, Fluffy, Elastica, and Echobelly would serve as more appropriate role models for the latter.) The Spice Girls have been used to sell soft drinks, but they have also encouraged girls to stand up to their boyfriends and to prize female friendships. Girl Power may be a superficial, individualistic marketing device and riven with contradictions but its interpretation by teenage fans has been liberating in effect. It has given credence to feminist ideas amongst pre-teen girls and even the term feminism has been revived.

The biggest obstacle which women face is simply that rock is seen as 'male' and the overwhelming majority of rock instrumentalists are men for whom playing rock music asserts masculine credentials. In order to play a rock instrument a woman has to cut her fingernails and get dirty, going against the norms of hegemonic femininity, which involves a socially manufactured physical, mechanical, and technical helplessness. Similarly, for a man, expressing sexuality on stage is relatively straightforward, whereas for a woman it is tricky because questions such as how to hold a guitar, what to wear, and how to stand are more problematic. Since becoming a rock musician requires seeing yourself as a bit unusual—an 'artist', a bohemian, a rebel against nine-to-five workaday normality—I would argue that, regardless of whatever else the rebellion is against, for women it is all that it is for men, plus an extra dimension—resistance to gender norms. If male rock musicians are rebellious, then women are doubly rebellious so that any factor which acts to nourish and sustain the revolt against hegemonic femininity will enhance the likelihood of women becoming rock musicians.

The second half of my book comprised an ethnographic examination of band membership, structured in terms of key 'career' stages: a band starting out, gigging, and becoming professional. Day-to-day band activity is structured around certain key features at each point. For the band at the first stage these include: acquiring equipment, songwriting, getting a 'set' together, and rehearsing; for the semi-pro band, they involve gigging, handling escalating financial outlay, and deciding whether to go fully professional, while for the professional band, they are recording and touring. These issues are not gender-specific, operating in male and mixed bands as well as female bands. However, gender continued to operate, as a largely constraining force, at each career stage since it is inextricably interwoven into these issues. For a female musician, the question 'How shall I present myself on stage?' is also 'How shall I present myself as a woman?' or 'How shall I perform the female gender?' Men and women playing rock are simultaneously performing both gender and sexuality, following existing scripts, creating new ones, and playing with them. But female musicians have less space in which to negotiate such scripts since, for example, men do not have to contend with the dual standard of morality which polices the expression of women's sexuality both on and off stage.

The most important gender constraints operating throughout each career stage are women's sexual relationships and their childcare responsibilities. For a variety of reasons, female musicians face a harder task than their male equivalents in balancing band involvement with sexual involvement. This is particularly the case for heterosexual women as men are less willing to be the wait-at-home partner whilst their woman goes off on tour. Similarly, having children handicaps female musicians far more than it does their male counterparts because pervasive ingrained social assumptions, that women are the childcarers who should put their men and children first, affect women's musical careers as they do those of all females.

In terms of their careers in indie/rock music, women face a series of obstacles which men do not. In particular they have to cope with a range of sexist responses: obstructive technicians, prejudiced promoters, patronizing DJs, unimaginative marketing by record companies, sexploitative media coverage, sexual harassment, and, most of all, simply not being taken seriously. The status 'woman' seems to obscure that of 'musician'. Moreover, the lack of women in powerful positions within the UK record industry seriously affects women musicians' opportunities and the general shape of their careers.

Furthermore, unlike men, women have to carefully juggle the demands of family and career, personal and public life. As I have shown, women are typically unable to commit themselves to rock careers in the wholehearted way in which men seem to do precisely because of these commitments elsewhere. In another way, though, women seem to be more committed than men to the rest of the band. The women I interviewed variously described their band as 'my marriage', 'my baby', 'my therapy', 'my life'. Delia told me that if she was not in a band she would kill herself. Paradoxically, it is this emotional commitment to the band as a unit which often militates against their *individual* rock careers. Feminist women are reluctant to use bands as vehicles for their personal climb to the top while all women's bands are potentially more fragile than male bands for the simple reason that it is far more difficult to find replacement musicians. That very knowledge binds a band, particularly a feminist one, in bonds of loyalty which can transform playing with another into an act of infidelity, and I think it is this, in particular, which makes feminist women's bands different from male ones.

However, despite these factors, some women do achieve the heights of commercial success, although often at great personal cost, which includes the sacrifice of relationships and the chance of having and bringing up children. The fact that very few female musicians make it to the top is largely because so very few get a foot on even the bottom rung of the ladder. The whole culture of rock bands is male-dominated and pervaded by a masculinist value-system which works against women because men dominate the space at gigs, in music shops, and in the studio. They control the technology of rock, often operating (not always deliberately) in a manner which excludes women, by the intensive use of technological jargon, for instance. In a mainly male environment, much behaviour can work to both express and create bonds between men at the expense of women. My interviewees told me the same sorts of stories of sexist jokes, wolf-whistling at women from the tour bus, and passing comments on women's bodies. Some of this is obvious but some is quite subtle. Rock bands are part of 'gender work', in which there are no stable monolithic genders, masculinity and femininity existing in a plurality of forms, each shifting, being constituted and reconstituted through time, and varying according to place. Because hegemonic masculinity is precarious, especially in the teenage years, and rock bands play an important part in helping to shore up and protect fledgling adult mascu-line identity, young women have been excluded. Walser (1993) argues that (to a degree) metal music works to repeatedly shore up or magically resolve the specific gender anxieties of a particularly powerless socio-economic age group, young working-class males, although as such fans get older they no longer need it. Moreover, one of the main themes that metal has dealt with lyrically is the perceived 'threat of women' who have to be excluded for such a resolution to work. Not only are young women actively excluded by male musicians, playing rock instruments does nothing towards resolving their own gender anxieties. Quite the reverse. As I have shown, it places their femininity in jeopardy.

Recent feminist scholarship has rightly been careful to take account of the dif-ferences between women in terms of colour, social, class, age, sexual preference, and so forth, differences which in the late 1960s and early 1970s were obscured behind the monolithic category 'woman'. In selecting my interviewees for this research I tried to include a wide variety of women and, where relevant to the specific issue being explored, I have attempted to discuss the ramifications of such differentiation. However, what stands out, above all, is that despite these differences in identity, structural location, style of music or instrument played, there are strong similarities in the stories that these women told. Although ageism, racism, homophobia, and classism affect them differently, women of all ages, colours, classes, and sexual preferences have in common the fact that they are women. Their separate individual experiences are linked since sexism and sexist practice impact on all of them, albeit with different inflections. Thus, virtually every interviewee reported problems in relation to music shops where they were treated in a negative manner by men *because they were women.*

Women's Music-Making

Music-making by either women or men is still under-researched. Because I have chosen to concentrate on women's, rather than men's, it is difficult without com-parative research to substantiate the comments made about men's bands by my interviewees. However, it is important that the *perceived* comparisons be docu-mented as they are interesting in their own right and even if they are merely dis-cursive they will inevitably have a dialectical impact on empirical reality. The all-female bands I interviewed tended to think there was something special and different about playing with women, rather than with men. It was stated that women were more supportive of each other in the learning process, gave each other care and encouragement. (This belief resonates with women's traditional 'enabling role' throughout history as formal and informal music teachers.[1]) Many women said they would never have had the confidence to join a band or learn how to play an instrument without this female context. I was told that women had more licence for experimentation and were less worried about making mistakes in an all-female band, for they were less likely to be judged. It was often argued that women listened to each other more carefully in rehearsals and on stage than men did, that they were concerned with the total sound rather than just their own part; that is, that they were both more attentive and more generous, less likely to be competitive, domineering, play loudly, and steal the limelight from other band members.

SARA WATTS : Men like to prove something. Whereas, if you play a simplistic line that works it actually lets something else be heard. Alright, it might not make *you* look impressive but it makes the song sound better as a whole. Many men don't appreciate that. Their main priority is to make *them*, as an individual, stand out as a top notch player.

CLAIRE (Atomic Candy): From my experience of seeing other bands—because we do know an awful lot of musicians—men are just so stupid together. I would say they're just out of touch with being able to talk to each other properly and get things sorted out. Or, if they can't be sorted out saying. . . . 'We'll agree to differ', they just end up fighting and punching each other and stupid shit and it doesn't get sorted. But I think women generally take time to talk about things more, say how they're feeling, what they're prepared to put up with and what they're not prepared to put up with. . . . We're not separatists or anything like that. We've just found that working together as women is more productive than working with blokes.

Bands can feel like gangs. This applies to men's bands as well, but many of the women I interviewed consciously rated the friendship aspect just as highly as the music and believed that they were less compartmentalized about their music and non-band lives than men were. Also, compared to men, women were supposedly less into technical aspects and the material clutter of music-making and more into the experience. Feminist bands have tended to be democratic: sharing the lifting and loading and the administration; letting everyone have their say over musical decisions; sharing record royalties out equally regardless of actual authorship, and so forth.

Many women had had the experience of playing in mixed and/or predominantly male bands and some of what these women argued resonated with my own experience of playing in these contexts. All the talk about female supportiveness, however, should not obscure the fact that female bands, like their male

---

[1] 'The definition of femininity as enabling carried on into debates about women's instrumental abilities in the nineteenth and twentieth centuries, such that many people who defended women classical and jazz instrumentalists appealed to notions of feminine sensitivity and cooperation in their playing. This musical expression of femininity as enabling is also perpetuated in the school, as exemplified in the comments of teachers and pupils . . . concerning girls' sensitivity and their cooperative attitudes in relation to music' (Green 1997: 1600).

equivalents, *can* be competitive, argumentative, undemocratic, and split into camps. This is particularly likely as a band makes its way along the career process since, at the professional stage for commercial bands, questions like 'Who contributed how much to this song?' potentially translate into a fortune, when 'sisterhood' can be severely stretched. I do not want to paint a simplistic picture of, on the one hand, totally harmonious all-female bands and, on the other, aggressive, competitive male bands. Some of my interviewees had experienced supportive, enabling relationships with male musicians, since obviously male musicians vary, as do the dynamics of mixed bands where there are differences of social class, 'race', age, and sexuality and also, crucially, differences in musical skills and gigging experience. However, after all these caveats, there will be some differences between male and female bands and, if the ones I have cited are generally true, the reasons are nothing to do with women's essential natures but are a reflection of social construction, because of the way men and women are differently constructed within society at present. In that sense, bands are gendered. Furthermore, all women are oppressed *because* of their gender, since they live in a society in which sexism surrounds them: in advertisements, in the music papers, on TV, in the pub, at venues, in music shops, at record company offices, and on the streets at night. This, then, is a shared experience amongst all female musicians and is liable to create some degree of empathy between them.

Gender inequality is bound to impinge on bands. Why should bands be different from the rest of society where women are often deemed inferior and treated so? Women in mixed bands have often had to be very assertive: 'There's a fair amount of equality but I think I've had to fight to get that space for myself in the band' (Katherine Garrett). Given that the indie/rock world is male-dominated and masculinist, women unsurprisingly tend to suffer from a lack of confidence in joining it, so that an all-women, and especially feminist, band will tend to be more understanding, empathetic, and supportive. Novice women's bands are likely to tolerate low levels of musicianship and create kinds of music different from male bands, partly as a consequence.

The Music

In doing this research, the music of some of the bands I have observed has variously excited, pleased, or inspired me. At other times I have been less musically enthralled, although the webs of social interaction comprising the bands, the audiences, and so forth have always been interesting. The women I interviewed played in such a diversity of genres that it would be impossible to analyse all of them in a book such as this. However, though the focus of this book has not been on the music itself, I shall make a few comments about music.

Some musical styles have been more open to women instrumentalists than others. Punk is particularly supportive for women because of its basic simplicity of musical form, the minimal musical skills required, the ethos of DIY, ama-teurishness, and iconoclasm. Women have also played jazz despite continuing attempts by male musicians to exclude them (Dahl 1984; Placksin 1985; Gourse 1995). Apart from well-known players like Carla Bley and Barbara Thompson, there is a thriving women's jazz scene in London run by Deidre Cartwright and Alison Rayner—'Blow the Fuse' at the Vortex. In contrast to punk, high skill levels are required. Experimental freedom is of the essence and the playing of a wide range of instruments beyond the guitar, drums, and bass of traditional rock and indie bands. A third area where women have preserved and increased a long-standing domain is folk/acoustic music because its 'unplugged' nature allows women to avoid the 'masculine'-coded forest of rock technology. In vivid contrast, the marked absence of women in metal bands is largely due to the fact that they are in style and instrumentation strongly coded as 'masculine'. Although increasing numbers of women go to metal gigs (Walser 1993), in the UK at least, unsurprisingly, female metal musicians remain rare. Lastly, dance music/techno is an area in which you might expect more women, because of its DIY ethos and because the traditional centrality of the guitar has been replaced by keyboards. However, largely because of its highly technical nature, dance is a field relatively closed to women.

In the late 1970s, there was a debate in feminist circles about the existence or possibility of a 'female music'. Although some feminist musicians, at the time, rejected electric music as intrinsically 'masculine' and would only play acous-tically, it was always easier to specify what 'female music' was not (loud, aggress-ive, heavy, throbbing, 'cock rock') rather than what it actually was. 'Women's music' was *supposed* to be more flowing, less structured, lighter, warmer, softer, but beyond that there was little agreement. The idea of a separate female aes-thetic (outside the culture created by men) has also been raised in other idioms, for example 'écriture feminine' in literature and in feminist art practice. Such ideas can be located within the wider theoretical debate between emancipat-ory equality feminism and a feminism which stresses 'difference' (Buikema and Smelik 1995). The argument of 'difference feminists' has sometimes been the essentialist position that women are innately different from men and thus pro-duce intrinsically different music. I would certainly take issue with this because there is nothing essentially masculine or feminine about any kind of music or instrument. Women are capable of rocking out as hard and as heavy as men who, likewise, can play the most gentle and sensitive kinds of acoustic music on the most delicate of instruments. The tradition of male pop groups shows that men's lyrics can be romantic and their vocals soft, while women's lyrics can be impersonal, rebellious, and aggressive. Existing gender differences have been culturally constructed. Moreover, a completely autonomous women's rock/indie music is impossible since women's music, like their writing, is in an inevitable dialogue with existing (male) musics. If too many of the conventions and codes of rock are broken (because they have been created by men) then one is no longer working inside that genre. Maybe that is one reason why many feminist musi-cians in the UK have more of a presence in experimental forms of jazz?

The non-essentialist 'difference' position is that women's music is unique because of their separate location within a patriarchy, in which, on a markedly unequal playing field, the 'feminine' is given a lower value than the 'masculine'. Thus women's participation in rock will always be seen as inferior because of rock's norm of masculinity. However, I would take issue with the very construction of these terms. A woman playing loud and aggressive guitar in a metal band is not playing in a 'masculine' way but merely in a loud and aggressive way. A man playing finger-picked gentle folk-songs is not playing in a 'feminine' way. Certainly, the women musicians I interviewed who played in a heavy style did not consider themselves to be 'masculine' or 'laddish' and strongly resented the notion that they should deny their own strength, loudness, and aggression because it is erroneously perceived as non-feminine, non-female, or non-feminist.

KIM MCAULIFFE : When we first started there were comments from extreme feminists, saying we shouldn't do it. But I think that's a load of rubbish. 'Cause we're into something that supposed to be so macho, showing that there's nothing women can't do. Why shouldn't we do it? We want to bloody do it! It's what we like doing. What right has anybody to say that you shouldn't be doing this? We don't flaunt our bodies or anything, we're just a band playing rock music . . . If you listen to one of our tracks, it doesn't sound like women playing. But, then again, what does women playing sound like? It just sounds like *someone* playing. I don't think it makes any difference if it's a male or female. It all depends on the actual person themselves and how they play.

ENID WILLIAMS : A lot of women . . . tend to play very sort of ethereal music, very spiritual. I like physical, lusty, earthy, passionate music. I was at a rhythm workshop a while back, and the woman who was taking it described the four-four snare drum beat as a white, male, militaristic, fascist, patriarchal rhythm, and I think that's a bit heavy, man!

For feminists who took this position, what demarcated feminist heavy rock from the male variety was how the noise was used and what the songs were about. The notion that women should play gentler music, they argued, is based on the sexist stereotype of conventional femininity. For this feminist punk performer, playing raucous music has been a way of escaping from gender socialization experiences:

VI SUBVERSA : It took a year before I turned my guitar volume up . . . because I was still scared of it, of making a noise to that extent. I turned the knobs down on my guitar for a whole year. And, then, suddenly I thought, 'Fuck it. I'm not going to do that anymore. . . . I get a buzz out of handling big energy and I think it can be subverted. . . . I've learnt how to make a big noise only recently, and I like it. And I'm not going to be told by any boy that I'm on their preserves and get off! . . . I don't feel that because I've got a big voice

I'm any less of a woman. . . . I mean, a woman lion can roar just as loud as a male lion. . . . For me it's undercutting a whole lot of conditioning . . . And, I believe, collectively, women have a right to this. . . . I feel it's some sort of celebration of something very animal and basic. . . . I understand the function of men making a lot of noise. . . . What I object to is that they do it on our backs, and at our expense, and keep us out. That's why the opposite of saying 'Get off our territory!' is I want every woman who wants to make a big noise to get on with it too.

Such women find it bad enough having male musicians and male audiences tell them that they should not (or cannot), play heavy rock, without feminists judging them and reiterating the message.

Within the question of what type of music should be performed, then, are played out some of the key paradoxes of contemporary feminism: 'It aims for individual freedoms by mobilising sex solidarity. It acknowledges diversity among women while positing that women recognise their unity. It requires gender consciousness for its basis, yet calls for the elimination of prescribed gender roles' (Cott 1986: 49). Insofar as women sometimes produce very different music from men this is a result of their different positioning within the sex-gender system: their experiences as women lead them to create the music. Some women I interviewed in the 1980s considered the Raincoats' music to be quintessentially 'female' or 'feminine', as have writers such as Reynolds and Press (1995). There are, clearly, reasons why women should have created this music but there is, however, no reason why men should not be able to play it. Indeed, the Raincoats had a succession of male drummers. Likewise, Reynolds and Press describe Throwing Muses as having a 'female rhythm', yet admit the importance of their male drummer in its creation. Rock's 'phallocentric rhythm' or 'phallic backbeat' is counterposed to 'poly-rhythmic percussion' which is seen as more 'female'. Yet a quick cross-cultural comparison explodes any idea that the latter is particularly 'female' in anything more than a momentarily socially constructed sense since African men make music which is characteristically polyrhythmic and they also tend to hold their guitars high up in a non-phallic way. Indeed, it was African music and reggae which the Raincoats drew on to help create their sound. On the other hand, as a number of my interviewees emphasized, within the Anglocentric genre of rock and indie bands there have been women's bands who could play exactly like male bands but there had not yet been any male bands who played like the Raincoats.

Whenever we use the terms masculine and feminine we risk perpetuating hegemonic gender ideology, giving the impression that women have a monopoly of, say, tenderness and men of aggression. There are clearly a number of masculinities and femininities in existence and gender constructions transmute through time in relation to wider socio-economic changes.[2] Why not describe a piece of music as delicate and intricate rather than as feminine?

[2] See Susan McClary's (1991) interesting exploration of this in classical music.

If the term 'female music' does not actually mean much, the term 'feminist music' is similarly misleading, for feminists have played many kinds of music. 'Womyn's music' (or 'Wimmin's music') was once a useful term for feminist popular music but it only covered a section of the wide range of music that they were playing (and attempting to subvert) during the 1970s and 1980s. What united feminists playing music was simply their feminism: a critical relationship towards gender construction, a commitment to social change, and a polemical musical practice.

Feminist Alternatives

Many bands with strong feminist identities in the 1970s and 1980s were fundamentally opposed to the values which they saw as underpinning the rock industry: hierarchy, competition, and superstardom. Instead, they espoused equality and cooperation and, in order to avoid compromising with the industry, developed a whole range of alternative strategies.[3] An outstanding example of this DIY approach was 1970s/early 1980s Jam Today, who set up their own record label (Stroppy Cow), producing, engineering, promoting, and distributing their own records. Alison Rayner: 'The idea wasn't just for our band. It was a feminist label with a specific kind of feminist politics: anti-capitalism and the straight music business, and the charts, and all that kind of stuff.' Members of Jam Today were also involved in setting up Women's Liberation Music Projects, a Women's Music Newsletter and women's music workshops. They also established an all-female PA company that enabled a decade of women-only bops to flourish. Jam Today acted as an important feminist role model, showing that it was possible for women to learn to do live sound engineering, carry heavy equipment around, and generally do anything and everything a man could within the music world. Women's Revolutions Per Minute (WRPM) also sprang out of this late 1970s feminist alternative culture and is still important today as the UK's sole independent feminist distributor of women's music. (See address in Appendix 3.)

Unlike most forms of work, music-making is immensely pleasurable and thus some bands are prepared to play for little or no remuneration and, as bands outnumber music venues, fierce competition can result which drives down payment from venue owners. Feminist Music Collectives, like many anarchist bands and also the Musicians' Union,[4] tried to limit such competition and to abolish it between bands at individual gigs, by rotating 'headlining' and insisting on equal

---

[3] I have explored these feminist alternatives in more depth in 'Feminist Musical Practice: Problems and Contradictions', in Bennett et al. 1993.

[4] The Musicians' Union has, for many years, fought sexual discrimination in orchestras and bands. It has also backed Women in Music and co-sponsored the Women's Music Festival in Chard since 1990 (Jempson 1993).

pay regardless of status or size of 'following'. Feminist bands explored new ways of working together based on cooperation and support rather than competitive individualism. They challenged the normative context of the rock environment, developing new ways of relating to audiences and to each other, trying to create space for personal relationships and for children. I would argue that it has been feminism which has developed the most radical alternatives within rock.[5]

However, the avoidance of conventional management and record company deals has deprived feminist bands of finance and, without the effective promotion and widespread distribution of major record companies, their records stood no chance of entering the charts. Whilst mass-market success is not the avowed aim of feminist bands, their staying outside the mainstream has caused their audience to be severely curtailed so that there has been a marked absence, for instance, of lesbian bands on the national media, whereas gay male performers and bands have had chart successes and appeared on television.

Faced with the ingrained sexual stereotyping and categorizing of the rock industry, many feminists have felt that too many compromises are involved in signing a record contract, which suggests a fundamental contradiction between being a feminist band and being a chart band. On the other hand, feminist musicians have shown that it is perfectly possible to establish a satisfying (if poorly remunerated) professional musical career, and a stable 'musician' identity, based primarily on gigging and session work. That is, there is a whole music world beyond *Top of the Pops*.[6] Moreover, in contrast to the numerous chart bands who have one or two hits and then vanish overnight, many of these women have been playing for a considerable time and aim to continue for the foreseeable future. Thus, questioning the very notions 'professionalism' and 'success', feminist musicians have tended to see mainstream chart success as involving inevitable compromises with their political beliefs (over clothes, appearance, music, behaviour) and so they have put forward alternative notions:

ALISON RAYNER : I love playing music. It's what I love doing best. I love being in a band. . . . I'm often very, very pleased with what we do. I think we've progressed a lot. I think I've improved as a musician over the years. We've been able to have a group where you can be fulfilled personally, where relations in the band are good, where you enjoy what you play, where you feel you are doing something that you really like doing.

---

[5] However, this alternative musical culture is nowhere near as developed in Britain as in the United States, where feminists have created a whole institutional network of women-only record labels (such as Olivia records, Women's Independent Distribution Network, and Redwood Records), recording studios, and distribution companies.

[6] Women are also involved in other musical worlds. Women instrumentalists have been, traditionally, significantly present in chamber ensembles and they are now increasingly joining orchestras (comment from Dai Griffiths; also Green 1997). Ruth Finnegan (1989) found that in Milton Keynes women far outnumbered men in choirs and, although the brass bands of the older generation were dominated by men, there was an increased proportion of girls in younger bands.

Feminism

'Feminism' is increasingly coming to mean a philosophical approach, whereas the 1970s Women's Liberation Movement was firmly committed to political action for social change. As has been well documented, the nationally organized 'women's movement' became fragmented by the belated recognition and assertion of the importance of the submerged 'differences' of class, 'race', and sexuality in the 1970s. Moreover, this emphasis on 'difference' has been increased by the emergence of postmodern feminists who have taken multiple subject positions and deconstructed the term 'woman'. The logical conclusion of the postmodernist feminist stance is that there are no 'women' and therefore there can be no political activity on their behalf. Hence, all feminisms become meaningless and a political paralysis results. Thus, 'postmodern feminist' could be seen as a contradiction in terms. Amongst others, Coppock, Haydon, and Richter (1995), and many authors in Bell and Klein (1996) have argued this position and I largely agree with them.

First, although I have looked at the body as a 'text' to a certain extent, in contrast to postmodernists I have also discussed bodies as messy unruly physical entities with interiors as well as 'surfaces', for instance, period pains, pregnancies, and breasts that get crushed by guitars. Whilst women do not reduce to their biology, bodies are of some import and we need to assert our 'difference' from men for tactical reasons as and when. For instance, the equipment used by bands has been designed by and for men. It could be redesigned for women. Amplifiers and speakers need not be so heavy and unwieldy, guitars could change shape, and mixing desks could be lowered. Venues can be made safer for women; it merely takes a commitment from management, and if women want clean and efficient changing rooms there is no reason why they should not have them.

Second, although I have urged the deconstruction of the terms 'masculine' and 'feminine', I deliberately retain the term 'woman'. A woman may see herself as *primarily* a teacher or a musician or a mother; she might be black or white, upper, middle, or working class, old or young, but it is as a woman that she experiences fear on the streets at night; it is the fact that she is treated as one of this category 'women' that prevents her from travelling fearlessly abroad on her own. More specifically, if she plays in a band she will be perceived as, and treated as, a woman and face a different set of expectations and judgements as a result. Although it is not the case that each and every woman is oppressed by each and every man, the world is organized in such a way that men *as a group* are privileged over women *as a group*. This does not mean that women are simply 'victims' or passive in the face of this oppression because the very shared knowledge of that oppression can be the source of empowerment and change. To paraphrase Marx, we are engaged in continuously creating the social world we inhabit, but not under conditions of our choosing: there is both 'agency' and 'structure'. Of course, the actual responses of individual women vary. Not every woman is engaged in active resistance; not every woman is a feminist and, even then, it is difficult not to compromise or collude at times. It is also the case that some men are actively engaged in anti-sexist practice. However, no matter what type of 'masculinity' a man can be said to 'perform', no matter how anti-sexist a man is, or oppressed he is in other ways (in terms of social class, 'race', sexuality, etc.), he is not going to be oppressed *as a woman* and he is going to be privileged *as a man*.

Some women musicians did indeed have excellent support from some men (other musicians, a youth worker, a teacher, a father, a husband, a boyfriend, a manager) but it is still the case that women musicians *as a group* suffer from a myriad of sexist assumptions, comments, harassment, prejudice, and so on from men as a group in the rock world, which works to undermine their confidence and impede their musical careers. Although some women successfully circumvent all of the obstacles, large numbers either do not leave the starting gate or fall at the first hurdle. To continue with this metaphor, it is from the start an unequal race, set up in a way that favours men rather than women. Some individual men do nothing to either help or hinder individual women and may think that the whole issue is irrelevant to themselves, but they are (unwitting) beneficiaries of a set-up that is skewed in their favour, in terms of a whole range of material and cultural resources.

Third, whilst I have applauded musicians playing with gender ambiguity and engaging in parody in order to demonstrate the social constructedness of gender, this could just remain at a superficial level where the politics gets lost in mere style. Seen from the perspective of the 1970s feminist generation, the political becomes *merely* the personal, a matter of individual choice rather than solidarity expressed through collective action to solve shared problems:

CAROLINE HUTTON : I look on k. d. lang and I think 'what the fuck were we doing for all those years that someone like k. d. lang is that successful?' It's all form and no content. So, a woman who looks like a young man is being successful. Well, fine. Good. But is she saying anything? Is she hell!

Moreover, if all gender is masquerade then how can the audience tell the difference between the parodic and the non-parodic? An 'innocent' reading constructs exaggerated femininity as simply femininity and misses the irony. It's all in the eye of the beholder and how much 'cultural capital' she or he has. For instance, both Madonna and Courtney Love could just be read as straightforward 'tarts'.

It is hard to know how to tell the difference between thoughtless, common or garden femininity and sophisticated femininity as masquerade. There is snobbery involved here too. There is clearly distinction of value between women's choices to wear precisely similar clothes according to whether they are ignorant and unenlightened or whether they have done cultural studies and read Lacan and made a deliberate and revolutionary choice to wear lacy low-cut bodices (Jeffreys 1996: 366).

Although ideally I would like gender to disappear, nevertheless it is clear that this is unlikely to happen in the foreseeable future and that, however much it is dismantled in theoretical terms, in everyday life a multitude of institutional practices are building it up again and, crucially, reconstructing the genders as markedly unequal with consequent oppressive effects for women as a group. These have to be recognized, analysed, and resisted in the name of 'women'.

Recent History

When I started updating my research, in 1995, a number of things initially struck me. In contrast to the 1970s and 1980s sample, the young women that I was interviewing generally called themselves 'girls' rather than 'women'; only a minority of women described themselves as feminist; and nobody claimed feminism as the main reason why they became a musician. Moreover, the very question 'Are you a feminist?' seemed suddenly problematic. In the 1980s, women answered simply 'yes' or 'no'. In the 1990s, it was either 'yes, but . . .' or 'no, but . . .' followed by a series of qualifications and reservations. Women tied themselves up in verbal knots trying to square the contradictions. Often a woman would start off saying she was not a feminist and end up saying she was, the main concern expressed being a fear of being seen as anti-men. Women believed fervently in sexual equality and equal opportunities but thought that feminists wanted more than equality, and that they took it 'too far' so that, ironically, rather than being anti-sexist, feminism is seen as epitomizing sexism. Confusion reigned. Many younger women said they were not sure what feminism meant and some revealed astonishing misconceptions. Marie: 'When somebody says "feminist" you imagine someone being really dirty and not washing their hair and not wearing make-up, not wearing nice clothes and not looking after herself and burning her bra and bonking every man in sight.' The band of 16-year-olds, Frances Belle, took a long pause before answering and obviously found this to be a difficult question:

AIMEE STEVENS : I think the image that jumps into your mind straightaway when they say 'feminist' is a skinheaded lesbian woman.

TERRI BONHAM : Probably going out and beating up men.

AIMEE STEVENS : Yeah, beating people with their handbags and stuff. But I don't actually know that much about it. We don't talk about that stuff at school or anything.

There was also a concern that feminism was seen by the public as old-fashioned, something a popular musician, especially, would therefore wish to avoid. Charley: 'A year or two ago I would have said 'yeah' and I guess I am [a feminist], but I suppose it's because it's become a really naff thing to say. I don't think about it anymore but, yeah, I am.'

Furthermore, feminists were seen as sexually puritanical and generally anti-fun. (In the early 1970s feminism was, conversely, seen as modern, progressive, youthful, exciting, and sexually adventurous.[7]) Lastly, many women musicians felt that a constant focus on being female was detrimental and served only to reinforce essentialist arguments and, thereby, sexism.

Sadly, in the 1990s, the negative associations of feminism, combined with homophobia, has also led to a resistance to women-only events or even 'women's events' in some places. For instance, 'I think it's fair to say that in Sheffield the word "women's events" is synonymous with "lesbian events" and that means that an awful lot of women *feel* disenfranchised and don't want to participate' (Moira Sutton).

Along with misunderstanding feminism, the young female musicians I interviewed in 1995 displayed a lack of knowledge of the 1970s feminist musical initiatives. This is not surprising as that history seems to have been forgotten and circumstances have changed. The struggle and work involved in just getting women's voices heard, setting up all-women bands, and fighting for women-only spaces are not contemporary issues. Today's struggles are different partly because of what feminism has already achieved and today's young female musicians are unwitting beneficiaries of that earlier history. I had, however, hoped to find some continuity on the local level, with one all-women band spawning another. Sadly, there was no evidence of this and often no sense of local female musical lineage. For instance, the only all-women band in Brighton in 1995 (Tampasm) had never heard of their feminist predecessors: early 1980s the Bright Girls and before them, the Devil's Dykes. Likewise, although many older (male) musicians remember Oxford's first all-women band the Mistakes, in 1995 the two all-women bands Beaker and Twist had no knowledge of that feminist history.

What did strike me, however, was the confidence and assertiveness of the young 1990s interviewees. I believe that this is in itself an effect of feminism, since it is now a familiar term and its ideas have spread throughout the world. As Naomi Wolf (1994) says, there has been a 'genderquake'. I have already mentioned the importance of feminist mothers amongst my 1990s interviewees and one could argue that *all* women have absorbed some aspects of feminism (like higher aspirations, and basic feminist assumptions of sexual equality) and that it has thus had lingering long-term effects. That is, most women *are* feminist despite not owning the word. It would be hard to find a young woman who did not believe in sexual equality, for instance. The teenagers and 20-year-olds that I interviewed in 1995 and 1996 were aware of sexism and of the particular obstacles which women faced although they did not wish to dwell on them. They were imbued with a spirit of 'we have every right to make music, too and we will brook no opposition'. Being in a band was a matter of individual determination. Indeed, it is not such a big deal to be playing in an all-women band today; it is more accepted and not the kind of militant political statement that it was in the 1970s. In strong contrast to the 1970s, even 16-year-olds are playing

---

[7] The situation seems a little different in the USA, where more bands espouse the term. The all-women band L7, for instance, started Rock for Choice with the Fund for the Feminist Majority.

in bands, whereas in pre-feminist days, the existence of schoolgirl bands (like Tampasm, Kid Candy, and Frances Belle) would have been inconceivable.

Feminism, then, has profoundly affected the outlook of contemporary young women, giving them self-confidence, high expectations, and determination. They *expect* to be treated equally in a way that my generation did not.

On the other hand, the amount of *actual* material and structural change is often exaggerated. Sex discrimination legislation and equal opportunities policies have not made women equal in terms of pay, power, and status. The world of work is gender-segregated and women lack equal opportunities, while in schools the 'hidden curriculum' of negative gender dynamics and harassment persists, unaffected by the 1970s legislation (Coppock, Haydon, and Richter 1995), and in the home there has been only a minimal redistribution of domestic labour. At the same time, since 1979, successive Conservative governments developed a flood of repressive social policies which further inhibit women's liberation. Women remain unequal: in the workplace, in political representation, in education, and in the home. There has also been an international 'backlash' mobilized against feminism (Faludi 1992; French 1992; Oakley and Mitchell 1997). As Kate Figes says,

> **We have bought the rhetoric of equal opportunity hook, line and sinker. Its policies, and our equality legislation, have been bolted on to a structure of institutionalized discrimination which still keeps women economically dependent on men and sees motherhood as a luxury rather than necessity. The rhetoric of equal opportunity has merely forced such discrimination to become covert where once it was unabashed and easier to detect.**
> **(Figes 1994: 6–7)**

And in relation to music-making, my research has shown that whatever the attitudes and outlook of today's young female musicians, they still have to contend with a barrage of obstacles because they are women.

Back in 1982, many of the women musicians I interviewed believed that by the late 1980s there would be as many women musicians as men. In retrospect, this seems extraordinarily optimistic. The numbers are increasing, but slowly. (Similarly, although the proportion of women at indie gigs is increasing and you even see women stage-diving these days, the majority of the gig-goers continue to be men. Indeed, this is even true at feminist bands' gigs.) The greater visibility of women playing instruments is of crucial importance, for most women musicians have been inspired by seeing other women play. In each passing decade the number of female role models increases. Gradually changes in other areas of young women's lives are having an effect on popular music-making. Feminist ideas have permeated every aspect of society: schools, magazines, newspapers, television, etc. In particular, increased sensitivity to gender issues in technical education has been having a slow but steady effect: young women are more confident on computers and with electrical equipment than in previous decades. The more sympathetic response to popular music within schools is giving girls an increased opportunity to learn rock instruments. This needs to be stepped up and all school students should be given the opportunity to learn to play instruments, use electronic musical equipment, and make videos. However, this in itself is not enough. As Lucy Green's research on music in schools shows 'pupils and teachers collude with each other in the perpetuation of the gender politics of music', confirming what is taken to be 'natural, normal common sense' (Green 1997). It often takes great courage for a girl to challenge 'common sense' and she will need support in the process. What is required in schools, then, is active intervention by teachers to disrupt the gendered status quo. In the teaching of music in schools, the contribution of women to popular music as instrumentalists (as well as singers) should be stressed. More than the inclusion of women players in the syllabus is required, however. The very issues that I have raised in this book should be discussed: the gender politics of music should be part of the schools curriculum. On the more practical front, all-female bands should be encouraged in schools and youth clubs. Just one enlightened, sensitive teacher or youth worker (female or male) who is dedicated to challenging the gendered musical status quo can have an immense effect in a particular locality, radically increasing the number of girls playing in bands. For example, in the mid-1990s, with only a handful of all-women bands in the whole of the city of Oxford, a local Oxfordshire village was sporting two bands composed of 15-year-old girls. As mentioned in Chapter 5, this was the result of one (male) youth worker's efforts.

Popular music is more important than is usually acknowledged, for it is actively constitutive of gender and sexual differences via the symbolic codes of the musical discourse. If we were to reach a point where as many women played rock as men, then rock would cease to be a male cultural discourse and would no longer be doing 'gender work' in relation to hegemonic masculinity. Women playing in rock and indie bands, therefore, are helping to render rock and indie more ambiguous in terms of gender and, thereby, to deconstruct the masculinity of the discourse.

I look forward to the day when there are as many women playing in rock bands as men, when gender will be as irrelevant to music-making as height. I await this not merely because I want to see an end to sexist constraints on women, but also because of the effects this would have on rock as a discourse. In playing styles, men would no longer be the yardstick against which women are measured. Playing rock would no longer denote masculinity if half the people playing it were women. Rock could still be about rebellion, but not necessarily a male one and the music would be sure to change. Lastly, virtually every woman that I interviewed told me of the tremendous pleasure, creativity, and fulfilment that playing in a band can bring.

JILL MYHILL : I love writing songs. I love doing gigs. I love recording . . . I love rehearsing. I love travelling . . . I really like the people I'm in a band with. Once you've done it, it's so exciting that you have to do it again.

Why should boys have all the fun?

Media Surveys: 1988 and 1996

Two media surveys confirmed the relative absence of women from rock bands, although I must emphasize that my argument does not rest on this content analysis. The surveys afforded simple snapshots of the situation during two particular weeks (commencing 2 April 1988 and 15 July 1996) and are used merely as an illustration. I watched music programmes on television, listened to a cross-section of Radio 1 programmes, and read the weekly and monthly music magazines and other magazines which contained a fair proportion of music coverage.

The national media reflect a number of separate, though overlapping, spheres of popular music. First, there is the world of rock and 'indie', represented in the album charts, the 'serious' music magazines, and in the specialist magazines catering for musicians and recording engineers. The local rock/indie band scene is part of this, as is the audience for evening Radio 1 programmes. This is a predominantly male domain and is perceived as 'harder' than the wider one of pop. Second, there is the world of 'pop': the singles chart, daytime radio, television programmes, and music magazines such as *Smash Hits* and *Top of the Pops*. Third, there are a number of much smaller specialist fields focusing on a particular genre of music, such as 'soul' and 'heavy metal'.

THE ROCK WORLD 1988

In 1988 roughly 10 per cent of performers on evening radio programmes were female and, of these, most were vocalists (see Table 1). In the 'serious' music magazines women's share of the text was low. In the *Melody Maker* women had

TABLE 1. Evening Radio Programmes: Performers by Gender, 1st week April 1988 (%)

	FEMALE	MALE
John Peel	11	89
Simon Mayo	10	90
Andy Kershaw	4	96

TABLE 2. The Music Press: Illustrations by Gender, 1st week April 1988 (%)

	FEMALE	MALE
Melody Maker	15	85
New Musical Express	17	83
Sounds	14	86
Q	13	87
Record Mirror	8	92
Underground	15	8

about 15 per cent of the coverage. In the *New Musical Express* roughly 47 per cent of the main feature articles were on women, in the *Record Mirror* 9 per cent, and in *Sounds* 0 per cent. Likewise, *Q* magazine, *The Face*, *Sky*, *i-D*, and *Underground* magazine were mostly concerned with male performers in terms of both articles and reviews. The proportion of illustrations depicting men and women was similar (see Table 2). Women formed only 15 per cent of the total number of performers in the Top 40 albums, again mainly vocalists. In the total of 79 performers, there were less than five women instrumentalists.

The specialist trade magazines were overwhelmingly directed towards male consumption, with male stars being used to test equipment and to talk about their technique and playing styles. In *Guitarist*, two out of eight feature articles were on women musicians, but this was exceptional. The feature articles in all the other magazines were about male musicians and nearly all the contributions to the letters pages came from men. Women's bodies were often used merely for their decoration or titillation factor in some of these magazines. A woman may be seen clutching a guitar who, judging by the length of her fingernails, is clearly not a guitarist herself. Second, in a number of advertisements the guitar was very clearly being used as a phallic symbol. In the magazine for drummers, *Rhythm* (aptly subtitled Brothers in Arms), the absence of women was total, which reflects the way in which drumming is seen as a very masculine activity. Most of the ads used famous drummers as their means of selling equipment. There was not a single woman pictured playing the drums.

THE POP WORLD 1988

In the broader world of 'pop', women performers featured more often. Compared to albums, a higher proportion of records in the singles chart were by women. Likewise, more records by women were played on daytime radio. However, what stood out clearly was that the majority of singles were still recorded by men; most of the women performers in the singles charts were vocalists; and the percentage of women playing instruments was very low.

On the Radio 1 Chart 40 on Easter Sunday 1988, about 25 per cent of the musicians were women. The vast majority of these were vocalists. The same sort of pattern was discernible in daytime radio play (see Table 3) and on TV (see Table 4). On *Top of the Pops* there was not a single woman playing an instrument. More-over, although women performers are typically singers, there are often more

TABLE 3. Musicians' Trade Magazines: Illustrations by Gender, 1st week April 1988 (%)

	FEMALE	MALE
Guitarist	11[a]	89
Guitar World	10[b]	90
International Musician	15	85
Music Technology	18[c]	82
Rhythm	1	99
Home and Studio Recording	—	100

[a] But one picture was of a non-musician.
[b] Of the eight pictures of women, only four were playing what are generally thought of as rock instruments: two were playing the flute and two the violin.
[c] If you take out those pictures where women were used for merely decorative purposes (gazing admiringly at men) then the figure was reduced to 9 per cent.

TABLE 4. Daytime Radio Programmes: Performers by Gender, 1st week April 1988 (%)

	FEMALE	MALE
Chartbusters	15	85
Steve Wright	22	78
Simon Bates	28	72
Gary Davies	20	80
Singled Out	25	75

male vocalists than female. In one week's worth of popular music on TV, the viewer would have seen 58 female and 64 male lead vocalists, 148 males playing instruments but only 8 women, 2 men doing backing vocals and 16 women. Overall, women represented 26 per cent of all TV performers, a figure very much in line with daytime radio programmes (see Table 5).

In the music magazines aimed at this end of the market, the preponderance of pictures of male musicians reflected the dominance of men within the music and the use of these pictures as pin-ups. In *Number One*, front and back covers sported male pin-ups, and there was a free badge picturing four male musician 'heart-throbs'. As in other magazines of this type, such as *Smash Hits*, the musicians were not seen playing their instruments, and the music itself was not discussed, the focus being on the performers as stars and personalities. In *Smash Hits Collection 1987: An A to Z of Pop*, women took a mere 12 per cent of the coverage. Lastly, the music coverage in girls' and women's magazines (*Look Now*, *Jackie, Girl, Over 21, My Guy, Blue Jeans*, and *Mizz*) was overwhelmingly about men. The women performers featured in these magazines comprised just the same few vocalists.

Turning to specialist musical genres, *Blues and Soul* (and *Black Music* and *Jazz Review*) devoted about 25 per cent of the main feature articles to women

TABLE 5. TELEVISION PROGRAMMES

	FEMALE	MALE
Top of the Pops (31.3.88)		
Lead vocals	4	6
Backing vocals	2	—
Instrumentalists	—	20
The Chart Show (1.4.88)		
Lead vocals	19	23
Instrumentalists	5	39
Roxy the Network Show (1.4.88)		
Instrumentalists	—	13
America's Top 10 (1.4.88)		
Lead vocals	11	13
Instrumentalists	1	19
Europe's Top Ten (1.4.88)		
Vocals	4	3
Instrumentalists	—	4
Meltdown (1.4.88)		
Lead vocals	—	1
Backing vocals	2	—
Instrumentalists	—	4
The Tube (3.4.88—repeat from 1983)		
Vocals	9	9
Instrumentalists	2	28
Daytime Live (5.4.88)		
Vocals	3	2
Instrumentalists	—	5
Daytime Live (7.4.88)		
Lead vocals	—	1
Backing vocals	1	—
Instrumentalists	—	4
Roxy the Network Show (5.4.88)		
Vocals	4	4
Instrumentalists	—	12

(predominantly vocalists). In *Echoes* (soul), roughly 15 per cent of the articles were about women performers and in *International Country Music News*, women were allocated no more than 25 per cent of the text. Unsurprisingly, the heavy metal magazine *Solid Rock* evidenced the greatest discrepancy. Of 236 pictures of musicians in the text, four were of women. Advertising pictures were exclusively male. The text was, I estimate, 99 per cent about male musicians (see Table 6).

TABLE 6. Specialist Genre Press: Illustrations by Gender, 1st week April 1988 (%)

	FEMALE	MALE
Blues and Soul	25	75
Echoes (soul)	17	83
International Country Music News	17	83
Solid Rock (metal)	2	98

TABLE 7. Q Magazine Album Reviews

	1988		1996	
	FEMALE	MALE	FEMALE	MALE
Solo	26	74	32	68
Single-sex bands	0	100	3	97

THE ROCK AND INDIE WORLD 1996

Astonishingly, in the two leading 'serious' music weeklies the proportion of women in the pictures remained as low as in 1988: *Melody Maker* 15 per cent and *NME* 12 per cent. The covers of both leading publications featured male bands and my estimate for the coverage of women musicians in the text was about 15 per cent. There was one interesting development. In each issue of *Melody Maker* in the mid-1990s there was a handful of ads asking for female instrumentalists. However, in terms of adverts for vocalists, gender differentiation is still apparent with some of the ads for female vocalists focusing on physical attributes more than musical talent e.g. a 'Female Jelly Baby' is requested in *MM* 8 June 1996 and no previous experience is necessary.

In *Q* magazine the proportion of feature article space allocated to women was significantly greater than eight years previously, although the majority of the features were still on men. Women's proportional presence in the album reviews had increased but not dramatically so (see Table 7).

Over half of the Top 40 albums had no female presence at all. Nearly half were by all-male bands but none were by all-female bands. Of the total number of instrumentalists involved (which I estimate to be somewhere between 80 and 100), there were only half a dozen women (similar to 1988). In all, there were only fourteen women involved in the Top 40 records (again, similar to 1988) (see Table 8). Gender composition in the UK Top Independent albums and singles was more marked than in the main album chart. In terms of singles, one all-male band, Oasis, claimed nine places and, in all, twenty-five out of the thirty albums had no female input whatsoever. There was one female solo album and three records with female vocals. There was only one female instrumentalist in the whole album chart. Women's place in the UK Top 30 independent albums was somewhat greater, yet there were still only half a dozen women playing instruments (see Table 9).

In *Guitar* August 1996, all the profiles were of male guitarists. There were eighty depictions of men playing guitars but only two of women and one of these

TABLE 8. UK Top 40 Albums (%)

	2.4.88	20.7.96
Band albums		
All female	0	0
All male	40	33
Male with at least one female[a]	15	18
Solo albums		
Female solo albums	15	18
Male solo albums	23	23
Mixed artists[b] and unknown		
	7	8

[a] Usually only one, and usually the vocalist.
[b] Mainly male.

TABLE 9. UK Top 30 Independent Charts 20.7.1996 (%)

	SINGLES	ALBUMS
Band		
All female	0	3
All male	80	60
Male with at least one female[a]	10	20[b]
Solo		
Female solo albums	3	3
Male solo albums	3	13
Unknown	4	—

[a] All but one were vocalists.
[b] Mainly 'female-fronted'.

seemed to be stereotyping the insecurity of women, by showing a scantily clad and worried looking woman under the sentence 'Don't Drop That Guitar' (an advert for security guitar straps). The back cover of the August 1996 issue of *Guitar School* magazine shows music equipment and a sexy woman clearly there for the *male* guitarist (to have sex with). The only sizeable picture of a woman in *Total Guitar* was located over the advertising line 'The best players play the best pickups': the scantily dressed woman is positioned as groupie. On the other hand, compared to 1988, there is an absence of blatantly phallic and naively macho 'cock rock' advertisements, such as the earlier 'Make it Big with an Aphex Aural Exciter' or 'Mega-Muscle', although there were still plenty of hairy chests and medallions in evidence.

In terms of text, only one magazine had a main feature article on a woman. *Guitar School* had a feature article on Sinead Lohan, whilst the other six articles

TABLE 10. Musicians' Trade Magazines: Illustrations by Gender, July/August 1996 (%)

	FEMALE	MALE
Guitar	2	98
Guitar School	5	95
Guitarist	4	96
Total Guitar	4[a]	96
Bass Player	4	96

[a] All playing acoustic guitar.

Table 11. The Phoenix Festival 1996

	%
The Main Stage	
Female bands	3
Male bands	68
Female artist with male backing band	6
Mixed bands	23
The Guardian—Stage Two	
Female bands	0
Female artist with male backing band	0
Mixed bands	15
Male bands/acts	85

were on men. However, her playing abilities were questioned. The title was 'I can play, really' and asks, 'Who says a woman's place is in the kitchen?' The (male) author later comments, 'As a "girl with a guitar", one might expect Sinead to opt for a dainty acoustic, but no, her current instrument is a black Godin Acousticaster.' Apart from a short piece on Suzi Quatro, *Bass Player* was virtually an all-male magazine. These magazines typically contained transcriptions of pieces for purchasers to learn to play, all of which were written by men, as were all the technical advice pages and playing advice. All the covers depicted male guitarists and a CD which came free with two of the magazines predictably featuring male players.

As can be seen, then, there has been little change in the gender composition of these magazines, in terms of the amount of space devoted to women in either the text or in illustrations (see Table 10). Any would-be or beginning female guitarist is still confronted with a solidly masculine world.

Finally, I decided to do a gender breakdown of the acts for one major festival and I chose the Phoenix 1996, the UK's first ever four-day festival (18–21 July). Bjork was headlining on the main stage on the Saturday night, but women's presence was not proportionally high (see Table 11). Women were particularly absent from the dance stages, where nearly all the DJs were male.

TABLE 12. UK Top 40 Singles (%)

	2.4.88	20.7.96
All-female bands	3	5
All-male bands	25	45
Mixed/male bands with at least one female	28	18
Female solo	32	8
Male solo	12	20

TABLE 13. TV Programmes[a]

	FEMALE	MALE
Top of the Pops (19.7.96)		
Vocals	8	8
Instrumentalists	3[b]	15
The Chart Show (20.7.96)		
Vocals	1	30
Instrumentalists	5	36

[a] Actual numbers.
[b] None was playing a traditional 'rock' instrument; instead they played keyboards, violin, and cello.

THE POP WORLD 1996

Compared to 1988, there was a surprisingly low number of female soloists in the mainstream singles chart: only three, as against thirteen in 1988. As in 1988, the vast majority of the women involved in any way in the chart were vocalists. In contrast to eight years previously, there were two all-women outfits in the 1996 chart but both were vocal groups and did not play instruments. In contrast, there were sixteen all-male bands. Identical to the 1988 album charts, over half of the top singles (25) had no female input at all. There were only four or five women playing instruments in the singles chart in 1988; in 1996 there seemed to be even less (see Table 12). When you compare women's presence on these two programmes with their equivalents eight years ago, the statistics are remarkably similar, indicating minimal change (see Table 13).

A female singer was on the cover of *Top of the Pops* monthly magazine and there were feature articles on two female singer-songwriters, three female vocal groups, and five female vocalists. That said, the majority of the magazine was devoted to male performers. The front cover of the July 1996 *Smash Hits* magazine pictured a male. Of the main features, four concerned male stars and only one was about a woman. Altogether, *Smash Hits* gave space to two female vocal groups, and three vocalists; the rest of the magazine was overwhelmingly about male performers.

As an additional check, I analysed Jools Holland's *Later presents Britbeat* (15 September 1996). There were nineteen women on this programme, which represented 19 per cent of the total. Of these nineteen women, ten were playing orchestral stringed instruments, one was a conductor, and two were backing vocalists. There were only six women playing rock instruments: two keyboard players and the four women in Elastica.

Alphabetical List of Interviewees

The names in inverted commas are pseudonyms because I carried out the 1980s interviews under conditions of confidentiality. However, I have since obtained permission to reveal some of the names. All of the 1990s interviewees are cited under their real names.

Aimee Stevens. Guitarist in the 1990s mainly female band Frances Belle (Eynsham, Oxfordshire). Age: 16.

Ali Smith. Saxophone and vocals in 1990s mixed band Diatribe. Age: 40. Later a member of Mothers With Attitude (Oxford).

Ali West. Keyboard player in 1980s all-female semi-professional feminist power pop band the Mistakes (Oxford). Age: 27.

Alison Rayner. Bass player in 1980s all-female professional jazz-Latin-rock band Jam Today (London). Age: 29. Later member of the Guest Stars and other bands.

Amelia Fletcher. Guitar and vocals in 1990s professional mixed indie pop band Heavenly (Oxford). Age: 29.

Andrea. Keyboard player in 1990s all-female semi-professional band Mambo Taxi (London). Age: 29.

'Angela'. Saxophone player and vocalist in 1980s post-punk band (Midlands). Age: 19.

Anna Power. Guitarist in 1990s all-female soul-funk dance band Sub Rosa (Nottingham). Age: 32.

'Anne'. Keyboard player in two all-female 1980s rock bands (York). Age: 28.

'Annette'. Percussionist in 1980s mixed reggae band (Oxford). Age: 20.

Barbara Stretch. Vocalist in 1980s all-female professional jazz-Latin-rock band Jam Today (London). Age: 20s.

'Becky'. Bass player in 1980s mainly-female new wave band (London). Age: 25.

'Beth'. Saxophone player in various 1980s bands (Birmingham). Age: 30.

'Brenda'. Vocals and guitar in 1980s professional mixed new wave band (London). Age: 29.

Bunty Murtagh. Guitarist in the 1980s all-female professional pop standards band the Mission Belles (London). Age: 39.

Candida Doyle. Keyboard player in 1990s mixed commercially successful high-profile professional pop band Pulp (Sheffield). Age: 33.

Candy Ballantyne. Keyboard player in 1980s mixed new wave band Jane Goes Shopping (Oxford). Age: 27.

Caroline Appleyard. Bass player in 1990s all-female metal band Treacle (Sheffield). Age: 26.

Caroline Hutton. Record distributor, Women's Revolutions Per Minute (Birmingham, 1990s).

Caroline Scallon. Saxophone player in 1990s mixed soul band Soul Devotion (Oxford). Age: 22.

Cerys Matthews. Vocalist in 1990s mainly-male professional band Catatonia (Wales).

Charley. Guitarist and vocalist in 1990s all-female indie band Frantic Spiders (London). Age: 24.

Charlotte Clark. Vocalist in 1990s all-female punk band Tampasm (Brighton). Age: 16.

'Christine'. Participant at 1980s young women's music workshop (Oxford). Age: 15.

Claire. Vocalist in 1990s all-female rock band Atomic Candy (Nottingham). Age: 31.

Claire Lemmon. Guitarist and vocalist in 1990s all-female semi-professional indie band Sidi Bou Said (London). Age: 20s.

Clare Howard. Drummer in 1990s all-female indie band Beaker and ex-Death By Crimpers (Oxford). Age: 25.

'Deb'. Sound engineer with 1980s all-female feminist pop band. Also vocalist (Brighton). Age: 23.

Debbie Smith. Guitarist in 1990s mixed commercially successful high-profile professional pop band Echobelly (London). Age: 28.

Dee. Vocalist in 1990s professional all-female vocal and dance group Every Woman (Sheffield). Age: 33.

Deidre Cartwright. Guitarist in 1980s professional all-female jazz-Latin-rock band Jam Today (London). Age: 20s. Later presenter of the TV programme *Rock School*. Plays in many contexts.

Delia. Guitarist in 1990s semi-professional all-female band Mambo Taxi (London). Age: 25.

'Diana'. Guitarist in various 1980s bands (London). Age: 20s.

Emma Anderson. Guitarist and vocalist in 1990s mixed commercially successful professional indie band 'Lush' (London). Age: 29.

Enid William. Bass player with 1980s professional all-female metal band Girlschool (London). Age: 27.

Fran. Bass player in various 1990s all-female bands in Nottingham: Mothers of the Future, Sub Rosa, The Very Good Rock'n'Roll Band.

Fran Rayner. Sound engineer with 1980s all-female professional feminist jazz-Latin-rock band Jam Today (London). Age: 20s.

Gail Greenwood. Bass player in 1990s professional mixed indie band Belly (America). Age: 36. Later played in L7.

Gayl. Bass player in 1990s semi-professional all-female indie band Sidi Bou Said (London). Age: 23.

'Gina'. Sound engineer with various 1980s bands (London). Age: 31.

Hannah Collett. Vocalist in the 1990s mainly female band Frances Belle (Eynsham). Age: 15.

'Harriet'. Keyboard player in 1980s all-female pop band (London). Age: 26.

'Heather'. Keyboard player in 1980s mixed pop band (Oxford). Age: 22.

'Hilary'. Guitarist in 1980s all-female rock band (Yorkshire). Age: 37.

'Hilda'. Drummer in 1980s all-female pop band Noisy Neighbours (Coventry). Age: 33.

Jackie Crew. Drummer in 1980s professional all-female jazz-Latin-rock band Jam Today (London). Age: 20s.

'Jane'. Guitar and vocals in 1980s all-female pop band (Yorkshire). Age: 26.

'Janice'. Keyboard player in 1980s all-female pop band (Yorkshire). Age: 34.

'Jayne'. Manager of various 1980s bands (London). Age: 30s.

'Jean'. Vocalist in various 1980s bands (Birmingham). Age: 28.

Jennifer Bishop. Bass player in 1990s all-female punk band Tampasm (Brighton). Age: 16.

Jill Myhill. Guitarist and vocalist in 1990s semi-professional all-women indie-rock band Valley of the Dolls (Reading). Age: 32.

'Joy'. Keyboard player in 1980s all-female pop band (London). Age: 30.

Jude Sacker. Keyboard player. Runs women's music workshop (Sheffield, 1990s).

Judy Parsons. Drummer in 1980s all-female pop band the Belle Stars (London). Age: 31. Previously with the Mistakes and the Bodysnatchers.

'Julia'. Guitarist in 1980s all-female pop band (Brighton). Age: 27.

Julie Ellison. Runs women's music workshop (Sheffield, 1990s).

Juliet Bowerman. Bass player in 1990s all-female indie band Twist (Oxford). Age: 25.

'Kassandra'. Guitar, keyboards, and vocals in 1980s semi-professional mainly female new wave band (London). Age: 20s.

Kate Wissenbach. Guitarist in 1990s all-female indie band Twist (Oxford). Age: 23.

'Kath'. Drummer in 1980s mainly female rock band (London). Age: 21.

Katherine Garrett. Guitar and keyboards in 1990s mixed professional pop band the Mystics (Oxford). Age: 23.

Kathryn. Guitarist and vocalist in 1990s all-female indie band Frantic Spiders (London). Age: 22.

Kim McAuliffe. Guitarist in 1980s professional all-female metal band Girlschool (London). Age: 28.

Laetitia. Synthesizer and vocals in 1990s professional mixed indie band Stereolab.

'Linda'. Administrator of 1980s women's music project (London).

Louise Hartley. Guitarist and bass player in 1990s mainly female band Kid Candy (Birmingham). Age: 18.

Manda Rin. Keyboards and vocals in 1990s high-profile professional mixed pop band Bis (Glasgow). Age: 17.

Mandy. Bass player in 1990s mixed professional indie band Ms45 (Liverpool).

Marcella Detroit. Guitar and vocals (Canada, 1990s). A professional musician with her mainly-female own band. Age: 40.

Margaret Thompson. Bassist in 1980s all-female professional band the Mission Belles (London). Age: 42.

Marie. Vocalist in 1990s professional all-female vocal group Every Woman (Sheffield). Age: 26.

Marion Asch. Guitarist in 1980s all-female professional band the Mission Belles (London). Age: 42.

Mary. Guitarist in 1990s all-female semi-professional rock band Atomic Candy (Nottingham). Age: 30.

Mary. Guitar and vocals in 1990s mixed professional indie band Stereolab.

Mary Genis. Semi-professional bass player in 1990s mixed reggae band Dread Warlock (Reading). Age: 41.

Melanie Woods. Drummer in 1990s all-female professional indie band Sidi Bou Said (London). Age: 26.

Miriam Cohen. Bass player in 1990s mainly-female band Kid Candy (Birmingham). Age: 18.

Moira Sutton. Studio manager: Red Tape Studios (Sheffield, 1990s).

'Naomi'. Participant in 1980s young women's music workshop (Oxford). Age: 15.

Natasha Atlas. Vocalist in 1990s mainly male professional indie dance band Transglobal Underground (London). Age: 32. Also solo performer.

'Roberta'. Music tutor at 1980s women's recording studio and music resources centre (London).

Ros Davis. Multi-intrumentalist in various 1980s all-women bands: Rash, Contraband, and the York Street Band (York) Age: 30s.

Rosemary Schonfeld. Founder of Ova Music Studio (recording studio and music resource centre for women and girls, now called Ovatones) (London, 1980s). Also member of acoustic duo Ova.

Sam Battle. Vocalist in 1990s all-female indie band Beaker (Oxford). Age: 22.

'Sandra'. Drummer in 1980s all-female pop band (Yorkshire). Age: 26.

Sara Watts. Guitarist in 1990s all-female metal band Treacle (Sheffield). Age: 20.

'Sarah'. Vocals and percussion in 1980s all-female pop band (Brighton). Age: 30.

Shareen. Guitar and vocals in 1990s mixed professional indie band Ms45 (from America).

Sharon. Vocalist in 1990s professional all-female vocal group Every Woman (Sheffield). Age: 24.

Skin. High-profile vocalist in 1990s professional band Skunk Anansie (London). Age: 28.

'Sophie'. Bass player in 1980s all-female rock band (London). Age: 22.

Steph Hillier. Sound engineer, ex-band manager, and record label manager (London, 1990s).

Sue Smith. Vocals and percussion in 1990s mixed band Aquabats (Oxford). Age: 46. Later in Mothers With Attitude.

'Suke'. Guitarist in 1980s all-female commercially successful pop band (London). Age: 28.

Suzanne. Vocalist in 1990s all-female professional vocal and dance group Every Woman (Sheffield). Age: 23.

'Sylvia'. Bass player in 1980s all-female pop band (Yorkshire). Age: 29.

Teresa Hooker. Guitarist in 1990s all-female band indie band Beaker and ex-Death By Crimpers (Oxford). Age: 26.

Terri Bonham. Bass player in the 1990s mainly female band Frances Belle (Eynsham). Age: 16.

Terry Hunt. Guitarist in 1980s all-female professional jazz-Latin-rock band Jam Today (London). Age: 28.

Val Lloyd. Drummer in 1980s all-female band rock band Tour de Force (London). Age: 20s.

Vanessa. Bass player in 1990s all-female rock band the Fabulous Jam Tarts (Birmingham). Age: 42.

'Veronica'. Keyboard player in 1980s mixed pop band (Oxford). Age: 22.

Vi Subversa. Guitar and vocals in 1980s mixed punk band Poison Girls (London). Professional. Age: 47.

Vicky Aspinall. Violinist in 1980s mainly-female professional new wave band the Raincoats (London).

Yolande Charles. Professional bass player with Marcella Detroit, ex-bass player with Paul Weller (1990s). Age: 25.

Some Useful Addresses

Women's Revolutions Per Minute (WRPM)
Caroline Hutton
36 Newport Road
Birmingham, B12 8QD
UK
Tel. 0121-449 7041
Fax 0121-442 2139
E-Mail: wrpm@mail.globalnet.co.uk

Women in Music
BAC
Lavender Hill
London, SW11 5TF
UK
Tel. 0171-978 4823
Fax 0171-978 7770
E-Mail:
106224.2125@Compuserve.com

Music, Gender, Education Newsletter
Rosemary Evans (editor)
MGEN, PO Box 14
Manchester, M23 0RY
UK
Tel. 0161-902 9893
E-Mail: revans@wmrc.u-net.com

Chard Festival of Women in Music
Six Gables
Otterford
Chard
Somerset, TA20 3QS
UK
Tel./Fax 01460-66115

Women's Jazz Archive
8 Chaddesley Terrace
Mount Pleasant
Swansea, SA1 6HB
UK
Tel. 01792 466083

Musicians' Union
60–2 Clapham Road
London, SW9 0JJ
UK
Tel. 0171-582 5566
Fax 0171-582 9805

Select Discography

Atlas, Natasha, *Halim*. 1996 (Nation NATCD 1087).

Belle Stars, the, *Sign of the Times*. 1982 (Stiff SEE 245).

Belly, *Star*. 1993 (4AD CAD 3002CD).
—— *King*. 1995 (4AD CAD 5004CD).

Bis, *The New Transistor Heroes*. 1997 (Wiija Records WIJCD 1064).

Bodysnatchers, the, *Let's Do Rock Steady*. 1980 (Two-Tone CHS TT9).
—— *Easy Life*. 1980 (Two-Tone CHS TT12).

Catatonia, *The Sublime Magic of Catatonia* (The Songs 1994–1995) 1996 (Nursery NYSCD 12X).

Detroit, Marcella, *Jewel*. 1994 (London Records 828491–2).
—— *Feeler*. 1996 (AAA Records AAACD1).

Echobelly, *King of the Kerb*. 1996 (Columbia ESCA 6439).
—— *Everyone's Got One*. 1997 (Fauve FAUV 003CD).

Girlschool, *Demolition*. 1980 (Bronze BRON 525).
—— *Hit and Run*. 1981 (Bronze BRON 534).
—— *The Best of Girlschool*. 1993 (DOJO CD 103).
—— *From the Vaults*. 1994 (Sequel NEMCO 642).

Guest Stars, the, *The Guest Stars*. 1984 (The Guest Stars GS10C 1984).
—— *Live in Berlin* (Eigelstein EF23).

Gymslips, the, *Rocking with the Renees*. N.d. (Abstract).

Heavenly, *The Decline and Fall of Heavenly*. 1994 (SARAH 623CD).
—— *Operation Heavenly*. 1996 (Wiija WIJC D1053).

Jam Today, *Stereotyping*. 1980 (Stroppy Cow).

Lush, *Ladykillers*. 1996 (4AD BAD 6002 CD).
—— *Lovelife*. 1996 (4AD CAD 6004 CD).
—— *Light from a Dead Star*. 1996 (4AD CAD 4011CD).

Mambo Taxi, *In Love with Clawfist*. 1994 (Hunk ACDC 007).

Mistakes, the, *Radiation/16 Pins*. 1981 (Twist and Shout TNS 2 1981).
—— *Live at the Caribbean*. 1982 (Mistakes Music MS1).

Mystics, the, *Who's That Girl?* 1995 (Fontana MYSDD 2 / 852 477–2).

Ova, *Ova*. N.d. (Stroppy Cow).
—— *Out Of Bounds*. 1981 (Stroppy Cow SC 666).

Passions, the, *Thirty Thousand Feet over China* 1981 (Polydor POLS 1041).

POISON GIRLS, *Hex*. 1979 (Xntrix).
—— *Where's the Pleasure*. 1982 (Xntrix XN2006/B).
—— *7 Year Scratch*. 1983 (Xntrix RM101).

RAINCOATS, THE, *The Raincoats*. 1979 (Rough Trade).
—— *Odyshape*. 1981 (Rough Trade).
—— *Moving*. 1983 (Rough Trade).

SIDI BOU SAID, *Bodies*. 1995 (Ultimate. Topp CD034).
—— *Obsessive*. 1997 (The Ultimate Record Co. TOP PCD053).

SKUNK ANANSIE, *Paranoid and Sunburnt*. 1993 (One Little Indian TPLP55CD).
—— *Stoosh*. 1996 (One Little Indian PPLP85CD).

STEREOLAB, *Stereolab*. 1992 (Too Pure. Pure CD11).
—— *Refried Ectoplasm*. 1995. Switched On Vol. 2 (Duophonic Ultra High Frequency Disks).

TRANSGLOBAL UNDERGROUND, *Dream of 100 Nations*. 1993 (Nation NRO 21 CD).
—— *International Times*. 1994 (Nation NATCD 38).

Various. *Making Waves*. 1981 (Girlfriend) featuring,

GYMSLIPS, THE,	(MISSION) BELLES, THE,
ANDROIDS OF MU, THE	AMY AND THE ANGELS,
GUEST STARS, THE	MINISTRY OF MARRIAGE,
REAL INSECTS	NANCY BOYS, THE,
ROCK GODDESS	SISTERHOOD OF SPIT.

Various. *Scaling Triangles*. 1971 (Treble Chants ASN 1):

SUB VERSE, SOLE SISTER, PETTICOATS, THE.

References

ARCHER, ROBYN, and **SIMMONDS, DIANA** (1986), *A Star is Torn* (London: Virago Press Ltd.).

ARNOT, MADELEINE, and **WEINER, GABY** (eds.) (1997), *Gender and the Politics of Schooling* (London: Hutchinson).

ASKEW, SUE, and **ROSS, CAROL** (1988), *Boys Don't Cry: Boys and Sexism in Education* (Oxford: Oxford University Press).

BALFOUR, VICTORIA (1986), *Rock Wives* (London: Virgin Books).

BATTERSBY, CHRISTINE (1989), *Gender and Genius* (London: The Women's Press).

BAYTON, MAVIS (1990), 'How Women Become Musicians', in Simon Frith and Andrew Goodwin (eds.), *On Record: Rock, Pop, and the Written Word* (New York: Pantheon).

—— (1993), 'Feminist Musical Practice: Problems and Contradictions', in Tony Bennett et al. (eds.), *Rock and Popular Music: Politics Policies, Institutions* (London: Routledge).

BELL, DIANE, and **KLEIN, RENATE** (1996), *Radically Speaking: Feminism Reclaimed* (London: Zed Books).

BENNETT, H. STITH (1980), *On Becoming a Rock Musician* (Amherst: University of Massachusetts Press).

BENNETT, TONY, et al. (eds.) (1993), *Rock and Popular Music: Politics, Policies, Institutions* (London: Routledge).

BENOKRAITIS, NIJOLE (1997), *Subtle Sexism: Current Practice and Prospects for Change* (London: Sage).

BINNEY, LYNNE, HARKELL, GINA, and **NIXON, JUDY** (1981), *Leaving Violent Men: A Study of Refuges and Housing for Battered Women* (London: National Women's Aid Federation).

BIRKE, LINDA, et al. (eds.) (The Brighton Women and Science Group) (1980), *Alice through the Microscope: The Power of Science over Women's Lives* (London: Virago).

BOURDIEU, PIERRE (1984), *Distinction: A Social Critique of the Judgement of Taste* (Cambridge, Mass.: Harvard University Press).

BROWN, HELEN (1995), *Expectations for the Future* (London: Health Education Authority).

BRUCE, ROSEMARY, and **KEMP, ANTHONY** (1993), 'Sex-Stereotyping in Children's Preference for Musical Instruments', in the *British Journal of Music Education*, 10/3.

BUIKEMA, ROSEMARIE, and **SMELIK, ANNEKE** (1995), *Women's Studies and Culture: A Feminist Introduction* (London: Zed Books).

BUTLER, JUDITH (1990), *Gender Trouble: Feminism and the Subversion of Identity* (London: Routledge).

BYRNE, ELIZABETH (1978), *Women and Education* (London: Tavistock).

CLARRICOATES, KATHERINE (1978), 'Dinosaurs in the Classroom: A Re-examination of Some Aspects of the "Hidden" Curriculum in Primary Schools', in *Women's Studies Quarterly*, 1/4.

COCKBURN, CYNTHIA (1981), 'The Material of Male Power', in *Feminist Review*, 9 Oct. 1981.

—— (1987), *Two Track Training: Sex Inequalities in the Youth Training Scheme* (Basingstoke: Macmillan).

—— (1991), *In the Way of Women: Men's Resistance to Sex Equality in Organizations* (Basingstoke: Macmillan).

—— and **ORMROD, SUSAN** (1993), *Gender and Technology in the Making* (London: Sage).

COHEN, SARA (1991), *Rock Culture in Liverpool: Popular Music in the Making* (Oxford: Clarendon Press).

CONNELL, ROBERT W. (1995), *Masculinities* (Cambridge: Polity Press).

CONNOLLY, RAY (1981), *John Lennon 1940–1980* (London: Fontana).

COOPER, SARAH (ed.) (1995), *Girls! Girls! Girls!* (London: Cassell).

COPPOCK, VICKI, HAYDON, DEENA, and **RICHTER, INGRID** (1995), *The Illusions of 'Post-Feminism': New Women, Old Myths* (London: Taylor & Francis).

COTT, NANCY (1986), 'Feminist Theory and Feminist Movements: The Past before Us', in Juliet Mitchell and Ann Oakley (eds.), *What is Feminism?* (Oxford: Blackwell).

COWIE, CELIA, and **LEES, SUE** (1981), 'Slags or Drags?', in *Feminist Review*, 9.

DAHL, LINDA (1984), *Stormy Weather: The Music and Lives of a Century of Jazz Women* (New York: Pantheon).

DAVIES, HUNTER (1969), *The Beatles: The Authorised Biography* (St Albans: Granada).

DEEM, ROSEMARY (1978), *Women and Schooling* (London: Routledge & Kegan Paul).

DELAMONT, SARA (1990), *Sex Roles and the School*, 2nd edition (London: Routledge).

DOBASH, REBECCA EMERSON, and **DOBASH, RUSSELL** (1980), *Violence against Wives: A Case against the Patriarchy* (Shepton-Mallet: Open Books).

—— —— (1992), *Women, Violence and Social Change* (London: Routledge).

EISENSTEIN, HESTER (1984), *Contemporary Feminist Thought* (London: Unwin Paperbacks).

EVANS, LIZ (1994), *Women, Sex and Rock'n'Roll: In Their Own Words* (Hammersmith: Pandora).

FALUDI, SUSAN (1992), *Backlash: The Undeclared War against Women* (London: Vintage Books).

FIGES, KATE (1994), *Because of Her Sex: The Myth of Equality for Women in Britain* (London: Macmillan).

FAULKNER, WENDY, and **ARNOLD, ERIK** (eds.) (1985), *Smothered by Invention: Technology in Women's Lives* (London: Pluto Press).

FINNEGAN, RUTH (1989), *The Hidden Musicians: Music-Making in an English Town* (Cambridge: Cambridge University Press).

FISHER, SUSIE, and **HOLDER, SUSAN** (1981), *Too Much Too Young* (London: Pan).

FORNAS, JOHAN, LINDBERG, ULF, and **SERNHEDE, OVE** (1995), *In Garageland: Rock, Youth and Modernity* (London: Routledge).

FRENCH, MARILYN (1992), *The War against Women* (Harmondsworth: Penguin).

FRITH, SIMON (1981), 'The Voices of Women', *New Statesman*, 13 November.

—— (1983), *Sound Effects: Youth, Leisure, and the Politics of Rock'n'Roll* (London: Constable).

—— (1984), *The Sociology of Youth* (Ormskirk: Causeway).

—— (1993), 'Popular Music and the Local State', in Tony Bennett et al. (eds.), *Rock and Popular Music: Politics, Policies, Institutions* (London: Routledge).

—— and **GOODWIN, ANDREW** (eds.) (1990), *On Record: Rock, Pop, and the Written Word* (New York: Pantheon).

—— and **HORNE, HOWARD** (1987), *Art into Pop* (London: Methuen).

—— and **McROBBIE, ANGELA** (1978), 'Rock and Sexuality', *Screen Education*, 29.

GAAR, GILLIAN (1992), *She's a Rebel: The History of Women in Rock & Roll* (Washington: Seal Press).

GARRATT, SHERYL (1984), 'All of Us Love All of You', in Sue Steward and Sheryl Garratt (eds.), *Signed, Sealed and Delivered: True Life Stories of Women in Pop* (London: Pluto Press).

GASKELL, JANE (1992), *Gender Matters from School to Work* (Milton Keynes: Open University Press).

GILL, JOHN (1995), *Queer Noises: Male and Female Homosexuality in Twentieth Century Music* (London: Cassell).

GOODEY, JO (1995), 'Fear of Crime: Children and Gendered Socialization', in Rebecca Emerson Dobash, Russell P. Dobash, and Lesley Noaks (eds.), *Gender and Crime* (Cardiff: University of Wales Press).

GOTTLIEB, JOANNE, and **WALD, GAYLE** (1994), 'Smells Like Teen Spirit: Riot Grrrls Revolution and Women in Independent Rock', in Andrew Ross and Tricia Rose (eds.), *Microphone Fiends: Youth Music and Youth Culture* (London: Routledge).

GOURSE, LESLEY (1995), *Madame Jazz: Contemporary Women Instrumentalists* (Oxford: Oxford University Press).

GREEN, EILEEN, HEBRON, SANDRA, and **WOODWARD, DIANA** (1987), 'Women, Leisure and Social Control', in Jalna Hanmer and Mary Maynard (eds.), *Women, Violence and Social Control* (Basingstoke: Macmillan).

—— —— —— (1990), *Women, Leisure, What's Leisure?* (London: Macmillan).

GREEN, LUCY (1997), *Music, Gender, Education* (Cambridge: Cambridge University Press).

GREIG, CHARLOTTE (1989), *Will You Still Love me Tomorrow? Girl Groups from the 50s on . . .* (London: Virago Press).

GRIFFIN, CHRISTINE (1985), *Typical Girls: Young Women from School to the Job Market* (London: Routledge & Kegan Paul).

GRINT, KEITH, and **GILL, ROSALIND** (1995), *The Gender-Technology Relation: Contemporary Theory and Research* (London: Taylor & Francis).

HALL, RUTH (1985), *Ask Any Woman: A London Inquiry into Rape and Sexual Assault* (Bristol: Falling Wall Press).

HALL, STUART, and JEFFERSON, TONY (eds.) (1976), *Resistance through Rituals: Youth Sub-Cultures in Post-War Britain* (London: Hutchinson).

HALSON, JACQUIE (1989), 'The Sexual Harassment of Young Women', in Lesley Holly (ed.), *Girls and Sexuality* (Milton Keynes: Open University Press).

HANMER, JALNA, and MAYNARD, MARY (1987), *Women, Violence and Social Control* (Basingstoke: Macmillan Press).

—— and SAUNDERS, SHEILA (1983), 'Blowing the Cover of the Protective Male: A Community Study of Violence to Women', in Eva Gamarnikow et al. (eds.), *The Public and the Private* (London: Heinemann).

—— —— (1984), *Well Founded Fear* (London: Hutchinson).

—— —— (1993), *Women, Violence and Crime Prevention: A West Yorkshire Study* (Avebury: Avebury Publishing Co. Ltd.)

HARGREAVES, DAVID J., and COLLEY, ANN M. (1986), *The Psychology of Sex Roles* (London: Harper & Row).

HEARN, JEFF, and PARKIN, WENDY (1986), *'Sex' at 'Work': The Power and Paradox of Organization Sexuality* (Brighton: Wheatsheaf).

HENDRY, LEO (1992), 'Sport and Leisure: The Not So Hidden Curriculum?', in John C. Coleman and Chris Warren-Adamson (eds.), *Youth Policy in the 1990s: The Way Forward* (London: Routledge).

HERON, LIZ (1985), *Truth, Dare or Promise: Girls Growing up in the Fifties* (London: Virago).

HESTER, MARIANNE, KELLY, LIZ, RADFORD, JILL (1996), *Women, Violence and Male Power* (Buckingham: Open University Press).

HEY, VALERIE (1986), *Patriarchy and Pub Culture* (London: Tavistock).

HOLLAND, DOROTHY, and EISENHART, MARGARET A. (1990), *Educated in Romance: Women, Achievement, and College Culture* (Chicago: University of Chicago Press).

JEFFREYS, SHEILA (1996), 'Return to Gender: Post-modernism and Lesbianandgay Theory', in Diane Bell and Renate Klein (eds.), *Radically Speaking: Feminism Reclaimed* (London: Zed Books).

JEMPSON, MIKE (1993), *The Musicians' Union 1893–1993: A Centenary Celebration* (London: Musicians' Union).

JENSON, JOLI (1992), 'Fandom as Pathology: The Consequences of Characterization', in Linda Lewis (ed.), *Adoring Audience: Fan Culture and Popular Media* (London: Routledge).

JONES, CAROL, and MAHONEY, PAT (eds.) (1989), *Learning Our Lines: Sexuality and Social Control in Education* (London: The Women's Press).

JOWELL, ROGER, et al. (eds.) (1992), *British Attitudes Survey, the 9th. Report*. SCPR (Aldershot: Dartmouth).

KELLY, ALISON (1981), *The Missing Half: Girls and Science Education* (Manchester: Manchester University Press).

KELLY, LIZ (1988), *Surviving Sexual Violence* (London: Polity Press).

Kemp's International Music Book (1995) (London: Showcase Publications Ltd.).

KITWOOD, TOM (1980), *Disclosures to a Stranger: Adolescent Values in an Advanced Industrial Society* (London: Routledge & Kegan Paul).

KITZINGER, JENNY (1995), 'I'm Sexually Attractive, But I'm Powerful: Young Women Negotiating Sexual Reputation', in *Women's Studies International Forum*, 18/2 (March/April).

KRAMARAE, CERIS (ed.) (1988), *Technology and Women's Voices: Keeping in Touch* (London: Routledge & Kegan Paul).

LAING, DAVE (1985), *One Chord Wonders: Power and Meaning in Punk Rock* (Milton Keynes: Open University Press).

LEES, SUE (1986), *Losing Out: Sexuality and Adolescent Girls* (London: Hutchinson).

—— (1993), *Sugar and Spice: Sexuality and Adolescent Girls* (London: Penguin Books).

LEIGH, SPENCER, and **FRAME, PETE** (1984), *Let's Go Down the Cavern: The Story of Liverpool's Merseybeat* (London: Vermilion).

LEONARD, D. (1980), *Sex and Generation* (London: Tavistock).

MAC AN GHAILL, MAIRTIN (1994), *The Making of Men: Masculinities, Sexualities and Schooling* (Buckingham: Open University Press).

—— (1996), *Understanding Masculinities* (Buckingham: Open University Press).

McCLARY, SUSAN (1991), *Feminine Endings: Music, Gender, and Sexuality* (Minneapolis: University of Minnesota Press).

McCRINDLE, JEAN, and **ROWBOTHAM, SHEILA** (1977), *Dutiful Daughters* (Harmondsworth: Penguin).

McDONNELL, EVELYN, and **POWERS, ANN** (1995), *Rock She Wrote* (London: Plexus).

McNEILL, MAUREEN (ed.) (1987), *Gender and Expertise* (London: Free Association Books).

McROBBIE, ANGELA (1978), 'Working Class Girls and the Culture of Femininity', in *Women Take Issue*, Women's Study Group (London: Hutchinson).

—— (1980), 'Settling Accounts with Subcultures', in *Screen Education*, 34.

—— (1991), *Feminism and Youth Culture: From Jackie to Just Seventeen* (Basingstoke: Macmillan).

MAHONEY, PAT (1985), *Schools for the Boys?* (London: Hutchinson).

NAVA, MICA (1984), 'Youth Service Provision, Social Order and the Question of Girls', in Angela McRobbie and Mica Nava (eds.), *Gender and Generation* (London: Macmillan).

NEGUS, KEITH (1992), *Producing Pop: Culture and Conflict in the Popular Music Industry* (London: Edward Arnold).

OAKLEY, ANN (1984), *Taking it like a Woman* (London: Flamingo).

—— and **MITCHELL, JULIET** (1997), *Who's Afraid of Feminism: Seeing through the Backlash* (London: Hamish Hamilton).

O'BRIEN, KAREN (1995), *Hymn to Her: Women Musicians Talk* (London: Virago Press).

O'BRIEN, LUCY (1995), *She Bop: The Definitive History of Women in Rock, Pop and Soul* (Harmondsworth: Penguin Books).

PLACKSIN, SALLY (1985), *Jazz Women: 1900 to the Present* (London: Pluto Press).

POLLOCK, GRISELDA (1988), *Vision and Difference: Femininity, Feminism and the Histories of Art* (London: Routledge).

RADFORD, JILL (1987), 'Policing Male Violence: Policing Women', in Jalna Hanmer and Mary Maynard (eds.), *Women, Violence and Social Control* (London: Macmillan).

—— and RUSSELL, DIANA E. H. (1992), *Femicide: The Politics of Woman Killing* (Buckingham: Open University Press).

RAPHAEL, AMY (1995), *Never Mind the Bollocks: Women Rewrite Rock* (Virago: London).

REAY, DIANA (1990), 'Working with Boys', in *Gender and Education*, 2/3.

REYNOLDS, SIMON, and PRESS, JOY (1995), *The Sex Revolts: Gender, Rebellion and Rock'n'Roll* (London: Serpent's Tail).

RHODES, DUSTY, and McNEILL, SANDRA (eds.) (1985), *Women against Violence against Women* (London: Onlywomen Press).

ROWBOTHAM, SHEILA (1973), *Women's Consciousness, Man's World* (Harmondsworth: Penguin).

SEGAL, LYNNE (1990), *Slow Motion: Changing Masculinities, Changing Men* (London: Virago Press).

SHARPE, SUE (1976), *Just Like a Girl* (Harmondsworth: Penguin).

—— (1994), *Just Like a Girl: How Girls Learn to be Women. From the Seventies to the Nineties* (Harmondsworth: Penguin).

SMITH, LESLIE (1978), 'Sexist Assumptions and Female Delinquency', in Carol Smart and Barry Smart (eds.), *Women, Sexuality and Social Control* (London: RKP).

SMITHERS, ALAN, and ZIENTEK, PAULINE (1991), *Gender, Primary Schools and the National Curriculum* (NASUWT and the Engineering Council).

Social Trends, 26 (1996) (HMSO).

SPENCER, LIZ, and TAYLOR, SALLY (1994), *Participation and Progress in the Labour Market: Key issues for women*. Research Services no. 35 (Sheffield: Employment Department).

SPENDER, DALE (1980), *Man-Made Language* (London: RKP).

—— (1982), *Invisible Women: The Schooling Scandal* (London: Writers and Readers).

—— and SARAH, ELISABETH (eds.) (1980), *Learning to Lose: Sexism and Education* (London: The Women's Press).

STAFFORD, ANNE (1991), *Trying Work: Gender, Youth and Work Experience* (Edinburgh: Edinburgh University Press).

STANKO, ELIZABETH (1985), *Intimate Intrusions: Women's Experience of Male Violence* (London: Unwin Hyman).

—— (1987), 'Typical Violence, Normal Precaution: Men, Women and Interpersonal Violence in England, Wales, Scotland and the USA', in John Hanmer and Mary Maynard (eds.), *Women, Violence and Social Control* (Basingstoke: Macmillan).

STANWORTH, MICHELLE (1981), *Gender and Schooling: A Study of Sexual Divisions in the Classroom* (London: Women's Research and Resources Centre Publication).

STEWARD, SUE, and GARRATT, SHERYL (1984), *Signed, Sealed and Delivered: True Life Stories of Women in Pop* (London: Pluto Press).

STREET, JOHN (1986), *Rebel Rock: The Politics of Popular Music* (Oxford: Blackwell).

THORNTON, SARAH (1995), *Club Cultures: Music, Media and Subcultural Capital* (Cambridge: Polity Press).

TOBLER, JOHN, and **GRUNDY, STUART** (1982), *The Record Producers* (London: BBC).

VERMOREL, FRED, and **VERMOREL, JUDY** (1985) *Starlust: The Secret Life of Fans* (London: Comet).

VICINUS, MARCIA (1979), 'Happy Times . . . If You Can Stand It: Women Entertainers During the Interwar Years in England', *Theatre Journal*, 31/3.

WAJCMAN, JUDY (1991), *Feminism Confronts Technology* (Cambridge: Polity Press).

WALKERDINE, VALERIE (1990), *Schoolgirl Fictions* (London: Verso).

WALSER, ROBERT (1993), *Running with the Devil: Power, Gender, and Madness in Heavy Metal Music* (Hanover: University Press of New England).

WEINER, GABY (ed.) (1985), *Just a Bunch of Girls: Feminist Approaches to Schooling* (Milton Keynes: Open University Press).

—— and **ARNOT, MADELEINE** (1987), *Gender under Scrutiny: New Inequalities in Education* (London: Hutchinson).

WEINSTEIN, DEENA (1991), *Heavy Metal: A Cultural Sociology* (New York: Lexington Books).

WHITE, EMILY (1995), 'Revolution Girl Style Now', in Evelyn McDonnell and Ann Powers (eds.), *Rock She Wrote* (Plexus: London).

WHITEHEAD, ANN (1976), 'Sexual Antagonism in Herefordshire', in Diana Barker and Sheila Allen (eds.), *Dependence and Exploitation in Marriage* (London: Longman).

WHYTE, JUDITH, DEEM, ROSEMARY, KANT, LESLEY, and **CRUICKSHANK, MAUREEN** (eds.) (1985), *Girlfriendly Schooling* (London: Methuen).

WILLIS, PAUL (1977), *Learning to Labour* (London: Saxon House).

—— (1978), *Profane Culture* (London: Routledge & Kegan Paul).

WILSON, DEIDRE (1978), 'Sexual Codes and Conduct', in Carol Smart and Barry Smart (eds.), *Women, Sexuality and Social Control* (London: RKP).

WOLF, NAOMI (1990), *The Beauty Myth: How Images of Beauty are Used against Women* (London: Vintage Books).

—— (1994), *Fire with Fire: The New Female Power and How it Will Change the 21st. Century* (London: Vintage Books).

WOLPE, ANNA (1977), *Some Processes in Sexist Education* (London: Women's Research and Resources Centre).

—— (1998), *Within School Walls: The Role of Discipline, Sexuality and the Curriculum* (London: Routledge).

Index

Bold numbers denote reference to illustrations

Index

Bold numbers denote reference to illustrations

TOBLER, JOHN, and **GRUNDY, STUART** (1982), *The Record Producers* (London: BBC).

VERMOREL, FRED, and **VERMOREL, JUDY** (1985) *Starlust: The Secret Life of Fans* (London: Comet).

VICINUS, MARCIA (1979), 'Happy Times . . . If You Can Stand It: Women Entertainers During the Interwar Years in England', *Theatre Journal*, 31/3.

WAJCMAN, JUDY (1991), *Feminism Confronts Technology* (Cambridge: Polity Press).

WALKERDINE, VALERIE (1990), *Schoolgirl Fictions* (London: Verso).

WALSER, ROBERT (1993), *Running with the Devil: Power, Gender, and Madness in Heavy Metal Music* (Hanover: University Press of New England).

WEINER, GABY (ed.) (1985), *Just a Bunch of Girls: Feminist Approaches to Schooling* (Milton Keynes: Open University Press).

—— and **ARNOT, MADELEINE** (1987), *Gender under Scrutiny: New Inequalities in Education* (London: Hutchinson).

WEINSTEIN, DEENA (1991), *Heavy Metal: A Cultural Sociology* (New York: Lexington Books).

WHITE, EMILY (1995), 'Revolution Girl Style Now', in Evelyn McDonnell and Ann Powers (eds.), *Rock She Wrote* (Plexus: London).

WHITEHEAD, ANN (1976), 'Sexual Antagonism in Herefordshire', in Diana Barker and Sheila Allen (eds.), *Dependence and Exploitation in Marriage* (London: Longman).

WHYTE, JUDITH, DEEM, ROSEMARY, KANT, LESLEY, and **CRUICKSHANK, MAUREEN** (eds.) (1985), *Girlfriendly Schooling* (London: Methuen).

WILLIS, PAUL (1977), *Learning to Labour* (London: Saxon House).

—— (1978), *Profane Culture* (London: Routledge & Kegan Paul).

WILSON, DEIDRE (1978), 'Sexual Codes and Conduct', in Carol Smart and Barry Smart (eds.), *Women, Sexuality and Social Control* (London: RKP).

WOLF, NAOMI (1990), *The Beauty Myth: How Images of Beauty are Used against Women* (London: Vintage Books).

—— (1994), *Fire with Fire: The New Female Power and How it Will Change the 21st. Century* (London: Vintage Books).

WOLPE, ANNA (1977), *Some Processes in Sexist Education* (London: Women's Research and Resources Centre).

—— (1998), *Within School Walls: The Role of Discipline, Sexuality and the Curriculum* (London: Routledge).